THE S. MARK TAPER FOUNDATION

IMPRINT IN JEWISH STUDIES

BY THIS ENDOWMENT

THE S. MARK TAPER FOUNDATION SUPPORTS

THE APPRECIATION AND UNDERSTANDING

OF THE RICHNESS AND DIVERSITY OF

JEWISH LIFE AND CULTURE

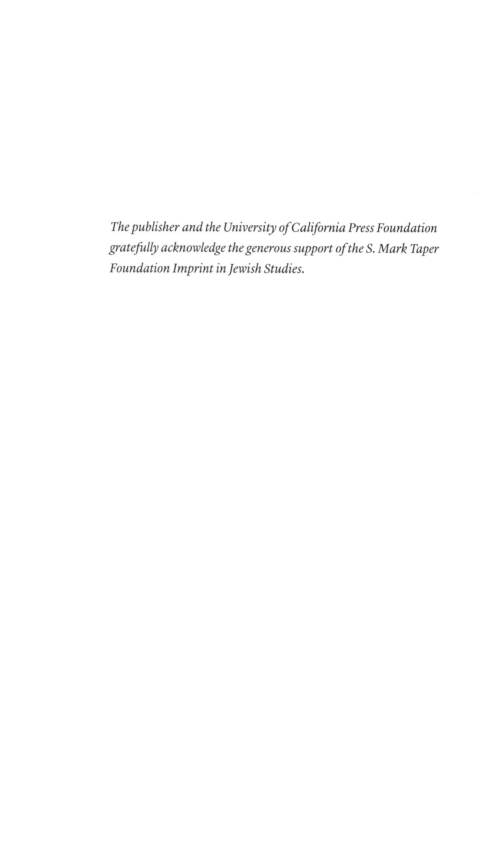

The publisher and the University of California Press Foundation gratefully acknowledge the generous support of the S. Mark Taper Foundation Imprint in Jewish Studies.

A Prophet Has Appeared

A Prophet Has Appeared

THE RISE OF ISLAM THROUGH CHRISTIAN AND JEWISH EYES

A Sourcebook

Stephen J. Shoemaker

 UNIVERSITY OF CALIFORNIA PRESS

University of California Press
Oakland, California

© 2021 by Stephen J. Shoemaker

Library of Congress Cataloging-in-Publication Data

Names: Shoemaker, Stephen J., 1968– author.
Title: A prophet has appeared : the rise of Islam through Christian and Jewish
    eyes : a sourcebook / Stephen J. Shoemaker.
Description: Oakland, California : University of California Press, [2021] |
    Includes bibliographical references and index.
Identifiers: LCCN 2020037017 (print) | LCCN 2020037018 (ebook) |
    ISBN 9780520299603 (cloth) | ISBN 9780520299610 (paperback) |
    ISBN 9780520971271 (epub)
Subjects: LCSH: Islam—Origin. | Islam—History—To 1500—Sources. | Islam—
    Relations—Christianity—History—To 1500—Sources. | Christianity and
    other religions—Islam—History—To 1500—Sources. | Judaism—Relations—
    Islam—History—To 1500—Sources. | Islam—Relations—Judaism—History—
    To 1500—Sources.
Classification: LCC BP55 .S5964 2021 (print) | LCC BP55 (ebook) |
    DDC 297.2/83—dc23
LC record available at https://lccn.loc.gov/2020037017
LC ebook record available at https://lccn.loc.gov/2020037018

Manufactured in the United States of America

29 28 27 26 25 24 23 22 21
10 9 8 7 6 5 4 3 2 1

In memory of PATRICIA CRONE

Contents

Acknowledgments

This is a book that I have been thinking about writing for a long time—probably since the first moment that I read *Hagarism* on 21 November 1997, while on a transcontinental flight from Atlanta to San Francisco to attend the AAR/SBL meetings. During those cramped, uncomfortable hours, I could at least delight in the process of an exhilarating intellectual discovery. The first chapters of this book opened up a new world of possibilities for studying the late ancient Near East, for me at least. I was struck both by how much the non-Islamic sources from the first century of Islam have to offer for understanding the earliest history of this new religious movement and simultaneously by the utter absence of these invaluable witnesses from any book that I had read or conversation that I had had about the beginnings of Islam. For someone trained in biblical studies and early Christian studies, such an omission was unfathomable. Of course, my encounter with that book has been a very productive one, inspiring a number of publications. Yet in light of the enormous value that contemporary witnesses have for understanding the formative history of a major world religion, the absence of a handy collection of the most important of these sources presented with historical commentary seemed to present a pressing need. Such volumes and studies are fairly common in biblical and early Christian studies and are extremely useful for both research and teaching.

So, it is with an aim toward filling this gap in the resources for studying the rise of Islam that I offer this collection of contemporary witnesses to the beginnings of Islam.

There are many individuals that I have to thank for their comments and advice in preparing this volume, but perhaps none more than my good friend and frequent collaborator and intellectual sparring partner, Sean Anthony. I decided to publish this book while browsing the book exhibit at another AAR/SBL, in San Antonio in 2016, and in the same moment, in a room ripe with possibilities, I began to consider where on earth I might find a home for such a volume. It was Sean who first connected this project with Eric Schmidt and the University of California Press. I knew Eric already, since UC Press publishes the official monograph series of the North American Patristics Society (Christianity in Late Antiquity) and I edit the society's official journal (*Journal of Early Christian Studies*). But I assumed that UC Press would not be particularly interested in publishing this study since they had just published a similar—and excellent—sourcebook of early Syriac writings on Islam by my friend and colleague Michael Penn. Yet Sean was in the course of publishing his brilliant new monograph on Muhammad with UC Press, and he mentioned my collection to Eric, who proved to be most enthusiastic about it, seeing my book and Michael's as complementary to one another, which I hope they will be. So, thanks to Sean's connection, a match was made, and a book was born. My great thanks to Eric and Austin Lim, Kate Hoffman, Teresa Iafolla and all the staff at UC Press, and also Jon Dertien and Gary J. Hamel at BookComp for all their help and efforts to facilitate the publication of this book.

I have to thank Sean especially for being in constant dialogue about this book over the years, and for carefully and critically reading the complete manuscript at a very late stage in its production. Guillaume Dye also helped with conceiving the book and read and commented on the manuscript as well, for which I am grateful: there are few people whose insights I value as much as Guillaume's. I also thank very much the two readers for the press, Naomi Koltun-Fromm and the other anonymous reader, for extremely helpful comments. I hope both will see much evidence of their constructive criticisms in the pages of this book. There are, of course, many others to thank for their contributions to this study, both big and small, and I only fear that in trying to name them I will leave someone important out. Several friends and colleagues read the initial proposal for the press, offering invaluable advice and assistance at the outset of this project, including, in addition to Sean Anthony, Michael Pregill, Gabriel Reynolds, John Reeves, and Philip Wood. I thank my colleagues at the University of Oregon, both in my home department and in our Mediterranean studies reading group, including especially Lisa Wolverton, David Wacks, Rick Colby, and David Hollenberg. My thanks to many others for answering questions or responding to emails about specific texts or ideas, including, but not limited to, David Brakke, Daniel Caner, Stephen Davis, Julien Decharneux, George Demacopoulos, Andrew Jacobs, Kristian Heal, Michael Penn, Christian Sahner, Beatrice St. Laurent, and Jack Tannous.

Perhaps in light of my opening remarks, the volume's dedication needs little explanation. Patricia was one of the most brilliant scholars that I have ever met—her work was an enormous inspiration to me, and she was an intellectual hero. I was first put into contact with Patricia by a common friend, Annette Reed, who, after a conversation at the North American Patristics Society in May 2004, passed along an offprint of an article that I had just published, "Christmas in the Qur'an." True to her constant intellectual generosity, Patricia emailed me very soon thereafter with many comments on the article, and we began to have regular exchanges via email. She read many of my publications while they were in progress, always with her trademark withering yet invaluable criticism, including *The Death of a Prophet* and early work on *The Apocalypse of Empire*. I had the great fortune to meet her in person while I enjoyed the boon of a membership in the School of Historical Studies at the Institute for Advanced Study, while writing *Mary in Early Christian Faith and Devotion*. I believe I owe a great debt to Patricia for making it possible for me to be there in the fall of 2013. She was approaching the end of her life at the time, and I count it as a great privilege that I got to spend several months regularly conversing with her and learning from her in person before her tragic death shortly thereafter. I dedicate this book, which is an extension of the work that she and Michael Cook began in *Hagarism*, to the memory of her scholarly brilliance.

Introduction

The present volume aims to fill a significant gap in the materials presently available for studying the beginnings of Islam. It gathers for the first time in a single volume the most important (in my judgment at least) non-Islamic witnesses for understanding the formation of the Islamic religious tradition during the first century of its existence. It has long been a standard practice in religious studies to employ contemporary sources external to a given religious tradition in order to study its early history, particularly during its formative era. It is thus unfortunate that even at this late date such an approach to earliest Islam remains effectively sidelined. The study of Christian origins, for instance, has long benefitted from concerted, critical attention to the testimonies of contemporary Greek and Roman writers about Christianity during the first two centuries of its existence. And although in the case of early Christianity these sources are both sparser and sparer than they are for early Islam, specialists on Christian origins have long recognized these external witnesses as among the most valuable sources that we have for understanding the formation of Christianity.

The observations from these outside voices regarding the emergence of Christianity afford "a unique perspective unavailable in other writings from the period," as Robert Wilken states in *The Christians as the Romans Saw Them*. There he also notes that "much of what the pagan critics say is 'true' but cannot be fitted into the Christian self-understanding. I am convinced that the perceptions of outsiders tell us something significant about the character of the Christian movement, and that without the views of those who made up the world in which Christianity grew to maturity, we will never understand what Christianity was or is. How something is perceived is an aspect of what it is. This is especially true in the social world, where the perception of others is an essential part of the reality people inhabit."[1] One hopes someday to see a similar attitude and greater openness to the range of the available data in the study of early Islam. With such intent I decided to publish this volume.

Of course, this book is not the first effort to bring these external sources to bear on the study of Islamic origins. That honor belongs, it would seem, to Sebastian Brock. In 1975 at an Oxford colloquium on first-century Islam, Brock delivered a brief communication that gestured toward the importance of non-Islamic sources for understanding the beginnings of Islam with a paper entitled "Syriac Views of Emergent Islam."[2] Henceforth, the study of Islamic origins would be changed. In effect, Brock's paper issued a challenge to the discipline to expand its data pool to include the witness of Christian sources contemporary with the events of earliest Islam. No longer could scholars of early Islam remain innocently ignorant of their invaluable testimony, content to reconstruct the rise of Islam on the basis of the Islamic sources alone. This challenge could, of course, simply be ignored, as it so often has been. Yet for those scholars who would embrace it and expand on it to include other non-Syriac and non-Christian sources, the resulting turn to integrate earliest Islam with its late antique milieu would prove transformative.

The first scholars to attempt an integration of these non-Islamic sources with study of formative Islam were Patricia Crone and Michael

Cook, whose path-breaking work *Hagarism: The Making of the Islamic World* also took shape at the same Oxford conference and appeared only two years later in 1977.[3] *Hagarism* proposed a bold reinterpretation of earliest Islam on the basis of these non-Islamic sources, yet its argumentation is deeply flawed by the uncritical credulity with which it approaches these non-Islamic witnesses while disregarding evidence from the Islamic tradition almost entirely, and the work was rightly criticized for this significant error, even among its most sympathetic readers.[4] But the overarching genius underlying its approach has nonetheless been unfairly marginalized and even maligned by far too many scholars of early Islam.[5] Indeed, in part because of the controversial nature of this book, and also the scholars who wrote it, the study of formative Islam has often proceeded largely in ignorance of the invaluable witness that these contemporary sources have to offer as we seek to understand the earliest developments within Muhammad's new religious movement. One can see this tendency, for instance, in any number of recent studies of Muhammad and the beginnings of Islam.[6]

Nevertheless, it remains essential that the evidence of these contemporary witnesses to the rise of Islam be fully integrated with the study of its earliest history. This is all the more so given the fact that the traditional Islamic accounts of the rise of Islam, as related in the earliest biographies of Muhammad, were composed only long after the events in question, and their accounts are notoriously unreliable and heavily determined by the beliefs and practices of Islam in the Abbasid Empire of the eighth and later centuries. Although these biographies relate copious and detailed information about Muhammad and the beginnings of his religious movement, as sources they are widely recognized as being highly tendentious and artificial. Yet most scholarship on Muhammad and the beginnings of Islam still looks to these sources to reconstruct the rise of Islam, believing them to preserve a reliable "historical kernel," even though the reliability of this kernel is merely asserted by scholarly fiat without a critical basis.

The Unique Value of the Non-Islamic Witnesses

According to the traditional narrative of Islamic origins, as stored in the collective memory of the Islamic historical tradition, Muhammad's new religious movement achieved its mature, traditional form before his death, which occurred, again following the Islamic historical tradition, in 632.[7] Islam's faith and practice were fully elaborated and perfected by this time, so that the classical Islam of the later eighth century and beyond was already in place and in no need of any further development. Likewise, the contents of the Qur'an were complete by this time, having been revealed to Muhammad and through him to his followers over the course of his prophetic career, so the canonical text reached its close with his death. The text of the Qur'an was thus already established in its final form, as it has come down to us in the present, even if its contents were only codified decades later and the final vocalizations added later still. Accordingly, Muhammad's followers received the Qur'an as a distinctive and uniquely authoritative scriptural tradition from the very start.

The message of the Qur'an and of Muhammad's preaching shares substantial similarities to earlier Jewish and Christian traditions, a fact that the Islamic tradition itself also recognizes. Yet Muhammad and the Qur'an brought their divine message specifically to the Arabs in Arabic and in the originally perfect form that the ancestors of contemporary Jews and Christians had corrupted. Thus, while there was a genetic relationship between religious cultures of Judaism, Christianity, and Islam, according to the traditional narrative, Muhammad and the Qur'an owe no debt to their religious predecessors. Instead, they have directly restored through divine revelation the true religion of Abraham, which he observed in Arabia, rather than the biblical Holy Lands, with his son Ishmael and his mother Hagar. Islam was therefore already by the death of Muhammad understood by his followers as a new, separate religious confession that revived an older faith and was clearly distinct from Judaism and Christianity with its own unique scripture and prophet.

Muhammad revealed his message and the Qur'an, according to tradition, in the Arabian Hijaz, the western part of the central Arabian Peninsula, in the cities of Mecca and Medina. Muhammad began to preach in his hometown of Mecca, which the Islamic tradition remembers as having been thoroughly pagan or polytheist in its religious belief and practice, although there is good evidence to suggest that this was not actually the case.[8] The tradition reports, nonetheless, that Mecca possessed a major pagan shrine, the Kaʿba, and pilgrimage to this sanctuary was an important part of the local Meccan economy. For this reason, and for others no doubt, the citizens of Mecca did not welcome Muhammad's new message of exclusive monotheism. Although he managed to attract some followers in Mecca, after about ten years he migrated with them to another city to the north, Yathrib (later renamed Medina) at the invitation of its inhabitants. This event, known as the *hijra*, the "flight" or "migration" to Yathrib/Medina is the event that traditionally marks the beginning of the Islamic tradition as well as the beginning of the Islamic calendar in the year 622 CE.

In Medina, Muhammad was accepted as the city's leader, and again he found himself among large numbers of Arab pagans, but in their midst was also a large Jewish community. Neither Mecca nor Medina, one should note, had any Christian community at all according to the Islamic tradition, and there is likewise no external evidence for a Christian presence in either location at this time. Muhammad made a pact with Medina's Jews, at least for a while, allowing them to be members of his new politico-religious community while retaining their traditional faith and practice, but according to tradition this was a short-lived experiment. It was also in Medina that Muhammad, soon after arriving, changed the direction of prayer for his followers away from Jerusalem, their original orientation, and established instead the Kaʿba in Mecca as the focus of Islamic prayer henceforward. Although at the time the Kaʿba was still in use as a pagan shrine, according to Islam it had been founded by Abraham and was thus an originally monotheist shrine that had subsequently fallen into pagan misuse. In 627 CE, Muhammad and his followers conquered Mecca and cleansed its shrine, restoring it to its monotheist roots, elevating it as the most sacred shrine of his new religion, and integrating it into an elaborate pilgrimage rite that he established in Mecca and its environs. Several years later, in 632 Muhammad died in Medina just as his followers were preparing to spread the dominion of their new monotheist polity beyond Arabia and into the Near East and Mediterranean world.

Such is the portrait of Islamic origins that we find in the traditional Islamic biographies of Muhammad: an Arabian monotheism proclaimed by an Arabian prophet through an Arabic scripture focused on an Arabian shrine deep within Arabia, with some Jewish presence and an absence of Christianity. Yet Muhammad's traditional biographies, the *sīra* traditions, as they are known, are widely recognized by modern historians as little more than pious imaginations about the beginnings of Islam that took shape in the collective memory among Muhammad's followers over at least a century after his death, at which time they were first collected and written down, around 750 CE. Relying on these traditional biographies as trustworthy sources for the beginnings of Islam is thus no different than if one were to write the history of first-century Christianity based on the second and third-century apocryphal acts of the apostles, something that no scholar of Christianity, by comparison, would ever even dream of doing.[9] Moreover, like these biographies of Muhammad, the early Islamic historical tradition first took shape only during the Abbasid Empire, and accordingly it betrays a pervasive bias against the Umayyad dynasty, the predecessors of the Abbasids who ruled as Muhammad's successors (caliphs) from 661 to 750 CE. Thus, the traditional Islamic accounts of the first century are regularly distorted not only by the pious memories of later generations, but also by a deliberate anti-Umayyad bias.[10]

The traditions of the Qur'an, for their part, almost certainly belong to the first Islamic century. Nevertheless they convey virtually no information concerning the life of Muhammad and the circumstances of his prophetic mission, let alone the early history of the community that he founded.[11] Indeed, it is this acute crisis of evidence for the history of Muhammad's new religious movement during the first century of its existence that makes attention to the witness of contemporary non-Islamic sources absolutely critical. Given the fundamentally unreliable nature of the early Islamic sources, one can highlight the problem clearly by simply reversing Jonathan Brown's argument that "to rely solely on these Christian sources would be like writing a history of the Soviet Union during the Cold War using only American newspapers."[12] Point taken, but certainly to rely solely on the early Islamic tradition in this case would be like writing a history of the Soviet Union during Cold War using only Soviet newspapers. It is thus perhaps not the best analogy for him to make, since that is effectively what Brown and so many other Islamicists generally have done when writing the history of early Islam.[13] For what it is worth, I more than suspect that an account based on the American news media would, in fact, prove more accurate than one drawn from the pages of *Pravda* or reports from TASS. Yet that is beside the point: surely any historian of the Cold War Soviet Union would use Soviet, American, and other sources together in a critical manner, and that is precisely what historians of formative Islam must also begin to do with more regularity and rigor.

Despite the frequent neglect of the non-Islamic sources in much scholarship, their study has by no means lain dormant since the publication of *Hagarism*. Fred Donner's volume on *The Early Islamic Conquests*, for instance, reconstructs the expansion of Muhammad's followers outside of the Arabian Peninsula through a synthesis of Islamic and non-Islamic sources, yielding admirable results in what remains the standard account of these events.[14] Donner's more recent study *Muhammad and the Believers* presents a compelling reconstruction of earliest Islam using both Islamic and non-Islamic sources.[15] Likewise Crone herself and Gerald Hawting have both published a number of excellent studies on earliest Islam using these sources.[16] I have myself also attempted two studies of early Islam that aim to synthesize evidence from the complete range of available sources.[17] And Sean Anthony's recent monograph *Muhammad and the Empires of Faith* offers an outstanding exemplary model of how the Islamic and non-Islamic source can be productively used in tandem.[18] Yet by far the most significant work on these non-Islamic sources is the magisterial inventory of these traditions in Robert Hoyland's *Seeing Islam as Others Saw It*.[19] Indeed, given Hoyland's near exhaustive catalog of these sources and their content, one might well wonder what is the need for the present volume. Likewise, Michael Penn's recent *When Christians First Met Muslims* provides interested readers with a ready sourcebook of the earliest Syriac writings on Islam.[20] In light of these two fine studies in particular, then, why would there be a need to publish this anthology of non-Islamic witnesses to the rise of Islam? Is not such a collection merely superfluous at this point?

In fact, this collection offers something quite different from these earlier publications. In contrast to Hoyland's tome, which includes at least some discussion of nearly every contemporary text that merely mentions Islam, I have instead focused on a limited number of sources, offering a curated selection chosen on the basis of their quality as witnesses to the rise of Islam. To merit inclusion in this volume, a source should ideally satisfy two criteria: (1) it must date with a high degree of probability from the first century of Islam; and (2) it must convey information concerning the religious beliefs and practices of Muhammad's followers. Mere mentions of the "Arabs," reports of battles, discussions of diplomacy and other political issues, and so on have been largely excluded. It should be noted, however, that I have made certain exceptions to the second point for a handful of important sources that are noteworthy for their very early witness to Muhammad and his new religious movement. Moreover, in contrast to Hoyland's book, the focus here is on the texts themselves, each of which we give in translation—something that Hoyland does only piecemeal and selectively. And while Penn's collection offers extensive translations from a range of sources, he limits his collection to only writings in Syriac and aims primarily to show how Syriac Christians responded to the rise of Islam. My objective, however, is to present something rather different. Each of the sources included in this volume holds significant value for understanding the early history of Muhammad's new religious movement itself. Moreover, while the Syriac tradition is of course vital for understanding the formation of Islam, as readers soon will see, it is by no means uniquely or singularly important. If one's goal is to use non-Islamic sources as important witnesses to the rise of Islam, then one must look beyond Syriac to the other linguistic communities of the late ancient Near East, including Greek, Hebrew, Armenian, Georgian, Arabic, and even Latin.

Readers familiar with some of my earlier publications will notice that this volume seeks to make some similar arguments about the nature of the religious movement founded by Muhammad that have already been raised in those studies. The main difference, however, lies in the approach. Rather than focusing on a theme—the end of Muhammad's life or apocalypticism, for instance, in this book we instead present all the relevant contemporary witnesses to the rise of Muhammad's new religious community from the non-Islamic primary sources themselves, allowing readers to encounter them directly. The result is not really a general reader for an introductory course on Islam (although, depending on the approach taken by the instructor, why not?). Instead, this volume seeks to encourage more attention to these sources and their historical witness to the rise of what would become Islam, especially in university classrooms where questions about Muhammad and the rise of Islam are engaged more specifically and narrowly. Yet I suspect that this anthology will also be of use to specialists in the study of early Islam and late antiquity, both graduate students and more advanced scholars, since most individuals working in these fields do not have facility in all the languages represented by the included texts. In many respects, I conceive of this volume as sharing much in common with Wilken's seminal volume *The Christians as the Romans Saw Them*, cited above, albeit with more direct attention to the texts themselves.[21]

As a further point of clarification, I would note that in the endnotes I frequently refer readers to my earlier publications for further clarification of various points. This pattern should not be taken as a sign of vanity—as if to suggest that only my work on these topics is worth consulting. Far from it: this is a matter of convenience. Since in these works I have already engaged a wide range of scholarship on a variety of matters, I refer readers to my publications in lieu of reproducing their arguments and references in the commentaries or notes of this volume. Readers can find in these publications discussions of the range of scholarly opinion on given topics along with references to other important works on these same subjects. To facilitate direct interaction with the texts, I have presented them in the following manner. Each text is preceded by a sort of basic introduction, providing the reader with the essential details of who wrote it, when, where, and why, insofar as we can know. These introductions will vary significantly in length depending on the nature of the text in question and how complicated such matters are in the current state of scholarship. The texts themselves will follow, and then I conclude each chapter with a historical commentary that seeks to explain what a particular source can tell us about the rise of Muhammad's new religious movement within the broader context of the late ancient Near East. In this way, I hope to provide readers with an approach to the texts that will enable them to form their own judgments about what they mean before reading my own comments.[22]

The Dome of the Rock and the Temple

One will quickly notice in reading through these texts that several themes recur, and interested readers can trace these themes across the sources by using the book's index. The repetition of these topics across a range of sources is of course highly significant. For historians, information reported independently by multiple sources written close to the events in question is the gold standard, and in many instances, the non-Islamic sources gift us with just such historical treasures. Perhaps the most persistent theme across these sources is an indication that Muhammad's followers held Jerusalem, and more specifically the site of the Jerusalem Temple, in the highest regard. I have written about this evidence at length in other venues, and it is particularly significant that the pattern of agreement among the non-Islamic sources on the importance of Jerusalem and its Temple is also confirmed by the early Islamic tradition.[23] As we noted above, it is widely acknowledged that Muhammad and his followers originally turned not to face Mecca and its shrine in their prayers, but toward Jerusalem instead. The Qur'an itself mentions a change in the direction of prayer in 2.142–44, although here it fails to mention either Jerusalem or Mecca by name. Of course, the later Islamic tradition is keen to apologize for this deviant original practice by insisting that a change was made very early in the movement's history and can even be harmonized, somehow, with prayer toward the Meccan Kaʿba. Yet when we consider the wide range of evidence from both the non-Islamic sources and the Islamic tradition itself, it seems that Jerusalem and its Temple, and not the cities of the Arabian Hijaz or any shrine therein, were at the center of the earliest Islamic sacred geography.

Three of the sources in this volume, one should note, do mention a particular shrine revered by Muhammad's followers, although it is not always clear from the reports where this shrine is located, and there is no indication whatsoever that it is in Mecca or even in the Hijaz. One contemporary Christian writer describes a desert location that they revered named "the tent of Abraham." According to this source, from time immemorial the desert nomads had venerated this site as a place of sacrifice established by Abraham while he was dwelling "in the remote and vast places of the desert." Another writer simply relates an account that he heard from several Christian men who visited the place where they "have the stone and the object of their worship" and observed their sacrifices there, yet without any indication of its location at all. Only a single source actually names this shrine the "Kaʿba," but, as we will see, according to the eyewitness testimony of this seventh-century Christian, the Kaʿba that Muhammad's followers turned to face was not in western Arabia; instead, it was to the east from Alexandria and to the west from Mesopotamia, seeming to indicate its location in the biblical Holy Land or somewhere close by.

For these reasons especially, the early interest that Muhammad's followers showed in restoring worship to the site of the Jewish Temple demands much greater prominence in discussions of Islam's formative history than it usually receives. Numerous sources, both Islamic and non-Islamic, identify the early efforts of Muhammad's followers to build a place of worship on the Temple Mount as a restoration of the Temple, and it appears that they established some sort of sacred structure there very soon after taking the city. The Dome of the Rock, thus, it would seem, was not the first place of worship that they built on the Temple Mount: instead it represents the culmination of their early building activities there. Such attention to these events in the non-Islamic sources is not altogether surprising, since they would have been highly visible to anyone in Jerusalem. Yet the non-Islamic sources also tell us with regularity that Muhammad's followers understood their efforts to restore worship to the Temple Mount as a restoration of the Jewish Temple itself. One could perhaps dismiss this report from a couple of sources, supposing that a Jewish or Christian author had leaped to this conclusion based on the location in which Muhammad's followers were building. But persistence of this witness across many independent sources suggests that there is more to these reports than just naive assumption—all the more so given that the Islamic tradition confirms that restoration of the Temple seems to have been a central aim of Muhammad's new religious movement.

The Islamic tradition, and particularly its eschatological traditions, frequently identifies the Dome of the Rock with the Temple and (following Jewish tradition) the sacred rock at its center as the Foundation Stone of creation, on which the Ark of the Covenant previously rested in the Holy of Holies of the Jewish Temple.[24] Presumably Muhammad's followers did not understand the Dome and its predecessors as an actual restoration of the Temple, since, among other reasons, there was no resumption of the Temple's sacrificial cult. Instead, they seem to have envisioned what amounted to an ersatz Temple intended to restore dignity and worship to this this most holy place, which for nearly six hundred years had lain as "the abomination of desolation" (Mark 13.14). The true Temple, presumably, was soon to be restored by God in the events of the eschaton, the end of the world, which Muhammad and his followers expected to arrive in the immediate future. Indeed, the eschatological links between the Dome of the Rock and the anticipated restoration of the Temple in the Islamic tradition signal the apocalyptic context of Jerusalem's liberation by Muhammad's early followers, as do the peculiar rituals that they are said to have performed to reverence the sacred Foundation Stone in the Dome during its early years.

Two separate Islamic sources describe the ritual practices that Muhammad's early followers initially observed inside the Dome of the Rock, and these rites stand in sharp contrast with later, traditional views of the Dome and its significance. It is true that both sources are relatively late, from the eleventh and thirteenth centuries, and are not always historically reliable on every point. Yet the ceremonies that the texts describe are so anomalous with the later traditions of the Dome of the Rock and subsequent Islamic practice that they must reflect primitive rites that were observed only during the early decades of the shrine's existence. Indeed, it is extremely difficult to imagine their observance at any later date, and there is moreover no good reason to suspect that someone invented a completely fictitious set of detailed rituals for the Dome of the Rock that deviate so significantly from later Islamic tradition and practice.

According to these reports, the shrine and its Rock were served by three hundred ritual attendants, as well as two hundred gatekeepers, ten for each of its gates, and a staff of Jews and Christians who cleaned the sanctuary and provided glass and wicks for its lamps and goblets.[25] The Dome was open for public worship only on Mondays and Thursdays; on other days only its attendants were allowed inside. The rituals for these two days commenced the evening before, the customary beginning of the day in Jewish and Christian liturgical time, as the Dome's attendants prepared a complex perfume that would sit overnight. On Monday and Thursday morning, the attendants purified themselves with ritual washing and put on special ceremonial garments. Following these preparations, they rubbed the sacred Rock at the Dome's center with perfume and burned incense all around it, thereafter lowering the curtains that surrounded the Rock "so that the incense encircles the *Ṣakhra* [the Rock] entirely and the odour [of the incense] clings to it."[26] Once the Rock and its surroundings were suffused with intense fragrance, the curtains were lifted, and a crier went out to the market calling the faithful to come to the Rock for prayer. The public was then allowed in to pray in the presence of the sacred Rock and its intense fragrance, but only for a brief time, allowing for just two prayer cycles or perhaps at most four according to one account. The meaning of these rituals is admittedly not entirely clear, and unfortunately the texts describing them offer no explanation. To my knowledge, only Moshe Sharon has ventured an interpretation of these practices, which he explains in relation to Jewish traditions about the Temple and its impending eschatological restoration, an understanding of the Dome of the Rock that is loudly echoed in the Islamic eschatological tradition.[27]

The Community of the Believers:
An Inter-confessional Abrahamic Movement?

The genetic link between the Dome of the Rock and the Jewish Temple coincides with the related importance of a renewed Abrahamic identity at the heart of Muhammad's new religious movement. On this basis, Muhammad and his followers were determined, it would appear, to liberate the biblical Holy Land of their Abrahamic patrimony from the sinful Romans who were illicitly occupying it. Several sources in this volume indicate the importance of reclaiming the Promised Land of the Abrahamic inheritance as a key tenet of this nascent faith, especially the *Chronicle* of Sebeos (chapter 6) and the *Secrets of Rabbi Shimʿōn b. Yoḥai* (chapter 12). Yet again, like the Temple traditions just discussed, this theme is also evident in the Qurʾan and the early Islamic tradition, as noted in the commentaries on these two sources in particular. Likewise, the complex relationship between Muhammad's new religious community and the Jewish religious tradition stems from their common roots in the idea of Abrahamic descent. There is little question that in its early history Muhammad's religious movement was closely linked to Judaism, and it welcomed Jewish members into its community even as they retained their Jewish faith, practice, and identity. The Islamic tradition itself reports this fact and is often at pains to apologize for this embarrassing early accommodation of the Jews. The only question, in fact, for the historian is how long Muhammad's new religious community continued to welcome Jews *as Jews* to full membership, without expecting their conversion to a new, different religious faith.

According to the Islamic historical tradition, this inclusion of the Jews was a brief experiment by Muhammad, attempted early on as a sign of his tolerance and willingness to compromise, but he quickly abandoned it once he recognized their perfidy. Yet we should not take this account simply at face value, since, as noted, the Islamic historical tradition is keen to minimize this awkward moment from its past: it was a problematic memory for a faith that by the time these histories were finally written had come to distinguish itself sharply from Jews and Judaism, which it often viewed quite negatively. To the contrary, there is strong evidence to suggest that the confessional boundaries of the religious community that Muhammad founded remained fluid much longer than the Islamic historical tradition could comfortably remember. Indeed, as Donner has recently argued, convincingly in my opinion, Muhammad's new religious community was open not only to Jews but Christians as well, who were included as full members of the community while remaining in their original faith for decades beyond Muhammad's death. As Donner observes, this primitive community does not seem to have identified itself as new religious confession called Islam whose adherents were Muslims. Rather, Muhammad's followers took up the name "the community of the Believers," as indicated by the Qur'an, which regularly designates those who follow the faith that it enjoins as "Believers."

According to Donner, then, Muhammad and his followers did not initially conceive of themselves as "a separate religious confession distinct from others" during the first several decades of the movement's existence.[28] Instead, the earliest "Islamic" community appears to have been a loosely organized confederation of Abrahamic monotheists "who shared Muhammad's intense belief in one God and in the impending arrival of the Last Day, and who joined together to carry out what they saw as the urgent task of establishing righteousness on earth—at least within their own community of Believers, and, when possible, outside it—in preparation for the End."[29] This new religious movement was not, as Donner explains, so much "a new and distinct religious confession" as a "monotheistic reform movement" committed to advancing personal and communal piety in the face of a swiftly approaching final judgment.[30]

There is widespread scholarly agreement that in its early stages Muhammad's religious movement was indeed something like this, at least for a time, as evidenced by the so-called "Constitution of Medina."[31] A broad consensus exists among scholars of early Islam that this document is a very early source, probably from the lifetime of Muhammad himself, since its content has such pronounced discontinuity with the ethnic and religious boundaries established in later Islam. The Constitution of Medina preserves an agreement between Muhammad and the Jews of Medina (as well as Medina's other inhabitants), wherein certain Jewish tribes were incorporated within Muhammad's new religious polity, even as they were allowed to retain their Jewish identity and follow the Jewish law and scripture. In defining the relations between two groups identified as the Believers (*Mu'minūn*) and the Muslims (*Muslimūn*), the Constitution declares the Jews to be "a people with the Believers, the Jews having their law and the Muslims having their law. [This applies to] their clients and to themselves, excepting anyone who acts wrongfully and commits crimes/acts treacherously/breaks an agreement, for he but slays himself and the people of his house."[32] In addition, the Jews are expected to "pay [their] share," while the Constitution's only doctrinal condition mandates profession of belief "in God and the Last Day."[33] As one can see, the Constitution outlines precisely the sort of inter-confessional community that Donner proposes, and so we may conclude that Jews were included as members of the community of the Believers alongside the newly converted "Muslim" Believers while remaining in their faith, at least for some period of time in its early history.[34]

Donner identifies similar evidence for inclusion of Jews and Christians within the early community of the Believers in the Qur'an as well. The Qur'an frequently refers to the "people(s) of the Book" (the *ahl al-kitāb*) in very positive terms, often seeming to indicate that these peoples, Jews and Christians in particular, were part of the Qur'an's religious community. Qur'an 2.62 and 5.69, for instance, identify those Jews, Christians, and Sabians "who Believe in God and the Last Day" as part of the community of Believers: as the Believers, they have nothing to fear or regret. Faith in God and the last day again emerges in these passages as the requirement for membership in the community, and confession of these two tenets "secures salvation" and "transcends the communal distinctions between Jew, Sabian, Christian, etc."[35] Similar notions regarding Jews and Christians appear in numerous other Qur'anic passages, as Donner demonstrates, indicating that there must have been some Jews and Christians within the community of the Believers, even as they continued to retain their identities as Jews and Christians. The only requirements for salvation, according to the Qur'an, seem to be belief in the God of Abraham and faith in the approaching eschaton, together with moral behavior.

The early Believers thus professed a simple creed that transcended membership in a particular monotheist community. Muhammad, for his part, appears to have served primarily as an "arbiter" among the members of this inter-confessional community and their spiritual guide, rather than a prophet with a new dispensation. Accordingly, the Qur'an expects that Jewish and Christian members of the community will remain faithful to their own "covenants," which will bring them salvation together with the other the Believers at the swiftly approaching last day.[36] It is true that many passages in the Qur'an speak negatively of the Jews and Christians, but as Donner rightly observes, in these instances the Qur'an is usually quite specific in censuring only some—and not all—of the peoples of the Book.[37] Presumably, these negative remarks about Jews and Christians are directed against those members of those communities that refused to associate themselves with the Believers, while the very positive references describe those Jews and Christians who were among the Believers.[38] Robert Hoyland likewise concludes that the earliest evidence reveals Muhammad's religious movement as "a single politico-religious community uniting different religious denominations under the 'protection of God' to fight on His behalf. The only requirement was that every signatory 'affirm what is in this document [the Constitution of Medina] and believe in God and the Last Day,' accept God and Muhammad as the ultimate arbiter for all parties, 'help one another against whomsoever fights the people of this document' and contribute to the war effort." This policy, Hoyland suggests, extended under the early caliphs, who were leaders of a religious polity comprising members of various "different religious affiliations whose overriding aim was the expansion of the state in the name of God and who shared a belief in the One God and the Last Day."[39]

Michael Penn and Jack Tannous have both recently introduced a wealth of data from the seventh century that seems to confirm that Muhammad's early followers and many contemporary Christians embraced such religious complexity and hybridity in the manner that Donner and Hoyland describe.[40] Nevertheless, it is surprising to find that, despite such convergence, Tannous seeks to separate his findings from any proposal that Muhammad's new religious movement was confessionally complex and included Jews and Christians who remained in their faith yet recognized his prophetic leadership. Tannous urges readers to reject the idea that Muhammad's new religious movement "stemmed from a consciously inclusive ideology," "an explicitly ecumenical ideology," and "a top-down ideology of religiously motivated tolerance."[41] The insistence here on some sort of deliberate intention greatly misses the point, I think. Muhammad (along with others in his movement) was not, I suspect, consciously and explicitly articulating an "ecumenical ideology" from the top down. Nor were deeply held theological principles about inclusiveness and tolerance at play: Donner himself does not introduce either concept in his work, and the very suggestion of these ideas by Tannous is highly anachronistic and makes a straw man out of the hypothesis.[42] To the contrary, the confessional complexity of Muhammad's early community was almost certainly an ad hoc mixture of closely related monotheisms struggling together to further the cause of righteousness and piety in advance of the approaching eschaton. And those who stood in the way of their devout polity and its divine mission were met with violence.

Likewise, Tannous sees the Qur'an's attacks on the Christian doctrine of the Trinity as incompatible with this hypothesis, an objection that others have brought as well. Yet, too often, it seems to me, judgments against this hypothesis on the basis of Christian Trinitarianism seem to have already accepted the critique that such belief is not truly monotheistic, which is not in fact accurate.[43] Moreover, in the same volume, Tannous notes at some length that there is considerable "evidence for confusion about, lack of knowledge of, and disregard for Prophetic and Qurʾānic teaching in the early decades of Muslim rule in the Middle East." He further observes that other than perhaps a small number of scholars, "significant numbers of the Prophet's community only took a real interest in his example and message long after he and those who knew him, or knew him best, had died."[44] Indeed, the near absence and ignorance of the Qurʾan among Muhammad's followers for most of the seventh century seems widely acknowledged. As Nicolai Sinai, for instance, writes: "the Quran may well have reached closure as early as 650, but nevertheless remained absent from Islamic history until c. 700, when it was secondarily co-opted, without much revision, into an existent religious tradition."[45] Even Theodor Nöldeke had to acknowledge that "as far as the Koran is concerned, the ignorance of the average believer in the early years of Islam was beyond imagination."[46] Nevertheless, the fact that the broader community seems to have been largely ignorant of the Qurʾan's contents for so long does not mean, one should note, that we cannot continue to look to this collection as our best witness to the religious beliefs of Muhammad and his earliest followers as they crystalized in the collective memory of the Believers during the seventh century. Whether the Qurʾan was broadly received as authoritative within the earliest community is a separate issue from the fact that this text is indeed the earliest collection of religious teaching from the new religious movement that Muhammad founded, whose followers ascribed its contents in some sense to their founder.

Accordingly, we should expect that the Qurʾan's anti-Trinitarian passages—which, one should note, are also balanced by other passages that appear to seek convergence with Christian views about Christ[47]—would have had little impact on the confessional boundaries of Muhammad's early religious community. From such a perspective, we should not necessarily assume that the divinity of Jesus was initially a deal breaker, as it were, for inclusion within Muhammad's new religious movement.[48] Only as the community gradually evolved into a distinctively Islamic confession of faith did this doctrine emerge as a primary boundary between Christianity and Muhammad's new revelation of monotheism. Indeed, the emphasis on Muhammad's unique status among the prophets also seems to be a later development, not present in the Qur'an, which seems to regard all prophets as equals.[49] If, then, we envision a group of monotheists—Jews, Christians, and Arabs—gathered together initially under the banner of Muhamad's preaching of God and the last day, it is easy to imagine how the doctrines of the Trinity and the divinity of Jesus could over time have become contentious issues, especially between Jewish and Christian members of the community. It would appear that, in this case, the momentum was, for whatever reason, ultimately in favor of a lower Christology, which I suspect must have been more palatable to the majority of the movement's members. Jesus, his messiahship, his miraculous birth, and other Christian traditions were less problematic and so could all be retained. The Trinity and Christ's divinity, however, were proscribed because they chafed against the monotheism that was central to the group's identity. Still, Christ's prominence in other aspects of the Islamic tradition, in eschatology, mysticism, and reverence his mother, for instance, reflect what was clearly a significant Christian contribution to the formation of the community of the Believers.

Thus, I think that we should not look for anti-Trinitarianism or a rejection of Christ's divinity at the beginnings of Muhammad's movement; instead, we should see these positions as products of the "sectarian milieu" within which Islam was forming its confessional identity. These were not positions that Muhammad or the Qur'an took from some shadowy, historically improbable group of Judeo-Christians hiding somewhere in the Hijaz. Rather, the Qur'an's Christology emerged from the mixture of monotheisms shared among the early Believers. As the community moved to exclude belief in Christ's divinity and a triune God, Christian Believers must have faced a choice: either break with Muhammad's community in favor of the Christian faith or adjust their beliefs about Jesus according to the evolving nature of the new faith that they had embraced. I more than suspect that many Christian Believers may have opted for the latter option. In the face of eschatological conviction and political turmoil, one can easily imagine their willingness to believe that God had raised up a new prophet for these troubling times. Indeed, the fact that Christians over the centuries have in large numbers abandoned faith in Christ's divinity in favor of Muhammad and the Qur'an shows that this would certainly not be unexpected, especially as these Believers could remain a part of Muhammad's eschatological community of the righteous in order to meet the quickly approaching judgment of the Hour.

The Qur'an

It is certainly worth noting that the Qur'an's marginal status within the early community is affirmed by the witness of the non-Islamic sources, including all of those translated in this volume. The Jews and Christians of the seventh century seem to have had no idea at all that Muhammad's followers had a distinctive scripture of their own, and it would appear that, in effect, they did not. The first non-Islamic source to show awareness of an Islamic scripture was long thought to be the *Disputation between a Muslim and a Monk of Bēt Ḥālē*, but this text has now been dated to the later eighth or even early ninth century. Accordingly, unless I have missed something, this honor now belongs to both John of Damascus and the Roman Emperor Leo III, who seem to stand in a virtual tie.

John of Damascus, in a text composed during the 730s, describes certain writings attributed to Muhammad by his followers, some of which clearly correspond with parts of the Qur'an and others that do not.[50] Although John's text is polemical, to be sure, one should not write off his account of this new religious community and its sacred writings so quickly.[51] John was in a position to be extremely well informed about Muhammad's followers, their internal affairs, and the content of their faith. John's grandfather had been the financial governor of Damascus and Syria during the final years of Roman rule, a role that his father would assume after the transition to the rule of the Believers. John's father, Sarjūn ibn Manṣūr, served as secretary for each of the first Umayyad caliphs—from Muʿāwiya (661–80) to ʿAbd al-Malik (685–705), with responsibility for taxation and the caliphal treasury. John himself later followed his father into the caliphal administration, serving also as secretary and financial officer for ʿAbd al-Malik before he departed for Jerusalem early in the eighth century to live out the remainder of his life as a monk.[52]

Accordingly, one must recognize that "John was well-positioned to have gathered some of the best information about Islam that could be acquired [in Damascus]."[53] Indeed, it is likely that John would have been better informed than most Muslims regarding the affairs of the caliphate, including any official doctrines or scriptures that they were attempting to promulgate. John mentions four writings ascribed to Muhammad by his followers by name, and he seemingly identifies each of these as individual writings that are not yet parts of a single work. Three of these writings have names identical or very similar to certain suras of the Qur'an: "the writing of the Woman, the Table, and the Cow" (suras 4, 5, and 2 respectively). Nevertheless, John's description of the writing of the Woman does not correspond at all with the Qur'anic sura "the Women."[54] As for the fourth writing that he mentions, "the Camel of God," most of what John ascribes to this writing does not find parallels in the Qur'an, although we do find traces of similar traditions elsewhere in early Islamic literature. It appears that John had before his eyes some sort of Qur'anic "apocryphon" with this title that has since vanished, except perhaps for a few traces in the Qur'an.[55]

As for emperor Leo III, several Christian historical writers of the ninth and tenth centuries report an exchange of letters between Leo III (717–40) and the Umayyad caliph ʿUmar II (717–20), a report that we now know ultimately derived from a vanished chronicle by the eighth-century polymath Theophilus of Edessa that was their collective source.[56] And as it turns out, letters from each of these two rulers to the other have in fact come down to us, preserved within their respective tradition: Leo's letter survives in Christian sources, while ʿUmar's has come down through Islamic channels. Scholars of course are not so naive as to assume that we have in these two documents writings from the actual hands of Leo and ʿUmar themselves. Nevertheless, there is now a fairly broad consensus that what has come down to us in this correspondence "is an amalgamation of several letters written either by the two leaders, or two persons living in the early eighth century."[57] Indeed, the Letter of Leo III to ʿUmar II, which is the writing that concerns us, survives in the Armenian *Chronicle* of Łewond, a text written in the later eighth century.[58] Thus, there seems to be little room for any doubt that the Letter of Leo III to ʿUmar II, whoever wrote it, is a Christian critique of Islam composed in the early eighth century, most likely sometime before 730, as Peter Schadler persuasively argues, approximately the same time, then, that John of Damascus was writing.[59]

In his letter, "Leo" reports that the Qur'an was produced by "a certain al-Ḥajjāj, who was appointed governor of Persia by you, who gathered all your ancient books and wrote another according to his taste and distributed it throughout all your lands. For such a thing was quite easy to accomplish with a single people with a single language, as it was in fact done—excepting only a few works of Abu Turab [i.e., ʿAlī ibn ʾAbī Ṭālib], for al-Ḥajjāj was not able to destroy them completely."[60] This al-Ḥajjāj was a highly influential and notorious figure of the age, who served the caliph ʿAbd al-Malik and his son al-Walīd (705–15) as viceroy of the caliphate and governor of Iraq. According to a number of reports from the Islamic tradition as well as other contemporary Christian sources, it was al-Ḥajjāj, working in the service of ʿAbd al-Malik, who first composed the Qurʾan, rather than Uthmān or one of the other early caliphs, as the canonical Sunni narrative relates. Leo III's near contemporary report of the Qurʾan's composition under al-Ḥajjāj offers strong support for this tradition against the other reports in the early Islamic tradition. Likewise, John of Damascus's description of the writings attributed to Muhammad by his followers certainly does not sound much like the Qurʾan that we have today.[61] Accordingly, for a variety of reasons, as I have explained elsewhere, it seems most likely that the Qurʾan was in fact composed under al-Ḥajjāj's supervision and authority.[62] This final version was imposed on the Muslim citizens of the caliphate by imperial authority around the turn of the eighth century, displacing other earlier versions that were rounded up and destroyed by the government authorities, as both Leo III and the Islamic tradition relate.

Prior to these two Christian texts, both from around 730, no other writer shows any awareness *at all* that Muhammad's followers have a sacred book of their own. This long silence should certainly give us pause, and it raises significant questions about the history and status of the Qurʾan during the first Islamic century. Sinai's curt dismissal of this evidence as "of course easy to impugn" is thus worryingly cavalier.[63] The Jews and Christians of late antiquity were peoples for whom the authority of a sacred book was paramount. Surely, they would have been curious and inquisitive as to whether these newly arrived Abrahamic monotheists had a scripture of their own. And yet they show complete ignorance of any distinctive corpus of scripture claimed by Muhammad's followers until the middle of the eighth century. For instance, Hoyland, in his massive catalog of non-Islamic witnesses to early Islam, identifies at least sixty such sources from the first Islamic century—not all of which we could include, or indeed, would want to include in the present volume.[64] Yet none of these sources contains any mention whatsoever of an Islamic sacred writing used in any capacity at all, let alone something called the Qur'an. This lengthy collective silence is quite telling: such silence, as they say, speaks volumes.

Although the hypothesis of an early multi-confessional religious community is admittedly not entirely unproblematic, it nonetheless presents a much more persuasive synthesis of the earliest evidence than the traditional Islamic accounts provide. It is by far the best explanation of the nature of the earliest community and its development in light of the full range of the available evidence that I have found. In the pages to follow, one will find that Donner's hypothesis correlates well with many of the reports coming from contemporary non-Islamic sources, which is certainly one of its great strengths, although, as we will see, this is certainly not the case in every instance. Indeed, one of the topics on which there is some significant difference of opinion in the non-Islamic sources concerns the attitudes that Muhammad's followers took toward other religious confessions, their members, their sacred places, and holy objects once they established their hegemony. Some sources, as we will see, such as the *Chronicle* of Sebeos (chapter 6) and the *Secrets of Rabbi Shim'ōn b. Yoḥai* (chapter 12), seem to require something like Donner's hypothesis to explain their accounts. Yet according to other voices from this era, Muhammad's followers were not always tolerant of other confessions and would treat them quite badly. It is not entirely clear how to reconcile this discrepancy, yet, as proposed in the commentaries below, it may simply be a matter of different policies in different places—or even more likely, perhaps, a matter of an official policy from the movement's leadership that was not always followed out in every place on the ground. The region was, after all, an active theater of war for most of this era, and incidents of violence beyond official policy unfortunately are not at all uncommon in such circumstances.

Apocalypticism and Martyrdom, Conquest and Conversion

Another important theme that we find in these sources, one that we have already mentioned, is apocalypticism and eschatological expectation. Belief that divine judgment and the end of the world were at hand characterized the age that saw the rise of Islam more generally and likewise stood at the core of the religious message espoused by Muhammad and believed by his earliest followers.[65] Recent research on the beginnings of Islam has shown that Muhammad and his earliest followers in fact almost certainly were expecting the eschaton, the end of the world, at any moment, seemingly in their own lifetimes. Indeed, this belief appears to be connected with their fervor to liberate the biblical Holy Land and Jerusalem from occupation by the infidel Romans.[66] The fact that Jerusalem and its Temple Mount remain center stage for the events of the end times even in contemporary Islam is a sure sign of Jerusalem's eschatological importance in the worldview of Muhammad and his earliest followers. Likewise, the Believers' keen interest in restoring worship to the Temple Mount almost immediately after the liberation of Jerusalem, mentioned above, relates to their apocalyptic expectations, as indicated by the eschatological links between the Dome of the Rock and the anticipated divine restoration of the Temple. Several of the sources in this volume indicate the eschatological impulse at the heart of this new religious movement, including some indications of messianic expectation.

When the Jews and Christians responded to the rise of Islam and sought to make sense of the dramatic changes that they faced, they too often turned to the apocalyptic genre. Such a response is hardly surprising, since, as we noted, apocalyptic expectations were already at a peak when Muhammad's followers first entered the Mediterranean world. The present volume includes several examples of this broader apocalyptic trend in the literature of the age. Christians also responded to the rise of Islamic hegemony by returning to the traditions of martyrdom and martyrology, and we include two examples of this phenomenon in this volume. Nevertheless, this revival of martyrdoms becomes more characteristic of the Christian response to Islamic dominion just after the period we have in view, during the later eighth and ninth centuries. In these years the martyr's *Passion* suddenly reemerged as a popular literary genre, especially, but by no means exclusively, among the Chalcedonian communities of Syria and Palestine who had remained faithful to the imperial church. There are nearly a dozen such Melkite martyrdoms from the Umayyad and early Abbasid periods, hardly an explosion but clearly evidence of a newfound interest in this topic that had been so essential in the formation of early Christian identity.[67] Closely related to these martyrdoms is the matter of conversion to and from Islam, which often plays a pivotal role in the martyr's ultimate demise. Some of the texts in this volume highlight the complexities of religious identity and conversion in this period, describing the struggles of individuals who sought to navigate the confessional boundaries by occasionally moving back and forth between the Believers and Christianity. Certainly, many Christians understood there to be a boundary between these communities. And as we will find, there is evidence from the sources to suggest that even in these early years conversion to Islam may not have always been voluntary and that apostasy from Islam could be a capital offense.

The non-Islamic sources also occasionally give some details about the internal affairs of the early community of the Believers that would not otherwise be known as clearly from the traditional Islamic sources alone. Several of the sources relate important information about the military activities of Muhammad's followers during their invasion of the Roman and Sasanian empires, material that has been put to good use especially in Donner's book on the conquests mentioned above as well as Hoyland's recent study *In God's Path*. Likewise, the Syriac writer John Bar Penkaye (chapter 17) provides an invaluable contemporary account of some of the events of the Second Civil War among the Believers, while the *Passion of Peter of Capitolias* (chapter 19) gives some insight into how the early caliphs handled religious dissent. Yet one of the most striking aspects of these non-Islamic sources is their collective witness to a tradition that Muhammad was still alive and leading his followers as they took possession of the biblical Holy Land, the Promised Land of their Abrahamic inheritance. Although one might at first be tempted to dismiss such reports as a misunderstanding of Muhammad's role in the community as outsiders first learned about this new political and religious movement, the evidence is not so easily cast aside. At least eleven non-Islamic sources from the seventh and eighth century report this information, in almost every case independently. Even a stray Islamic source also describes Muhammad as still alive and leading his followers as they left the deserts of Arabia and set off to engage the armies of the Romans and Persians.[68]

Indeed, the evidence indicating Muhammad's longevity into the period of his community's expansion into the Near East is of extremely high historical quality, even if it is contradicted by the much later accounts of the end of his life in the traditional Islamic biographies. These biographies, however, were again written only more than one hundred years after his death, on the basis of a very narrow tradition purporting to derive from an oral transmission all the way back to the life of Muhammad himself. By comparison, then, the traditional Islamic accounts of the end of Muhammad's life are historical sources of especially poor quality, even if they are the officially sanctioned narratives of the Islamic tradition. We must therefore give serious consideration to the well-attested countertradition that Muhammad was still alive at the time of the invasion of the Roman Near East. Clearly such a tradition was in broad circulation during the early Islamic centuries, indeed as early as 634 it would seem. Yet this does not mean that we must revise the date of Muhammad's death from 632 to 635. Rather, the larger and more significant point is that we do not in fact know nearly as much about Muhammad and his life—or death—as scholars have long assumed. In this regard, one of the main things that students of early Islam can learn from studying the witness of these contemporary non-Islamic sources, then, is how unreliable the traditional Islamic narratives of the faith's origins and the life of its founding prophet often are as historical sources and move accordingly to treat them with greater suspicion and skepticism in reconstructing the early history of Muhammad's new religious movement.

Some Terminology

Before turning to the texts, it would perhaps be useful to conclude with a word about nomenclature, particularly regarding the names given to Muhammad's followers during this period, not only by the sources in this volume but by modern scholars as well. In the translations, we have generally reproduced the names the sources give to Muhammad's followers, even when these may be considered derogatory. *Saracens* is the most common term in the Greek and Latin sources, following a late classical tradition. In the Syriac world, however, the most common term used to describe them is the *Tayyāyē*, a word that is often translated simply as "Arabs." Nevertheless, as Fred Donner rightly notes, *Tayyāyē* is "a standard Syriac designation for nomads—a word that cannot be considered an effort to replicate Arabic *al-ʿarab*, and should not blithely be translated as 'Arab,' which decidedly rings of conceptions of ethnic nationalism that arose only in the nineteenth century."[69] "Arab" is to be avoided as a translation all the more so since Arab identity seems to have developed only as a result of the process of Islamicization at the end of the seventh century and was not an operative concept for Muhammad's early followers. *Tayyāyē* is, in effect, the Syriac (and, through borrowing, Persian) equivalent of "Saracens" rather than "Arabs."[70] Accordingly, we have translated this word as "Nomads" rather than "Arabs," since the latter would be inaccurate and anachronistic. To use instead the transliteration *"tayyāyē,"* as we effectively do with Saracens, would likely be too unfamiliar and awkward for many readers. Thus we have opted for "Nomads," which, while not perfect, at least partly serves the purpose of highlighting the problematic nature of the underlying terminology. One Syriac author in this volume uses the term *"mhaggrāyē"* to describe Muhammad's followers, a term used more commonly in later Syriac sources. Although some scholars would interpret this term as "Hagarene" in reference to the Ishmaelite identity of the Nomads, the term much more likely reflects their self-designation as *Muhājirūn*, or "Emigrants," a common term in the Qur'an and the early Islamic tradition.[71]

No less complex is how to name the religious movement founded by Muhammad during first decades of its existence. Of course, this movement would eventually yield the religious tradition that came to be called Islam, and therefore one could opt to name the faith Islam and its adherents Muslims from the very start. Yet to do so obscures an important historical point: it is not at all clear that the faith and practice of Muhammad and his earliest followers was identical with the religious faith that would eventually emerge as Islam. Indeed, the development of this faith tradition from the religious movement founded by Muhammad and observed by his followers during the seventh century into the classical Islamic tradition of the later eighth century and beyond is precisely what interests the historian of religion. There is little evidence, in fact, that Muhammad and his earliest followers referred to the members of their community as Muslims or their religious beliefs and practices as Islam.

The first external reference to the community of the Believers as Muslims or Islam does not occur until 775 CE, in the Syriac *Chronicle of Zuqnin*, while the first Islamic reference outside of the Qur'an appears only in an inscription on the Dome of the Rock, which nonetheless quotes from the Qur'an (3.19). Yet the latter instance is itself problematic: in the Qur'an, *Islam*, which means "submission," refers to the attitude a Believer is expected to take toward God rather than being a term of communal self-designation.[72] Perhaps the use of this verse in the inscriptions of the Dome of the Rock may have had the intent of naming group identity for Muhammad's followers in relation to the other Abrahamic monotheists of the medieval Near East. Nevertheless, the usage of this term in the Qur'an itself offers no basis for this claim. In effect, then, the first non-Qur'anic evidence with clear reference to Muhammad's followers as Muslims is found in inscriptions from the early eighth century—more than one hundred years after Muhammad's *hijra* and the founding of the community.[73]

Moreover, in the earliest Islamic sources it seems that the term *Muslim* refers only to a subset within the broader "community of the Believers," the name most commonly used by the Qur'an and the early tradition for Muhammad's followers. Prior to the third quarter of the first Islamic century, Donner maintains that the term *Muslims* referred merely to one subgroup among the early "Believers." As much is indicated, for instance, by several Qur'anic passages that appear to distinguish two such overlapping groups within the early community. As Donner explains, in the early history of the community of the Believers, the name *Muslim* came to apply to those non-Jews and Christians who had newly converted to monotheism as a result of Muhammad's teaching and joined his confessionally diverse confederation of Abrahamic monotheists. While Jewish and

Christian Believers could continue to be identified as such, converts from "paganism" to Abrahamic monotheism could no longer be known by their former confession: "pagan Believers" obviously would not work. Yet when Muhammad's followers later began to distance themselves from Judaism and Christianity and establish a confessionally distinct monotheist sect, *Islam* and *Muslim* were thus the terms adopted to distinguish this new monotheism from the Jews and Christians that it once welcomed.[74]

Accordingly, we have tried assiduously to avoid using the terms *Muslim* and *Islam* in reference to the new religious movement founded by Muhammad in this volume, preferring instead "Believers" or "community of the Believers" when some sort of name is necessary. We have done so precisely because it is hoped that these texts will problematize for readers the easy historical slippage between later Islam and this early religious community, which seems to have held different beliefs and practices. There have been similar efforts, for instance, to identify terminology for naming the religious movement of Jesus and his earliest followers, which was likewise quite different in nature from the Christian faith that would eventually emerge from it. Scholars have often experimented with such designations as "the Jesus movement" for this early stage or "the Way."[75] Nevertheless, given that the profound differences between the nature of the primitive community and later Christianity are widely recognized in scholarship, such careful terminology seems less necessary in the study of Christian origins than it currently does in Islamic origins.

In the main, I have opted to refer to the religious group in question as Muhammad's new religious movement; the community that Muhammad founded; Muhammad's followers; the faith and practice of Muhammad's religious movement/community, and other similarly vague yet more accurate descriptors. Such terms allow us to remain as open as possible to the nature of the religious phenomenon in view and its subsequent development. Some more skeptical scholars, I should note, have criticized me in this regard for placing too much confidence in Muhammad's importance within this nascent religious community. Muhammad's role in this religious movement and his significance for its early adherents in fact remain very open questions. Certainly, his status as a final prophet does not seem to have been fully formulated yet; his unique status among the prophets was certainly a later development, not evidenced in the Qur'an, which appears to regard all prophets as equals.[76] Muhammad's earliest followers seem to have understood him instead as one prophet standing in a long line of many equals whom God had called to warn of the impending last day and to spread a message of submission to God's commandments, which enjoined a rather generic version of shared late-ancient piety, as quickly as possible to as many people as possible in advance of the impending end of the world.[77] Accordingly, I have little doubt that from its earliest days the community of the Believers looked to Muhammad as its political and religious leader, even though its members did not yet accredit Muhammad with a new religious dispensation or unique prophetic authority. Indeed, I think it is safe to assume that the members of the community of the Believers believed that by following Muhammad's leadership and guidance, they would soon attain individual and collective salvation in the arrival of the last day.

There is one important term that we use throughout this study that may be unfamiliar to many readers who are not more familiar with the academic study of religion. This is the technical term *the eschaton*, originally a Greek word taken from the discourse of early Jewish and Christian apocalypticism.[78] *The eschaton* literally means "the end," and in this context we mean of course, the end of time, the end of history, the end of the universe, to be followed in Jewish, Christian, and Islamic belief, by the divine judgment and the eternal reign of God. Thus, the related term *eschatology* refers to the topic of the end-times, and beliefs and teachings related to this subject.

Finally, we should add a brief note on transliterations from Arabic. In cases where an Arabic word or name has a clear form in English, we have used this rather than transliterating the Arabic: Muhammad instead of Muḥammad; Qur'an instead of Qur'ān; Hijaz instead of Ḥijāz; sura instead of sūra, and so on. In cases where there is no clear equivalent in English, we have transliterated the Arabic using the American Library Association and the Library of Congress standard, which is commonly used and yields forms that are generally easy to recognize and remember.

1   *The Teaching of Jacob the Newly Baptized*
(July, 634 CE)

This early seventh-century text, often known by its Latin title, *Doctrina Iacobi nuper baptizati*, purports to relate several lengthy debates that took place among the Jews of North Africa in response to their forced baptism under Heraclius in 632.[1] In it, the members of this community debate whether they should embrace the conversion to Christianity that has been forced upon them. Not surprisingly, then, most of its contents have nothing at all to do with Muhammad or his new religious movement. Nevertheless, as the dialogue progresses, recent events in Holy Land eventually intrude and give what is the earliest account of the emergence of Muhammad's followers onto the world stage. The *Teaching of Jacob* is therefore one of the most important sources for understanding the earliest history of what would eventually become Islam. The text locates these alleged debates in July of 634, thus at the very moment when Muhammad's followers had first begun to enter the Roman Near East. Specific concern with the recent forced baptism and numerous references to other contemporary political events seem to confirm that the text was indeed composed sometime very close to this date, a matter on which there is a strong scholarly consensus.[2]

The text's author is a certain Joseph, who was one of the partic-ipants in the debates. Nevertheless, its central character is Jacob, a Jewish merchant from Palestine who, along with the others, had been forced to receive baptism while on an ill-timed business trip to Africa. As the text begins, Jacob addresses the other Jews who have been forced into baptism and declares that he has now come to recognize the truth of Christianity through a miraculous vision and careful study of the scriptures. Following an extensive instruc-tion and dialogue with his audience, Jacob successfully convinces these "newly baptized" Jews to embrace with their hearts the faith that they had recently received through compulsion. Several days later, however, and about halfway through the text, a new character appears: Justus, the unbaptized cousin of one of Jacob's pupils who has just arrived from Palestine. Justus is dismayed that his cousin and so many other Jews agreed to accept their Christian baptism, and he decides to debate the issue anew with Jacob before the group.

Not surprisingly, given that this is a Christian text, Jacob ulti-mately persuades Justus to convert as well. Yet, despite this rather predictable outcome, the text offers an incredibly rich source for understanding the history of the eastern Mediterranean at the piv-otal moment just after the Sasanian occupation and the Roman reconquest of the Near East, and right as Muhammad's followers were beginning to enter the region. Of course, Christian writing on Jews and Judaism is notoriously unreliable, frequently governed by caricatures and stereotypes with little relation to any historical reality. Accordingly, one might be tempted to discount this source along with any information that it purports to relate about the reli-gious cultures of the Mediterranean world in the early seventh cen-tury. Nevertheless, easy dismissal of the text and its contents on such grounds would be unwarranted; to the contrary, by nearly every measure the *Teaching of Jacob* appears to be a trustworthy source on such matters. In contrast to many other contemporary Christian writings on Judaism, the *Teaching of Jacob* presents a knowledge-able and realistic portrayal of late ancient Judaism and Jewish life such that it is, as David Olster remarks, "the exception that proves the rule."[3] Indeed, Olster concludes that its depiction of late ancient Judaism is so accurate and nuanced that it must have been composed with a Jewish audience in mind by an author who was himself a con-verted Jew.[4] Likewise, the *Teaching of Jacob* shows significant knowl-edge of Palestinian geography as well as contemporary events in North Africa, adding credibility to its purported origin within a com-munity of Palestinian Jews who found themselves in North Africa at this inopportune moment.[5]

The main passage that concerns us occurs in the aftermath of Jacob's debate with Justus, after the latter has converted. Here Justus relates the contents of a letter that his brother Abraham had recently sent him from Palestine with an update of current events. In it, Abra-ham describes the recent arrival of the Saracens who had entered the Holy Land under the leadership of a new prophet: obviously, this is Muhammad, although he is not specifically named. For good mea-sure, Abraham tells us that he personally investigated these new developments and confirmed them by speaking with individuals who had met this prophet.

The Teaching of Jacob the Newly Baptized V.16[6]

Justus answered and said, "Indeed you speak the truth, and this is the great salvation: to believe in Christ. For I confess to you, mas-ter Jacob, the complete truth. My brother Abraham wrote to me that a false prophet has appeared. Abraham writes, "When [Sergius] the *candidatus* was killed by the Saracens, I was in Caesarea, and I went by ship to Sykamina.[7] And they were saying, 'The *candidatus* has been killed,' and we Jews were overjoyed. And they were say-ing, 'A prophet has appeared, coming with the Saracens, and he is preaching the arrival of the anointed one who is to come, the Messiah.' And when I arrived in Sykamina, I visited an old man who was learned in the Scriptures, and I said to him, 'What can you tell me about the prophet who has appeared with the Saracens?' And he said to me, groaning loudly, 'He is false, for prophets do not come with a sword and a war-chariot. Truly the things set in motion today are deeds of anarchy, and I fear that somehow the first Christ that came, whom the Christians worship, was the one sent by God, and instead of him we will receive the Antichrist.[8] Truly, Isaiah said that we Jews will have a deceived and hardened heart until the entire earth is destroyed. But go, master Abraham, and find out about this prophet who has appeared.' And when I, Abraham, investigated thoroughly, I heard from those who had met him that one will find no truth in the so-called prophet, only the shedding of human blood. In fact, he says that he has the keys of paradise, which is impossible." These things my brother Abraham has written from the East.

Commentary

Several things are especially important in this account, including reference to the murder of the *candidatus* Sergius of Caesarea by the invading Saracens, an event known also from other sources.[9] More significantly, however, Abraham's letter reports that this prophet is coming with the Saracens, suggesting that Muhammad is still alive at this time, and he is proclaiming the imminent arrival of the Messiah. This is the first of several witnesses from the seventh century reporting that Muhammad was still living and leading his followers as they first entered the Roman (and Sasanian) Empire. Lacking knowledge of the much later reports to the contrary from the Islamic historical tradition, one would certainly read this passage as indicating that Muhammad was indeed still alive and "coming with the Saracens."[10]

As for the letter's report that Muhammad was "preaching the arrival of the anointed one who is to come, the Messiah," there is some question as to whether or not Muhammad may or may not have heralded the impending arrival of a Messiah who would follow him. Clearly, the *Teaching of Jacob* here mirrors the powerful apocalyptic charge that Muhammad's message held as well as the eschatological expectations of his earliest followers. The Qur'an and other early materials from the Islamic tradition indicate quite clearly that imminent eschatology, a conviction that the end of the world was at hand, was central in Muhammad's preaching and the faith of his followers.[11] Yet it is also possible that the Messiah's promised advent reflects the Jewish context of this source, in which the apocalypticism of Muhammad and the Believers has been refracted through the lens of Jewish eschatological expectations. For a Jewish audience, the eschaton's impending arrival meant that the Messiah soon would appear along with it.[12] As we will see, the *Secrets of Rabbi Shim ̄on b. Yoḥai*, a late ancient Jewish apocalypse also included in the present volume, similarly reports that Muhammad and his followers were expecting the Messiah's immediate advent.[13] Indeed, Muhammad's new religious movement emerged within a religious landscape that was highly charged with eschatological expectations among Christians, Jews, and even Zoroastrians.[14]

At the same time, however, we should not rule out the possibility that the report is accurate, and that Muhammad and his early followers were in fact awaiting the arrival of some sort of messianic figure. In such a case, their expectation of the imminent second coming of Jesus Christ, the Messiah, emerges as a likely possibility. Jesus is regularly named the Messiah in the Qur'an (e.g., 3:45, 4:157, 171–72, 5:17, 72, 75, 9:30–31), and the Qur'an itself expects Jesus to return just before the Hour, as one of its signs. The most important passage associating his return with the Hour's arrival is 43:57–61. According to its canonical vocalization, the final verse of this passage proclaims that the subject of the Qur'an's revelation is nothing less than "knowledge of the Hour [i.e., the eschaton]; doubt not concerning it" (43:61), a reading that, in its own right, seems to highlight the imminent eschatology that prevailed within Muhammad's teaching and his new religious movement. Yet, according to an early alternative vocalization, the canonical form "knowledge (*'ilm*) of the Hour" should instead be read as "a sign (*'alam*) of the Hour."[15] Since Jesus is the subject of the immediately preceding verses, by this reading he remains the subject of verse 61, so that Jesus the Messiah is identified as "a sign of the Hour; doubt not concerning it and follow me."

As Sean Anthony and Muhammad Ali Amir-Moezzi have both noted (among others), there is good reason to suspect that this alternative vocalization was in fact the primitive one.[16] This variant reading not only makes better sense of the passage, but it also comports with our understanding of the early development of the Islamic apocalyptic tradition. Elsewhere, for instance, the Qur'an portends that Jesus will be present for the Final Judgment, when he will serve as a witness against the people of the Book (4:159), a passage that seems to confirm the variant reading. Moreover, this noncanonical reading's dissonance with the later Islamic tradition and its agreement with major tendencies identified by David Cook in the early apocalyptic tradition also vouch for its antiquity. Christ's return at the eschaton is attested in a number of early *ḥadīth*, whose antiquity is highly probable, since it is unlikely that later Muslims would have successfully forged traditions so discordant with other orthodoxies of what eventually became "classical" Islam.[17] Indeed, as David Cook observes, Jesus was in all likelihood the first messianic figure in Islam. Otherwise, it is once again difficult to understand why his return occupies such a prominent role in Islamic eschatology to this day. The fact that the later tradition shows significant concern to diminish his primary eschatological role further seems to indicate the antiquity of this tradition.[18] Accordingly, it appears that expectation of Christ's return at the eschaton was likely proclaimed in the Qur'an and was a part of the primitive kerygma of its community's faith. Thus, Abraham's report that this prophet was preaching the Messiah's arrival appears to find confirmation in the Qur'an and the early Islamic apocalyptic tradition.

Abraham also indicates that he consulted "an old man who was learned in the Scriptures" for his opinion on this new prophet. The sage replied that "he is false, for prophets do not come with a sword and a war-chariot," and he encouraged Abraham to look into the matter himself more carefully. Abraham then continues to relate the results of his inquiry: "When I investigated thoroughly, I heard from those who had met him that one will find no truth in the so-called prophet, only the shedding of human blood." For good measure, Abraham also reports that this prophet "says that he has the keys of paradise, which is impossible."[19] As Sean Anthony recently explains, Muhammad's alleged claim to possess the keys of paradise also seems to reflect an important belief held by Muhammad and his earliest followers, as Cook and Crone first noted in *Hagarism*.[20] Obviously, as Anthony notes, this claim is eschatological, yet no less important is its strong association with the military campaigns of the Umayyads in the early Islamic historical tradition. Several traditions link the Umayyad conquest ideology with the keys of paradise, which suggests that this motif in the *Teaching of Jacob* offers "an early testimony to the doctrine of *jihād* procuring believers access to paradise."[21]

On the whole, then, this testimony would appear to be a very high-quality witness to the earliest history of Muhammad's new religious movement. It is contemporary with the events that it describes, and it purports to derive its information from an eyewitness source in Palestine who had confirmed what he writes with followers of Muhammad who had met him. To be sure, we cannot be entirely certain that all of this is indeed factual, but nevertheless, on the face of things, this is one of the best sources that we have for understanding the beginnings of Islam, and much that it relates can be confirmed in one fashion or another by other sources, both non-Islamic and Islamic. On the basis of this source, then, Muhammad's earliest followers appear to hold the belief that they were living in the end-times, and that the eschaton would soon arrive, along with the Messiah, most likely understood—on the basis of comparison with early Islamic materials—as the second coming of Christ. It is a new religious movement that, moreover, seems to be deeply intertwined with elements of the Jewish and Christian traditions and was also intent on conquest. Therefore, we have in the *Teaching of Jacob* evidence that as the Believers left the deserts of Arabia behind them, they entered the Promised Land with an eschatological fervor rooted in Jewish and Christian tradition that was joined to a conviction that the Believers were obligated to spread the dominion of their faith through warfare, a pious militarism that would ultimately be rewarded with entry into paradise. And, according to its report, their Prophet was still with them, leading them as they entered the Holy Land. With the possible exception of this last point, Abraham's description of Muhammad's new religious movement is really not particularly controversial, or at least, it should not be. Indeed, as will be seen in the following sections, other sources, both Islamic and non-Islamic, bear out much of what he reports.

2 *Synodical Letter* (late 634 CE)
Homily on the Nativity (25 Dec. 634 CE)
Homily on Epiphany (6 Jan. 636 or 637 CE)

SOPHRONIUS OF JERUSALEM

To Sophronius of Jerusalem fell the difficult lot of shepherding the Christians of Jerusalem as Muhammad's followers invaded and began to occupy the Holy Land. Sophronius ascended to the patriarchal throne in 634, several years after the death of his predecessor Modestus, who had led the church of Palestine through the difficulties of occupation and captivity at the hands of the Persians from 614 to 628. In actuality, Modestus served during this tumultuous period as patriarchal vicar in Jerusalem for the sitting patriarch Zacharias, who had been taken captive to Iran along with a large portion of Jerusalem's Christian population. Zacharias died while in captivity, and when Heraclius arrived in Jerusalem in March of 630 to restore the True Cross, which also had been seized, Modestus was formally appointed as the new patriarch.[1] Nevertheless, Modestus served for less than a year, dying on 17 December of the same year and leaving a new vacancy in the see of St. James that would last for nearly four years.[2]

Although Sophronius at some point became a monk at the monastery of St. Theodosius near Jerusalem, he spent much of his life living elsewhere in the Roman Empire, together with his close friend John Moschus. For much of the Persian occupation, he was in North Africa with his protégé Maximus the Confessor. Sophronius only returned to Palestine in 634, to repatriate the remains of his friend John Moschus. It was John's wish to be buried at Sinai if possible, but if that proved impossible, then at the monastery of St. Theodosius instead. When Sophronius reached Ashkelon with John's remains, he found that already the "Hagarenes" had overrun the land, making passage to Sinai impossible. Instead, he headed for Jerusalem, where he arrived in September 634 and deposited his friend's remains at St. Theodosius.[3]

Shortly thereafter, Sophronius found himself elevated to the patriarchal throne, in circumstances that remain somewhat murky. As he writes in his *Synodical Letter*, which he sent shortly after his election to the patriarchs Sergius of Constantinople and Honorius of Rome, the patriarchate came upon him "through the great compulsion and force of the God-loving clerics and pious monks and faithful laymen, all the citizens of this holy city of Christ, our God, who forced me by hand and acted upon me tyrannically . . . with what judgments I do not know or understand."[4] Clearly Sophronius was not eager for the job but capitulated to the will of the faithful out of a sense of duty. And assuming that this is not just some sort of humility *topos* (which is not uncommon on such occasions), one can certainly understand why: by this time Muhammad's followers had entered Palestine and were bringing chaos and confusion upon his flock.

As patriarch, Sophronius must have played a key role in the city's surrender and likely would have had to collaborate at some level with these new rulers until his death, seemingly in 638.[5] Indeed, according to later tradition, Sophronius personally received the caliph ʿUmar in Jerusalem and showed him around the city, as we will see in the final text included in this volume (chapter 20). After his death, Sophronius was not immediately replaced, owing to theological controversies over the question of whether Christ continued to have a human will after the Incarnation, and there is no known successor until the end of the seventh century. Only much later, at some uncertain date, Patriarch Anastasius II (691?–706) assumed the throne, following a long interregnum with Stephen of Dora, one of Sophronius's lieutenants, and then John of Philadelphia serving as patriarchal vicar in the absence of a properly appointed patriarch.[6]

Only two of Sophronius's patriarchal homilies refer directly to the unfolding events of the invasion of Muhammad's followers, his *Homily on the Nativity*, which was delivered in Jerusalem for Christmas 634, and his *Homily on the Epiphany*, which seems to have been delivered later, possibly on 6 January 636 or 637. Below we have translated the relevant sections of both homilies as well as the most important passage from his *Synodical Letter*.

Synodical Letter 2.7.3[7]

I bring an equally profuse appeal to you [i.e., Sergius of Constantinople and Honorius of Rome], that you will make persistent and ceaseless supplication and plead to God on behalf of our Christ-loving and most serene rulers, who obtained the rudders of the empire from God, so that God himself, the merciful lover of humankind, who has power equal to intention, will be appeased by your prayers which are acceptable to God, and he will favor them with very many years and grant them the greatest victories over the barbarians and trophies, and crown them with their children's children and fortify them with divine peace, and grant them strong and mighty authority over all the barbarians, but especially the Saracens, shattering their pride. On account of our sins they have now unexpectedly risen up against us and are seizing everything as booty with cruel and savage intent and godless and impious bold-ness. Therefore we beseech you blessed men ardently to make the most intense supplications to Christ, so that when he has graciously received these from you, he will quickly cast down their wanton acts, full of madness, and will present them, worthless as they are, as a footstool for our God-given rulers, as it was before, so that those who rule the kingdom on our earth may prosper once they have finished with the clamors of war, and may their entire polity prosper with them also, fortified by their mighty scepter and har-vesting the clusters of grapes that bring forth mirth through their peaceful order.

Homily on the Nativity[8]

19. But let the inspired Magi and shepherds take themselves to God-welcoming Bethlehem, and let them have the star as a companion and a fellow traveler. And let them behold the wonder beyond all wonders and contemplating the wonder let them be astonished. And let them sing with the angelic choir and bring as gifts the offerings of the Magi, saying "Glory to God in the highest, and on earth peace among those whom he favors!" [Matt 2.14] without fear, without par-alyzing terror in their hearts or having to contemplate the madness of Herod. Instead, filled with divine thoughts, they behold the new-born wrapped in swaddling clothes and lying in the God-bearing manger, the one who is the Savior of the universe, truly Lord and God ineffably. And if he was concealed in a covering of flesh for us who are fleshly, it was because we are not able to see the pure divinity nude of human flesh and a body.

20. Nevertheless, we, unworthy to behold these things on account of our countless sins and grievous offenses, are prevented from being on the roads to go there. Unwillingly, indeed, against our will, we are forced to remain at home, not because we are bound

together closely in the flesh but bound together through fear of the Saracens.

23. For when [Adam] was expelled from the delight of Paradise and cast out from such great pleasure, he nevertheless saw Paradise with his eyes, for he was settled across from it. But he could not return there, since he saw the flaming and twirling sword that was guarding the entrance to Paradise and depriving him of such yearning, on account of the transgression that he dared to commit [cf. Gen 3.24]. So we too are settled next to God-welcoming Bethlehem and restrained from rushing over there, not seeing a twirling and flaming sword but the sword of the savage and barbaric Saracens, which, filled with every diabolical cruelty, striking fear and bringing murder to light, keeps us banished from this blessed vision, forcing us to stay home and not allowing us to go forth.

27. For he [Christ] is the one who says explicitly and defines this clearly for us: "Not everyone who says to me, 'Lord, Lord' will enter into the kingdom of heaven, but only the one who does the will of my Father in heaven" [Matt 7.21]; and "If you love me, you will keep my commandments" [John 14.15]; and "You are my friends if you do what I command you" [John 15.14]. Therefore, if we would do the will of his Father, having the true and orthodox faith, we should blunt the Ishmaelite sword and turn away the Saracen dagger and shatter the Hagarene bow. And we should look upon holy Bethlehem not from afar but should behold up close the wonders in it and see Christ working miracles and cry out to him with the angels the hymn "Glory to God in the highest, and on earth peace among those whom he favors!" [Matt 2.14], shouting with the loudest voice and making ourselves acceptable to him.

41. But we have the burning desire and thirst of David to see this water, like the much-praised David, and to refresh the soul with

this singular sight, but we are kept away from this vision by fear of the Saracens. For now the army of the godless Saracens, like that of the Philistines then, has taken divine Bethlehem and does not allow us passage to enter it [cf. 2 Kgdms 23.14–16]. But they threaten slaughter and destruction if we should go forth from this holy city and dare to draw near to our longed for and holy Bethlehem.

42. Therefore, and not without sadness we observe this commemoration remaining within the gates [of Jerusalem] and celebrate this feast in this holy church of the Theotokos.[9] Therefore exhort and pray for and entreat your intense longing for Christ our God, so that, insofar as we are able, we will make ourselves straight and make ourselves shine through repentance and purify ourselves through penitence and refrain from committing deeds that are hateful to God. For thus if we should live as is loved by and pleasing to God, we would laugh at the fall of our Saracen enemies and would observe their near ruin and witness their final destruction.

43. For their blood-thirsty sword will enter their hearts and their bow will be shattered and their arrows will be fixed in themselves.

Homily on the Epiphany 10[10]

But the contrary circumstances compel me to think about our way of life, for why are they waging war among us? Why do barbarian raids abound? Why do the Saracen armies rise up against us? Why have destruction and plunder proliferated so much? Why is there endless shedding of human blood? Why are the birds of the sky devouring human flesh? Why have the churches been torn down? Why is the cross mocked? Why is Christ, the giver of every good thing and the provider of this our great joy, blasphemed by mouths of heathens, and he cries out to us most rightly: "Because of you my name is blasphemed among the nations" [Isa 52.5], which is the most onerous of all the dreadful things that have befallen us. For on account of this the God-hating and wretched Saracens—clearly the abomination of the desolation that was prophetically foretold to us [Dan 11.31; cf. Mark 13.14]—run about through places where they are not allowed, and they plunder cities, mow down fields, burn villages with fire, set flame to the holy churches, overturn the sacred monasteries, stand in battle against the Roman armies, and they raise up trophies in combat and add victory to victory. And increasingly they mock us and increase their blasphemies against Christ and the church and speak iniquitous blasphemies against God. And these adversaries of God boast of conquering the entire world, recklessly imitating their leader the Devil with great zeal, and emulating his delusion on account of which he was cast down from heaven and assigned to the gloomy darkness. These things the vile ones would not have accomplished, nor would they have gained so much power as to do and utter these things lawlessly, unless we first insulted the gift and first defiled the purification, and in this way aggrieved the giver Christ and incited him to wrath against us, even though he is good and takes no pleasure in evil, being the font of mercy and not wanting to see the ruin and destruction of humankind. But truly we bear responsibility for all these things ourselves, and no ground will be found for our defense.

Commentary

At the time of his accession, as reflected in his *Synodical Letter*, it seems that Sophronius was optimistic that the Roman Empire would soon expel these invaders from the Holy Land and restore order, expressing hope that the emperor will purge these barbarians from the Holy Land. As he draws this important missive to a close, he asks for prayers that God will make these "vile creatures" the "footstool of our God-given emperors," as they had been before. These hopes seem to have quickly faded by the time he delivered his *Homily on the Nativity* on 25 December 634: the homily reveals that already by this time Muhammad's followers were in effective control of Jerusalem's immediate environs, so that it was not possible to travel the roughly ten kilometers from Jerusalem to Bethlehem for the Nativity feast. Instead, Sophronius had to give his Christmas homily in Jerusalem. Thus, it would appear that already by this early date Roman authority had vanished from the Holy Land, leaving the invading armies of the Saracens unchecked as they assumed control of the countryside. Damascus had already fallen, almost at the very same moment that Sophronius assumed the patriarchate, and soon the cities of Palestine would follow.

By 635 Palestine, Jordan, and southern Syria were completely under the control of Muhammad's followers, with only the exception of Caesarea and Jerusalem. Caesarea would hold out until 640, but Jerusalem capitulated in the spring of 637 according to the most widely accepted chronology. Nevertheless, Heribert Busse makes an excellent case, using Christian and Islamic materials together, for dating Jerusalem's fall to early in 635.[11] Indeed, the events of the invasion of Syria and Palestine are generally so confused in the Islamic sources that their chronology is "impossible to reconstruct with confidence because the traditional Muslim sources provide conflicting reports that cannot be reconciled satisfactorily."[12] Although I find Busse's arguments for an earlier surrender convincing, any date, including the consensus dating, remains quite uncertain.

The *Homily on the Nativity* is important especially because it shows the progress that Muhammad's followers had made in taking control of the Holy Land already by the end of 634. Indeed, this homily seems to favor an earlier date for the capture of Jerusalem, as Busse proposes, since, according to Sophronius, by the end of 634 the environs of Jerusalem were entirely under Saracen control: One would imagine that in such circumstances the city could not have held out for very long, let alone for more than two years. In this homily Sophronius also expresses hope that God will soon deliver the people of Jerusalem from these recent invaders, although in contrast to the *Synodical Letter* quoted above, he no longer expects such liberation to come through the intervention of imperial forces. Rather, since God had allowed the Saracens to come upon his people for chastisement, as a result of their collective sin, their deliverance will be secured through collective repentance, through moral, doctrinal, and liturgical reform. As David Olster rightly observes of Sophronius's homilies, his "call for unity in the face of the Arab threat was not to join together in resistance, either passive or active, but to express Christian unity through the liturgy."[13]

The *Homily on the Epiphany* echoes the same themes, while drawing explicit attention to the outrages that these invading Saracens were committing against the Cross, the churches and monasteries, Christ, and the name of God. Yet, as Robert Hoyland notes, even in this homily, likely one of his latest, "the appearance of the Arabs is not of interest in itself—Sophronius assumes that it is just another in a very long succession of Arab raids—it is its significance that counts, its indication of Jesus's dissatisfaction with his people."[14] Although there may be no explicit expectation of Roman political restoration in this homily,[15] at the same time, it does not seem that Sophronius yet has the sense that the Saracens and their hegemony were here to stay.

One should additionally note that Sophronius does not mention Muhammad by name, nor does he indicate that his followers, who had fallen upon the Holy Land, observe any particular religious faith. Instead, he refers to them primarily as Saracens, but also as Ishmaelites and Hagarenes, and while he calls them "godless" and accuses them of blasphemies, we probably should not read too much into this: presumably, he is referring to their savagery and depravity rather than any particular religious convictions. Even though Sophronius does not tell us very much about the motives or convictions of these invaders, his comments have a special value as some of the earliest eyewitness testimony regarding the arrival of Muhammad's followers in the Near East and the violence and disruption that this occasioned, coming in this case from no less of a source than the Patriarch of Jerusalem.

3   *A Syriac Fragment Concerning the Believers' Invasion of Syria* (637 CE)

This fascinating yet very fragmentary document is the first text to make explicit reference to Muhammad by name. Indeed, it is even earlier than the Qur'an, at least as a written document, by any estimation of the Qur'an's origins. For this reason alone, we have included it in this collection, even though it tells us relatively little about the beliefs and practices of Muhammad's followers. The text consists of twenty-three now faded lines written on the front fly-leaf of a sixth-century Syriac manuscript containing the Gospels of Matthew and Mark.[1] As Andrew Palmer notes, this brief description of the Believers' invasion of Palestine appears to be the notes of a parish priest who recognized the historical significance of the events unfolding around him and decided to make a record of them for posterity, following a common practice of making such notes on the blank pages of Gospel manuscripts.[2]

Syriac Fragment Concerning the Believers' Invasion of Syria[3]

... Muhammad ... the priest Mar Elias ... and they came ... and from ... strong ... month ... and the Romans [fled?] ... And in

January [the people of] Homs made an agreement in exchange for their lives, and many towns were destroyed in the slaughter by [the Nomads of] Muhammad, and many people were killed and captives [were taken] from Galilee all the way to Beth [ZK . . . WT' . . .].[4] And the Nomads [ṭayyāyē] set up camp near . . . , and we saw everywhere . . . and the olive oil which they brought and . . . them . . . And on the [twenty-sixth] of May, [the *sakellarios*][5] went as usual . . . from the vicinity of Homs, and the Romans pursued them. . . . And on the tenth [of August] the Romans fled from the vicinity of Damascus . . . many [people], about ten thousand. And at the turn [of the year] the Romans came. And on the twentieth of August in the year [nine hundred and forty-]seven there assembled in Gabitha . . . the Romans and many people were killed, from the Romans about fifty thousand. . . . In the year nine hundred and for[ty] . . .

Commentary

This fragment describes a series of engagements between the Romans and Muhammad's followers, culminating in the battle of Gabitha-Yarmuk, at which the Roman army was routed in 636. As the text's first commentator, William Wright, notes, "It seems to be a contemporary notice" of these events, written by an eyewitness.[6] It describes widespread violence, death, and destruction at the hands of these newly arrived Nomads. Otherwise, it is of fairly limited historical significance, particularly since it is so garbled in its present state. The text identifies the year 947 of the Seleucid calendar as the date of this battle, which corresponds to 636 CE, and since it seemingly refers to the following year in its final line, scholars have generally dated this fragment to the year 637 CE.

4   *Letter 14* (634–40 CE)

MAXIMUS THE CONFESSOR

By almost any measure, Maximus the Confessor is the most important and influential Christian theologian of the seventh century. Accordingly, most of his writings engage the rarified topics of Christian theological discourse; yet, in a single instance Maximus makes one of the earliest mentions of Muhammad's religious movement's emergence onto the world stage. Although Maximus tells us much less than we would like to know, his witness is nonetheless especially valuable, particularly given his background. Maximus was born in Palestine, and at a young age he entered one of its oldest monastic communities, the monastery of St Chariton. There he met Sophronius, who served as his mentor for the remainder of his life. Maximus therefore knew Palestine and its religious communities well.[1] His brief reference to Muhammad's followers comes in one of his letters, *Letter 14*, addressed to a certain Peter the Illustrious, who was a Roman official in Numidia. The letter is generally dated to the period between 634 and 640, when Maximus seems to have been in Carthage.[2] That Maximus refers here to the Believers' invasion of the Near East—rather than the Persian conquest—is generally agreed based on his identification of the invaders as people who lived in the desert.

Letter 14[3]

But I remind you, who are guarded by God, to be vigilant and pray according to the command of the Lord that we will not be overcome by the snares of all the temptations that surround us from every side. For if we are vigilant and sober, I know that we will guard ourselves against the tricks of the demons. And if we pray, we will gain for our aid the divine grace that battles along with us and makes us victorious against every opposing power and protects us from error and ignorance. This is especially what we must do now, when, even without a command, nature, taking into account the circumstances, teaches us to seek refuge in God. For what is more precarious than the evils that beset the world today? What is more terrible to those who understand than the things that are happening? What is more pitiable or fearsome for those who endure them? To see this barbarous people from the desert overrunning another's lands as if they were their own! And to see this civilized polity devoured by savage and raging beasts, who have the mere appearance of only the form of a human beings! And to see the Jewish people, who have long delighted in the flow of human blood and know only how to please God through slaughter of a creature, who because of this are filled with rage to be more conspicuous in wealth of wickedness than those acclaimed for iniquity, who think that they serve God by doing what is hated by God, who alone are the most faithless of all the peoples on the earth. And therefore they are most ready to welcome the enemy forces, ushering in, by every way and means, the advent of the evil one, and revealing by what they are doing the arrival of the Antichrist, since they ignored the true Savior.

Commentary

The most significant information to be taken from Maximus's extremely terse report is his indication—or perhaps, accusation—that the Jews were collaborating with these invaders. Likewise, he identifies these events as a sign that the eschaton had drawn nigh, and the advent of the Antichrist was imminent. Maximus's report of Jewish collusion with the invaders is intriguing, given the fact that other sources, Christian, Islamic, and Jewish, seem to confirm the inclusion of Jews who retained their Jewish identity among Muhammad's followers, at least in the earliest decades of his religious movement. Nevertheless, Maximus is hardly neutral on this point: his terse account of Jewish collaboration with the invaders seethes with an abundant anti-Jewish invective. Therefore, one cannot entirely exclude the possibility his accusation of Jewish collusion was engendered by his polemical agenda.[4] Yet, given significant other evidence indicating Jewish participation in the nascent community of Muhammad's followers, as well as the fact that such Jewish collaboration seems to be the factor giving rise to his anti-Jewish polemic in this context, one is inclined to give some credence to this particular detail.

5   *Chronicle* (ca. 640 CE)

THOMAS THE PRESBYTER

This chronicle appears in an assemblage of seemingly disparate texts gathered together in an eighth-century manuscript now in the British Library, a collection previously known in earlier scholarship as the *Chronicle to 724*.[1] The rather disparate contents of this manuscript include a variety of different historical texts as well as a fragmentary geographical treatise, all of which scholars had previously regarded as an unrelated set of miscellaneous historical documents. Recently, however, Andrew Palmer has convincingly argued that the various components fit together as a sort of anti-Chalcedonian "World Chronicle," compiled by a Miaphysite priest from Rashaina named Thomas, sometime directly after Muhammad's followers invaded Mesopotamia in 639–40.[2] Several of the writings undoubtedly predate Thomas's collection, and while the final three sections appear to be his own work, these clearly draw on a number of earlier historical sources. The compilation's tenor is sharply anti-Chalcedonian, attacking specifically the ecclesiastical policies of the emperor Heraclius (610–41), whom the latest reference in the *Chronicle* describes as being in his thirtieth year. Since Heraclius ruled for thirty-one years, and the *Chronicle* does not mention either his death or any other event after this year, its composition in 640 seems quite likely.[3]

Chronicle[4]

In the year 945, indiction 7, on 4 February, on Friday, at the ninth hour, there was a battle between the Romans and the Nomads of Muhammad [*ṭayyāyē d-mḥmṭ*] in Palestine, twelve miles east of Gaza. And the Romans fled and left behind the patrician, the son of YRDN, and the Nomads killed him. And around four-thousand poor peasants of Palestine were killed: Christians, Jews, and Samaritans. And the Nomads devastated the entire region.

Commentary

Although this account is very brief and perfunctory, with little information about the religious belief and practice of Muhammad's followers, it is especially significant as the first fully coherent text to identify Muhammad specifically by name. Hoyland concludes that "its very precise dating inspires confidence that it ultimately derives from first-hand knowledge. The account is usually identified with the battle of Dathin, which Muslim historians say took place near Gaza in the spring of 634."[5] This battle is generally thought to be the same battle referenced in the *Teaching of Jacob* (chapter 1), and the "patrician" who is left behind and killed in this text is commonly identified with the *candidatus* Sergius mentioned in the *Teaching of Jacob*.[6] One should also note that like many of the very early sources we have seen, including the *Teaching of Jacob*, Sophronius of Jerusalem, and the Syriac fragment translated above, the arrival of Muhammad's followers in Syria and Palestine brought great death and destruction upon these lands and their inhabitants. So far, the arrival of Muhammad's followers does not seem to have been a very peaceful transition.

6 *The Armenian Chronicle of 661 attributed to Sebeos*
(640s CE)

For many years, scholars misidentified this next writing as the *History of Heraclius* by a certain Bishop Sebeos, a long-lost chronicle mentioned by several medieval Armenian historical writers. Today the document is regarded as an anonymous chronicle covering the period from the 480s to 661, with a special focus on events in Armenia between 572 and the mid-650s.[1] Nevertheless, despite this new scholarly consensus that the chronicle is anonymous, we will continue the practice of referring to it as the history of "Sebeos," which by now has become fairly common.[2] Several features indicate the chronicle's composition at the beginning of the 660s: its description of the beginnings of Muhammad's new religious movement derives from eyewitness testimony, it speaks of certain events from 652 as if they had just taken place, and it concludes with Muʿāwiya's victory in the First Civil War among Muhammad's followers (656–61), in a fashion that Robert Hoyland describes as "stop-press news." All of this suggests its composition very shortly after 661. The chronicle's extraordinary account of the rise of Muhammad's religious movement, however, is itself significantly earlier than this. For this material, Sebeos relies directly on an earlier source, a now lost record of these events that was composed in Jerusalem sometime in the 640s. Therefore, we place this report among the earliest sources in this volume, just after Maximus's letter from the end of the previous decade.[3]

Sebeos's history is in general one of the most valued historical sources for events in the Near East during the early seventh century. As James Howard-Johnston estimates its worth, "Sebeos' contribution to our knowledge of the ending of classical antiquity is greater than that of any other single extant source."[4] As a historian, Sebeos earns the highest marks. Critical study of the chronicle reveals that Sebeos made extensive use of earlier documentary sources (including especially the source just mentioned), that he chose these sources very wisely, and that his editing of these sources appears to be minimal. Moreover, Sebeos presents this all in a historical narrative that, in comparison with other contemporary historians, is remarkably free from bias. Excepting only two specific incidents, Sebeos describes the events of this period with an impartiality that few if any among his peers were able to equal.[5] Sebeos's account of the beginnings of Muhammad's religious community is beyond question one of the most important. He is, as Hoyland notes, "the first non-Muslim author to present us with a theory for the rise of Islam that pays attention to what the Muslims themselves thought they were doing."[6]

The Armenian Chronicle of 661[7]

42. I will tell of the offspring of Abraham, not from the free one, but the one born from the handmaid, in whom the true divine word was fulfilled: "his hands against all, and the hands of all against him" [Gen 16.12].

When the twelve tribes of all the clans of the Jews went forth, they gathered at the city of Edessa. When they saw that the Persian army had fled away from them and had left the city in peace, they shut the gate and fortified themselves within it. And they did not allow the army of the Roman Empire to enter among them. Then the king of the Greeks, Heraclius, gave the order to lay siege to it. And when they realized that they could not resist him in battle, they sought peace from him. Opening the gates of the city, they went and stood before him. Then he ordered them to go and remain in their own dwelling place, and they went away. Travelling on desert roads, they went to Tachkastan, to the sons of Ishmael.[8] They called on them to help them and told them of their hereditary kinship in the testament of the Scripture.[9] Yet although they were able to persuade them of their close kinship, they could not achieve agreement within their multitude, because their religious practices divided them from each other.

At that time a man appeared from among these same sons of Ishmael, whose name was Muhammad, a merchant, who appeared to them as if by God's command as a preacher, as the way of truth. He taught them to recognize the God of Abraham, because he was especially learned and well informed in the history of Moses. Now because the command was from on high, through a single command they all came together in unity of religion, and abandoning vain cults, they returned to the living God who had appeared to their father Abraham. Then Muhammad established laws for them: not to eat carrion, and not to drink wine, and not to speak falsely, and not to engage in fornication. And he said, "With an oath God promised this land to Abraham and his descendants after him forever. And he brought it about as he said in the time when he loved Israel. Truly, you are now the sons of Abraham, and God is fulfilling the promise to Abraham and his descendants on your behalf. Now love the God of Abraham with a single mind, and go and seize your land, which God gave to your father Abraham, and no one will be able to stand against you in battle, because God is with you."

Then they all gathered in unanimity "from Havilah to Sur, which is opposite Egypt" [Gen 25.18]. And they went from the desert of Paran [cf. Gen 21.21], twelve tribes according to the tribes of their patriarchs. They separated the 12 thousand men, like the sons of Israel, into their tribes—one thousand men in each tribe—to lead them into the land of Israel. And they went forth, camp by camp, each according to their family lineage: Nabaioth, Kedar, Nabdeel, Massam, Masma, Idouma, Masse, Choddad, Thaiman, Ietour, Naphes, and Kedma. These are the tribes of Ishmael [cf. Gen 25.13–16]. They reached Araboth of Moab in the territory of Reuben [cf. Jos 13.14; Deut 34.1], for the Greek army was camped in Arabia. And coming upon them unexpectedly, they struck them with the sword and put to flight Theodore, the brother of the emperor Heraclius. And after returning they made camp in Arabia.

And when all the remnants of the people of the children of Israel assembled, they joined together, and they became a large army. And after that they sent a letter to the Greek king, and they said as follows: "God gave that land to our father Abraham and to his descendants after him as a hereditary possession. We are the sons of Abraham. You have occupied our land long enough. Leave it in peace, and we will not come into your land. Otherwise, we will demand that possession from you with interest."

But the emperor did not accept this and did not respond agreeably to their demand, but he said: "This land is mine, and the lot of your inheritance is the desert. Go to your land in peace." And he began to raise an army, about 70,000, and he appointed one of his trusted eunuchs as a general for them and ordered them to go to Arabia. . . .

. . . We heard this from men who had been taken as captives from Arabia to Khuzistan. And having been eyewitnesses of these things themselves, they told us this account.[10]

43. I will also speak about the plots of the seditious Jews, who when they secured an alliance with the Hagarenes for a little while, devised

a plan to rebuild the Temple of Solomon. And when they found the spot that is called the Holy of Holies, they rebuilt it with a fixed edifice, a place for their prayers. And when the Ishmaelites became envious of them, they drove them out from that place and called the same house of prayer their own. The former then built there a place for their prayers in another spot at the base of the Temple. And there they hatched their wicked plot, desiring to fill Jerusalem from end to end with blood in order to eradicate the Christians from Jerusalem.

Commentary

Although Sebeos's account is somewhat at odds with the later Islamic historical tradition, at the same time it is not completely irreconcilable with it. According to Sebeos, just prior to the birth of Muhammad's community, a group of Jewish refugees settled among the Nomads. These Jews explained to the "sons of Ishmael" their common descent from Abraham, seemingly in an effort to "convert" them. Although these Nomads were persuaded of their kinship with the Jews, they were for the most part reluctant to adopt the religious practices of Judaism. This all changed rather suddenly, however, with the appearance of a man named Muhammad among them. This Muhammad was a merchant, according to Sebeos, and based on the general quality of his sources and his report, we may take this description as highly probable information about the historical figure of Muhammad. One should add that Muhammad is also identified has having been engaged in commerce in another Christian source from the later seventh century not included in this volume, the *Chronicle* of Jacob of Edessa, whose letter concerning the direction that Muhammad's followers faced to pray is translated below (chapter 18). This same Jacob in his *Chronicle* records next to the year 617/8 CE that "Muhammad went down for trade to the lands of Palestine, the Arabias, and Phoenicia of the Tyrians."[11] Thus, it would seem that Muhammad was indeed a trader, and perhaps his trade brought him to the lands of Syro-Palestine.

Inspired by Muhammad, these "Ishmaelites" rose up together with the Jews in order to retake possession of the promised land of their inheritance, the Holy Land. We certainly need not imagine that the specific catalyst for the emergence of Muhammad's new religious community was a group of Jewish refugees from Edessa, as Sebeos indicates, although, one must admit, it is oddly specific information from an extremely high-quality source. Nevertheless, if one were to look for some sort of historical kernel at the basis of this tale of Jewish inspiration, undoubtedly it reflects the important influence of Jews and Judaism on the rise of Muhammad's new religious movement, as witnessed especially by the *Constitution of Medina*. Why the author of the chronicle's source identifies the origin of this influence with the Jewish community of Edessa remains a mystery. Although Sebeos reports that "religious practices" initially kept the two communities divided, with Muhammad's emergence as a leader, "they all came together in unity of religion," presumably including both the Jews and the sons of Ishmael together. Indeed, the message that Sebeos ascribes to Muhammad's teaching shows deep compatibility with fundamental elements of Jewish faith and practice. They must worship the one true God of their common father Abraham and observe a religious law that included dietary restrictions and rejection of lying and fornication. Only the prohibition of wine stands out as unusual in regard to Jewish practice, and while Sebeos seems to report accurately here concerning a tenet held by many in the early community of the Believers, one should also note that the ban on wine and other alcoholic beverages was not always widely observed among members of the community of the Believers during the first century of its history.[12] One imagines, accordingly, that this principle was likely more flexible for some members in Muhammad's following than Sebeos here seems to suggest.

At the heart of Muhammad's message, according to Sebeos, was a call for his followers, sons of Isaac and Ishmael together, to rise up and reclaim the promised land of their Abrahamic patrimony in the biblical Holy Land. Muhammad enjoins here the "sons of Abraham" collectively, and not only the sons of Ishmael, to take back their land from the occupying Romans. They come together from Havilah to Sur and from Paran, lands identified by late ancient Christian authors with Arabia Deserta, the desert region between Nabataea and Mesopotamia. Sebeos then describes the deployment of the Ishmaelites in preparation for battle using biblical terms that deliberately evoke the Israelites and their invasion of the promised land after the Exodus. The Ishmaelites defeat the Romans with a surprise attack in the region east of the Dead Sea, striking from Araboth of Moab—that is, the Wādī ʿAraba/Aravah, part of the Jordan Rift Valley that runs between the Dead Sea and Aqaba/Eilat and forms the border between modern Israel and Jordan. This location accords with the first engagements between the two armies in Transjordan, in a battle that seemingly marks the beginning of the Believers' campaign against Rome and Palestine.[13] Quite possibly, the event referred to here is the early engagement between Muhammad's followers and Rome at Muʿta, which is very near the Wādī ʿAraba. In any case, after their victory, "all the remnants of the people of the children of Israel assembled, they joined together, and they became a large army." The children of Israel, then, the Jews, were united with the victorious sons of Ishmael in Muhammad's call for them both, the sons of Abraham, to reclaim the land of their inheritance.

This report, from one of our best and earliest sources, seems to indicate something very much like an interconfessional community of the Believers, as proposed by Fred Donner and Robert Hoyland as well, a religious movement that initially welcomed Jews and even Christians to full membership in the community, requiring only a simple profession of faith in "God and the last day." Undoubtedly it is no coincidence that the first objective of these Abrahamic Believers was to liberate their sacred patrimony in the biblical Holy Land and especially its sacred center in Jerusalem and the Temple Mount. Indeed, as noted in the introduction to this volume, the original direction of prayer for Muhammad's followers was, by all accounts, Jerusalem, and this practice seems to have continued beyond his lifetime.[14] Moreover, the Qur'an itself specifically indicates on several occasions that liberation of the Holy Lands and their restoration to Abraham's descendants were central tenets of Muhammad's new religious movement from the very start.[15] Sura 33.27 proclaims that "He made you heirs to their land [ardahum] (of the 'people of the Book') and their dwellings and to a land which you have not yet trodden," a land that the Qur'an elsewhere names "the Holy Land" (al-ard al-muqaddasa).[16] The explicit identification of this land as belonging to "the people of the Book" unmistakably indicates the biblical Holy Land in Palestine and Jerusalem is in view. Sura 10.13–14 similarly relates: "We destroyed generations before you when they acted oppressively while their apostles brought them proofs, yet they did not Believe. Thus do we repay a guilty people. Then we made you successors in the land [al-ardi] after them, so we may see how you behave."[17] Likewise, sura 21.105–6, citing Psalm 37.29 explicitly, promises, "Indeed, we wrote in the Psalms, after the remembrance, 'My righteous servants will inherit the land [al-arda].'[18] Truly in this is a delivery for the servants."

Each of these passages addresses Muhammad's followers as chosen by God to liberate the biblical Holy Land and take possession of it as rightful heirs. And so the Qur'an itself incites the Believers to rise up and seize the Holy Lands, a call that they embraced by rising up together to seize their Abrahamic inheritance. Uri Rubin also notes several early Islamic traditions witnessing to a primitive impulse to liberate the Holy Land from Roman occupation. Through careful and convincing analysis, Rubin argues that these traditions in fact reflect the earliest recoverable stratum of Islamic self-identity. They envision a religious community comprised of both Jews and Arabs, who "share the sacred mission of carrying out the divine scheme, which is to renew the ancient Exodus and to drive the Byzantines out of the Promised Land. The messianic goal is shared with the Arabs not only by contemporary 'Judeo-Muslims,' but also by the Biblical Children of Israel," who are expected "to assist the Muslims in the eschatological anti-Byzantine holy war."[19] Although it is true that many of the traditions identified by Rubin survive only in more recent sources, their aberrant identification of the biblical Holy Land as the main focus of the Believers' religious aspirations, in contrast to the more traditional focus on Mecca and Medina as the Islamic Holy Land, surely signals their early formation.

Before they began their invasion, however, Sebeos tells us that Muhammad and his followers first sent a letter to the Roman emperor, in which they explained to him their claim to the promised land as Abraham's heirs. Accordingly, they asked the Romans to depart from their land peacefully, while threatening to seize what belongs to them by force if necessary. The emperor, of course, refused their request and maintained that the land belonged to him. The desert, he explained to these children of Abraham, is their inheritance, and he suggested that they should depart thence instead. Of course, they ignored his advice, and the Believers' invasion of Palestine ensued immediately. Details of the first military engagements between Muhammad's followers and the Romans and Persians follow, which we have omitted from the translation above.[20] The section concludes, however, with a notice that the information just related about the beginnings of Muhammad's religious community derives from eye-witness reports made by those taken captive: such captives, as Jack Tannous observes, served as one of the main vectors for transmission of religious knowledge between communities during the early Islamic period, citing this particular example as a case in point.[21]

Since this notice derives, it would seem, from Sebeos's earlier Palestinian source, we should emphasize again that this report of the formation of Muhammad's new religious movement was apparently committed to writing in Jerusalem in the 640s, during the reign of ʿUmar or ʿUthmān, and it was purportedly compiled based on eyewitness testimony of these captives.[22]

This same early Jerusalem source also relates that just as soon as the Believers had reclaimed their promised inheritance, they quickly set about restoring worship at the site of the Temple. According to Sebeos, the Jewish members of the community of the Believers took the initiative on this front. They built a place for worship at the location of the former Holy of Holies, which according to tradition is the Foundation Stone of the Creation. When the Ishmaelites grew envious, they seized the sanctuary for themselves, and the Jews were forced to build another edifice nearby to serve as their own house of prayer. This section then concludes with an anti-Jewish polemic, which accuses the Jews of plotting—unsuccessfully—to have the Christians slaughtered by blaming them for the slaughter of two pigs in their house of prayer.

One must note, however, that the Foundation Stone of the Creation, on which the Ark of the Covenant had originally rested within the Temple's Holy of Holies, is in fact the very same rock that presently sits at the center of the Dome of the Rock.[23] The Dome of the Rock, however, the earliest surviving Islamic monument, does not appear to be the first edifice that the Believers erected on the site of the Jerusalem Temple. Rather, it marks the culmination of their building efforts, which began soon after they captured Jerusalem. As we will see, Sebeos's report of such early building activity on the Temple Mount is not unique, and many of the sources that follow describe similar efforts by the Believers to restore worship to the Temple Mount shortly after they took control of Jerusalem. Indeed, certain early Islamic sources converge with these non-Islamic witnesses to reveal a strong interest among the early Believers in restoring the Temple in some fashion. Their early reverence for the site of the Temple and interest in restoring worship there seem to have been directly linked to their imminent eschatological expectations, and the Dome of the Rock stands today as an enduring monument to the Temple piety of Believers. Although James Howard-Johnston proposes to identify the building described by Sebeos with the al-Aqsā mosque,[24] this is very unlikely. Sebeos—who is echoed on this point by many other sources in this volume—specifically indicates that this structure was built at the site of the former Temple, which is simply not consistent with the location of the al-Aqsā mosque. Yet the large rock in the center of the Temple Mount was well known in Jewish and Christian collective memory to have stood within the Temple's Holy of Holies.[25] Accordingly, Sebeos must instead describe some sort of precursor to the Dome of the Rock, which, in contrast to the al-Aqsā mosque, stands over the site of the Temple's Holy of Holies.

7   *The Spiritual Meadow*, Appendix to the Georgian Version (ca. 640 CE)

JOHN MOSCHUS

John Moschus was a close friend of Sophronius, whom we met in chapter 2, and presumably also Maximus the Confessor. As young men, Moschus and Sophronius belonged to the same monastery in Palestine, Saint Theodosius, near Jerusalem. There Moschus became Sophronius's mentor, and the two remained lifelong friends. Together they traveled throughout the Mediterranean world, visiting its many monastic communities and spending long periods of time at Mount Sinai (ca. 583–93), in Alexandria (ca. 578–82 and 606–15), and finally ending up in Rome. Moschus's *Spiritual Meadow*, which he wrote toward the end of his life in Rome, is a collection of pious tales about the many holy men that they encountered in their sojourns. These brief narratives, more than two hundred in number, offer an unequalled glimpse of religious life in Egypt, Syria, and Palestine just before Muhammad's followers began their invasion

The total number of anecdotes that Moschus collected, however, is not entirely certain. The modern edition of the Greek text includes 219 tales.[1] Nevertheless, Photius, the ninth-century patriarch of Constantinople (d. 886), notes in his *Bibliotheca* that he had seen two versions of the *Spiritual Meadow*, one containing 304 chapters and another containing 342, and he warns his readers that "the narratives will not be found in equal numbers in all copies of the text."[2] Moreover, scholars have identified a number of surviving tales from this period that seemingly once belonged to this collection but are not included in the critical edition. Accordingly, the most recent English translation of the *Spiritual Meadow* includes 231 stories.[3] As Phil Booth observes of the collection, its "open, delinearized narrative" invited later scribes to add their own narratives and subtract others, so that it is often rather uncertain which tales were gathered by Moschus and which were added or excised at a later date.[4]

The Georgian translation of Moschus's invaluable collection is rather truncated in comparison with the Greek versions, including only ninety-one tales. Nevertheless, one tenth-century Georgian manuscript of the *Spiritual Meadow* appends to these a collection of thirty additional "edifying stories."[5] Although the Georgian version of these anecdotes seems to have been translated from an Arabic intermediary, there is little doubt that they were originally composed in Greek, seemingly not long after Moschus completed his own collection. And despite their mediation through Arabic, there is every indication that the translations faithfully reflect their Greek originals.[6] The appendix, in fact, consists of two separate collections that have been joined together. The first eleven begin with a title indicating that "these chapters were found on Cyprus, in the place called Theomorphou, which is like Paradise."[7] Not surprisingly, these narratives relate events that took place on Cyprus, and Greek equivalents are known for each of these.[8] Then, following the eleventh "edifying tale," the manuscript introduces a new title designating the remaining nineteen anecdotes as a separate collection of "Chapters of Miracles,"[9] and indeed, these stories relate various miracles. Several of these miracle tales are extant in Greek, and two more appear in Antiochus Strategius, *The Capture of Jerusalem by the Persians in 614*, an account of the Persian conquest and captivity composed in Greek shortly after the restoration of Roman sovereignty in Jerusalem in 628 that now survives only in Georgian and Arabic translations.[10]

In contrast to the first collection of eleven tales from Cyprus, which are completely anonymous, all but two of the nineteen miracle stories are attributed to specific individuals, as is generally the case in the *Spiritual Meadow*. Moreover, each narrative in this second collection indicates a relatively specific time and place for the events that it describes, so that the stories all have a "chronological homogeneity," falling within the period between Gregory the Great's papacy (590–604) and the reign of the emperor Constans II (641–68). Therefore, as Gérard Garitte concludes, these miracle tales are not a random collection of anecdotes but instead comprise a coherent and connected series of stories that had been gathered together sometime not long after the reign of Constans II, the latest date mentioned.[11] The final tale is attributed to "a priest of our lavra of Mar Saba named Michael,"[12] which seems to indicate that the collection was made by a monk in that monastery, seemingly sometime around the year 670.[13] As Booth notes, despite his anonymity, we can recognize that this author seems to have had a lot in common with Moschus: "he was interested in the monasteries of Palestine, and was perhaps a monk of St. Sabas; he knew Moschus' disciple Sophronius as patriarch of Jerusalem, and regarded him as a champion of orthodox doctrine; and he had travelled in the Latin West, to Rome and Ravenna." Moreover, Booth notes that the first of the collection's anecdotes regarding Gregory the Great (no. 12) was later incorporated into Gregory's first biography, which was written at the beginning of the eighth century.[14] Therefore, we may take even greater certainty that this collection was assembled not long after the reign of Constans II, in the middle of the seventh century. The story that follows is located during Sophronius's reign as patriarch of Jerusalem, and sometime shortly after the Believers' conquest of Jerusalem. This information, if accurate, situates the story sometime between 637 and 639: the fact that it refers to Sophronius as a person of recent memory for its audience would appear to confirm a relatively early date for this tale.

The Spiritual Meadow (Georgian Version), A19[15]

And this same person [Theodore, beloved by God and archdeacon of Theodore the Great Martyr, which is outside the gates of the city of Jerusalem[16]] told us and said: "The godless Saracens entered the Holy City of Christ our God, Jerusalem, with God's allowance, to discipline our wickedness, which is immeasurable. And running quickly they reached the place that is called the Capitolium [i.e., the Temple Mount]. They took some men, some by force and some willingly, to clean the place and to build that accursed thing, which is for prayer and which is called by them a mosque [*miżgit'a*]. And among them was John, an archdeacon of Saint Theodore the Martyr, for he was by trade a marble worker. And he was led astray by them for wicked gain, and he went of his own free will to work there: and he was very skilled with his hands.

And when the most-blessed man, Saint Sophronius, whom you recall, learned this, he sent to him on Friday. And he was brought to him, and he asked him, as a father and as the one who seeks the articulate lambs that God has bestowed on him, not to defile his hands utterly but to separate himself from such a vile endeavor. He persuaded him and said: "The Holy Anastasis will give you as much work as you like, at twice the price, only do not disobey my command. And do not harm yourself and do not become the cause of the corruption of many, when of your own freewill you build in that place that Christ cursed [Luke 13.35]. And do not oppose his commandments, he whom no one is able to oppose. Otherwise, you will not be able to work there and to remain under the yoke to which you have been appointed: indeed, not even a layman who is called a Christian should work there.' And thus he also similarly implored the deacons, his companions. Nevertheless, at that time he swore an oath and promised by the power of the precious Cross that he would no longer work there. And after two days he was found there again, for he was working in secret.

Nevertheless, when the good shepherd learned about this, he was troubled in his thoughts at his destruction and was seized by the zeal of Phinehas [cf. Num 25.6–13]. And he went and called him quickly. And he was pierced by the word of God as if by a sword and excommunicated from the Holy Church of Christ our God. Nevertheless, after he was excommunicated by the holy man of God, with the help of the Saracens, he entered his church by force. After a few days, however, he was working in the monastery that is called the Monastery of the Captives on the holy mountain, and he stood on a ladder.[17] And he was as far above the ground as [the height of] single man. And he stumbled and fell down to the ground. And he broke his leg and hurt his skin and body, and he was ill for a long time.

And the healing arts could do nothing useful for him. Then he confessed his wickedness and said: 'This befell me not on account of another cause, but for this reason, that I disobeyed a bishop. And this wrath came upon me, which has no consolation.' And he asked a certain one of his friends about this (a God-fearing man who is also the one who told us this): what could he do? Nevertheless, he suggested that he should take himself to the tomb of a saint, light a lamp, and anoint his wound from it and drink the rest. And he did thus, and he found a little relief, so that he was able to walk with a cane. And again he became prideful, and he forgot God's mercy. And he went to the holy altar and put his hand on the table, because he was not able to stand up. And not long thereafter, his wound began to fester and consumed his leg up to his thigh. And he was lost, and the wretch departed in great affliction."

Commentary

The anecdote is of particular interest for understanding the beginnings of Muhammad's new religious movement on two points. Most importantly, the story again indicates that the early Believers were intensely interested in building on the Temple Mount in order to restore some sort of worship and dignity to the site, which had lain in ruins since the later first century. We need not believe that Muhammad's followers literally ran to the Temple Mount immediately after taking the city, as the narrative indicates, but presumably we can have some confidence in its report that building a place of worship there was an urgent priority for the invaders following the conquest. Indeed, as already seen, other early sources independently confirm that the Believers began work on a sanctuary on the Temple Mount shortly after capturing Jerusalem.[18] From this we may conclude that restoring worship to the Temple Mount was an especially high priority for Muhammad's followers in the first decades of their history—and seemingly beyond as well. Although the Georgian text uses a calque on the Arabic *masjid* to describe this building, we should not assume, as some have, that this story refers to early work on the al-Aqsā mosque. In its root meaning, *masjid* simply means a place of prostration, or of worship or prayer, and thus it could apply to a wide range of sacred structures, particularly in this early period. One should also note that, as mentioned in the introduction, it seems that the Dome of the Rock was, in its earliest use, itself a place of prostration, where Believers would assemble twice each week to perform their prayer cycles. Therefore, while this source witnesses to the Believers' determination to restore worship to the Temple Mount soon after taking Jerusalem, it is not clear that we should align this report with any of its existing monuments.

Secondly, this tale could suggest that there were Christians in Jerusalem who were, for whatever reason, sympathetic to the Believers' cause, so much so that they were willing to assist in their efforts to restore worship to the Temple Mount. According to the text, this was so even when the ecclesiastical authorities were allegedly offering as much work as they wanted at twice the pay if they would refrain from helping the Believers to build on the Temple Mount. If this were indeed the case, such Christian cooperation could suggest that the Believers were in their earliest history a confessionally open community, much as Donner has proposed, open to Christians and other monotheists who professed belief in God and the Last Day.[19] Possibly we should see in the same light the peculiar remark that "with the help of the Saracens, he entered his church by force." Perhaps the Saracens made this happen by the force of their political authority over the city. Yet, at the same time, it seems to show an unexpected interest in the affairs of Jerusalem's Christians and their churches at this early stage.

8   *Homily on the End-Times* (ca. 640s CE)

PS.-EPHREM THE SYRIAN

Ephrem the Syrian is without peer the greatest writer of the Syriac
Christian tradition. He is its most esteemed theologian and ranks
as one of the most gifted (if not the most gifted) poet-theologians of
the entire Christian tradition. Ephrem lived during the fourth century on the frontier of the Roman Empire in northern Mesopotamia,
moving from Nisibis to Edessa in 363 as the Roman Empire's boundaries shifted to the west. Yet although Ephrem died in 373, new literary works bearing his name continued to appear in the centuries
that would follow. Owing to his peerless status, later forgers often
sought to attach their writings to Ephrem's fame, no doubt in hopes
of securing them broader circulation and unquestioned authority. In
the present case, we have what amounts to an apocalyptic vision of
the end of the world ascribed to the great Ephrem. Nevertheless, the
text's contents transparently reveal it as a composition of the seventh
century, most likely sometime during the 640s CE, at least in its current form. The last historical events to which the apocalypse refers
are the Near Eastern invasions by Muhammad's followers, which it
portends with the telling accuracy of a *vaticiunium ex eventu*—that is,

a prophecy written after the predicted events had already occurred. We will have more to say regarding the likely date of this apocalypse in the commentary that follows. It appears in this volume not only for its witness to the early history of the Believers movement and their polity, but also as one of the earliest exemplars of an apocalypse that incorporates the rise of their hegemony into its vision of the encroaching end of the world.

From the early sixth century onward, the religious cultures of the late ancient Near East bear steady witness to mounting expectations that the world would soon end. Many Christians, Jews, and even Zoroastrians of this era believed that they were living at the dawn of the eschaton, which would soon come upon the world, bringing history to an end or at least to a decisive cosmological turning point. These eschatological hopes, moreover, were in each case intertwined with the idea of a divinely chosen empire whose destiny would be to conquer the world before finally handing over power to God. Not surprisingly, in these Jewish and Christian eschatological scripts, Jerusalem is center stage, and its conquest is pivotal in the final events before the eschaton. There, in many accounts, the chosen emperor will ultimately hand over worldly power to God. These potent expectations of an imminent eschatological empire that would subdue the world and hand over authority to God are essential for understanding the rise of Muhammad's new religious movement, the Believers, which was simultaneously imperial in its ambitions and, so it would seem, fueled by a conviction that the world would soon end in the final judgment of the Hour. Not surprisingly, some of the best evidence for this apocalyptic backdrop to the emergence of Muhammad's new religious movement emerges from certain Syriac writings, one of which even appears to have directly influenced the Qur'an and, one assumes, the beliefs of Muhammad's earliest followers.[1]

The most famous and influential of these post-Islamic apocalypses is, without doubt, the *Apocalypse of Ps.-Methodius*, a text composed in Syriac sometime during the final decades of the seventh century that quickly spread into Greek and Latin and became one of the most popular and diffuse apocalyptic traditions of medieval Christianity. Nevertheless, *Ps.-Methodius* is primarily of interest for its place in the history of Christian apocalypticism and for gauging Christian reactions to hegemony of the Believers: there is little information regarding the faith and practice of the latter, which is our primary concern. Interested readers can easily find English translations of this apocalypse in several other publications.[2] Given its importance in the later tradition, however, it is perhaps worth pausing to present some brief remarks about this apocalypse before moving on to our translation of Ps.-Ephrem.

The *Apocalypse of Ps.-Methodius* draws its main inspiration from an earlier apocalyptic tradition about the Last Roman Emperor that presently survives as a part of the Latin version of the *Tiburtine Sybil*, and a fairly broad scholarly consensus dates this legend to the later fourth century.[3] According to the prophecy, the Last Emperor, through victory over the enemies of Christ, will inaugurate the events of the eschaton, and having vanquished his foes, he will travel to Jerusalem to lay down his diadem and royal garments, thus handing over rule to God. As Ernst Sackur carefully demonstrated, the historical figures and events referenced in this prophecy locate its production as well its expectation of the end-times during the era of Constantine and his sons.[4] The latest historical events to which the *Tiburtine Sibyl*'s Late Emperor tradition refers, as Paul Alexander likewise observes, belong to the end of the fourth century. These qualities, along with its prediction that sixty years after the rise of Constantine, Constantinople will no longer be the imperial capital, give us strong assurances that we are dealing with an apocalyptic legend from the later fourth century.[5] The Last Emperor's name is given as "Constans," which does not appear to refer to a specific historical individual. This is as one would expect, since this figure presumably has not yet appeared but is expected in the near future. "Constans" instead represents here, so it would seem, the root form of the various names given to the members of the Constantinid clan: Constantine, Constantius, and Constans, all of which bear effectively the same meaning: "resolute." In this regard the Last Emperor tradition of the *Tiburtine Sibyl* mirrors a parallel trend to advance a Roman imperial eschatology focused on Constantine and the Constantinids, evident especially in the contemporary writings of Eusebius of Caesarea, Lactantius, and Ephrem.[6]

The *Apocalypse of Ps.-Methodius* adopts the Last Emperor tradition present in the *Tibertine Sibyl*, although its author clearly has shaped this older tradition to fit the contours of his Syriac cultural milieu and the circumstances of rule by Muhammad's followers.[7] Most significantly in this regard, Ps.-Methodius retains a citation of Psalm 68.31 from its late fourth-century source: "Egypt and Ethiopia will hasten to offer their hand to God." In its original context, this verse provides a biblical prophecy forecasting the Last Emperor's conversion of the pagans to Christianity just before the end of the world, which the Sibyl juxtaposes in close parallel with a reference to Jeremiah 23.6 ("In those days Judah will be saved and Israel will dwell in confidence"), as a comparable witness to the Last Emperor's ultimate conversion of the Jews. Yet by the time Ps.-Methodius was writing, the conversion of the pagans had effectively been accomplished, and so a new significance had to be found for Psalm 68.31 if it were to be retained. What results is an extended exegesis of this verse that is so unusual and idiosyncratic that one can only ascribe it to a need to reinterpret a citation that had been inherited from an earlier model. Because the biblical passage had lost its original resonance through the passage of time, another meaning had to be found that could make it speak to a new and very different historical context.

In so doing, Ps.-Methodius takes this passage in a decidedly different direction from its original significance as a prophecy of pagan conversion. Indeed, its author explicitly rejects this traditional interpretation of the verse as found in the *Tiburtine Sibyl* and other late ancient sources as well. Instead, he interprets this verse as a forecast of the Last Emperor's abdication in Jerusalem, which in his reading will fulfill the Psalmist's prediction (in 68.31) that "'Kush [Ethiopia] will hand over power to God,' . . . for a son of Kushyat, daughter of Pil, king of the Kushites [Ethiopians], is the person [i.e., the Last Emperor] who will 'hand over power to God.'"[8] The impact of this new interpretation is profound over the extent of the apocalypse, determining a great deal of its remaining contents. As Alexander observes, the author, in order to justify this unprecedented and peculiar interpretation of Psalm 68.31, "dedicates the entire first half of the work to proof of the proposition that the 'Ethiopia' of the Psalmist was not, as some earlier members of the clergy had believed, the historical and contemporary kingdom of Ethiopia but the Roman (i.e., Byzantine) Empire."[9] As Sebastian Brock notes, the entire purpose of this strange genealogy that dominates the apocalypse is "to provide an eschatological exegesis of *Psalm* 68.31, 'Kush will surrender to God,' whereby Kush can be identified not as the Ethiopian kingdom of the author's own time, but with the Byzantine Empire."[10] Yet this novel interpretation of the Psalm seems so awkward, so forced, that its character becomes fully understandable only when one realizes that the author inherited a tradition already linking this verse with the Last Emperor's appearance that required him to rethink the verse's eschatological meaning. Ps.-Ephrem, however, presents us with a much more straightforward apocalypse of empires in the late ancient tradition, which in this case has updated this tradition to include the most recent imperial hegemons, the followers of Muhammad.

Homily on the End-Times, 2–5[11]

2. Therefore, my beloved ones, the end-times have arrived. Behold, we see the signs, just as Christ described them for us. Rulers will rise up, one against the other, and affliction will be upon the earth. Nations will rise against nations [cf. Mark 13.8], and armies will fall upon one another. And as the Nile, the river of Egypt, floods and covers the earth, countries will prepare for battle against Roman Empire. Nations will rise up against nations, and kingdom against kingdom [Mark 13.8]. And the Romans will go from place to place in flight, and the Assyrians [i.e., the Persians] will rule over part of the Roman Empire. The fruits of their loins will be enslaved, and they will also defile their women. And they will be sewing and reaping, and they will plant fruit in the land. And they will amass great riches and bury treasure in the land. But, just as the Nile, the river of Egypt, turns back from what it has covered, so too will the Assyrians turn back from the land to their own country. And the Romans will hasten back to the land of their inheritance [i.e. the Promised Land].[12] When wickedness has increased in the world, and the land has been defiled with fornication, the cry of the persecuted and the poor will ascend to heaven. Then justice will arise to cast them from the land [cf. Ps 12.5)] A holy wail will rise up; a cry will ascend to heaven.

3. A people will come forth from the desert, the offspring of Hagar, the servant of Sarah, who hold fast to the covenant of Abraham, the husband of Sarah and Hagar. Once set into motion, they will come in the name of the ram, the envoy of the Son of Perdition [cf. Dan 8.3; 2 Thess 2.3]. And there will be a sign in the heavens, which the Lord described in his gospel [cf. Matt 24.27]. It will shine forth among the bright stars, and the light of his face will gleam. Rulers will quake and tremble; the armies that they send forth will crumble. The nations of the earth will be terrified when they see the

sign in the heavens. And all nations and tongues will prepare for battle and come together. And they will wage war there and drench the earth with their blood.

4. And there the nations will be defeated, and a marauding nation will triumph. The marauders will spread across the land, over plains and mountaintops. And they will take women and children captive, and men both old and young. The grace of men will be destroyed, and the adornment of women will be removed. With mighty spears and lances, they will impale old men. They will separate a son from his father, and a daughter from her mother's side. They will separate a brother from his brother and a sister from her sister's side. They will kill the bridegroom in his bedroom and expel the bride from her bridal chamber. They will take away a wife from her husband and slaughter her like a sheep. They will remove an infant from his mother and chase the mother into captivity. And the child will cry out from the earth, and its mother will hear, but what will she do? For it will be trampled by the feet of horses and camels and infantry. And they will not allow her to turn to it, and the child will remain in the field. They will separate children from their mothers like soul from the body. She watches as they separate her beloved from her bosom. Two of her children to two masters, and she herself to another master, separated, and her sons with her, to be slaves to marauders. Her children will cry out with weeping, and their eyes burning with tears. She will turn toward her beloved, and milk will flow from her breast. "Go forth in peace, my beloved, and may God go with you, the one who accompanied Joseph during his servitude among foreigners [cf. Gen 37.28ff]. May he accompany you, my children, into the captivity to which you are going." "Farewell, our mother, and may God go with you, the one who accompanied Sarah into the house of Abimelech the Gadarite [cf. Gen 20.18]. May he accompany you until the day of resurrection." A son will stand and watch his father sold into slavery. The tears of both will flow, with one groaning before

the other. Brother will see brother slaughtered and thrown to the ground, and they will lead him too into captivity to be a slave in a foreign land. They will also slay mothers clutching their children to their breast. Shrill is the cry of the infants, groaning to assuage their distress. They will make their way through the mountains and blaze paths across the plains. They will plunder the ends of the earth and take control the cities, and the lands will be devastated, and the slain will multiply on the earth, and all nations will be subjugated before the marauding people. And when the nations have persevered in the land and they think that peace is soon to come, they will impose tribute, and everyone will fear them. And wickedness will multiply throughout the land and even conceal the clouds, and iniquity will envelop the creation and rise up smoldering to heaven.

5. Then the Lord in his wrath, because of the iniquity throughout the land, will stir up kings and mighty armies, for when he wants to purge the land, he sends men against men to destroy one another. Then righteousness will summon kings and mighty armies that are behind the gates that Alexander made. Many kings and nations will rise up behind the gates, and they will look to heaven and call upon the name of God. And the Lord will send a sign of his glory from heaven. And the divine voice will call out to those inside the gates, and at once they will be destroyed and will collapse at the divine command. Many armies will go forth, like stars without number, as multitudinous as the sand of the sea and more than the stars of heaven.

Commentary

This apocalypse, whose true author is unknown, seems to have been written not long after Muhammad's followers swept in and swiftly seized control of much of the Roman and Sasanian Near East, probably sometime around 640 or not long thereafter. Indeed, for the better part of a century, there was a solid consensus that this document, at least as we have it now, was composed sometime after Muhammad's followers entered the Near East. The text's first editor, T. J. Lamy, initially considered this homily an authentic work of Ephrem.[13] Nevertheless, in his review of Lamy's edition, Theodor Nöldeke observed soon after its publication that the clear reference to Muhammad's followers in this apocalypse precludes its attribution to Ephrem. Instead, the circumstances described in this part of the vision, according to Nöldeke, "clearly indicate the time of their emergence, around 640."[14] Shortly thereafter, Ernst Sackur reached the same judgment.[15] So too did the great Hungarian Orientalist, Michael Kmosko, who observed that this section of the apocalypse "clearly reflects the general panic and despair which followed the catastrophic defeat of the mighty army of emperor Herakleios."[16]

Nevertheless, in the same year that Nöldeke published his review, 1890, C. P. Caspari published a study in which he argued extensively that this apocalyptic homily was composed in 373 CE, even if he was unwilling to attribute the work to Ephrem on account of its style.[17] Caspari's interpretation fails to explain the clear references to the conquests of the sons of Hagar, however. Wilhelm Bousset sought to remedy this deficiency by proposing that the sections in question, sections three and four of the edition, were later interpolations of what was originally, in the remainder of the text, an apocalypse composed around 373. Regarding these sections, Bousset essentially agrees with Nöldeke and Sackur that they are a composition from shortly after the invasions by Muhammad's followers, only in his estimation they are an addition to a much earlier work. More recently, Harald Suermann has advanced a version of Bousset's interpolation hypothesis, suggesting that invasions of the Sabir Huns in 515 or the Chazars in 626 may have inspired the original apocalypse, although there is some evidence, he maintains, that the original text derives from the age of Ephrem the Syrian,

Nevertheless, Suermann, as the others before him, is quite clear in dating the apocalyptic account of the arrival of Muhammad's followers to sometime between 640 and 650.[18]

Therefore, although there has been some disagreement in the past as to whether the references to the arrival of the sons of Hagar in this apocalyptic homily are original, there has been effective unanimity that its apocalyptic vision of their appearance seems to have been composed in its current form sometime during the 640s. This remained the case until Garrit Reinink more recently proposed dating the entire composition somewhat later, suggesting its composition after 640 but before 683, since the text does not seem to be aware of the Second Civil War (*fitna*) among Muhammad's followers, which began in that year.[19] Still more recently, Robert Hoyland notes that while there has long been some consensus around 640 for dating this apocalypse, perhaps its references to the payment of tribute and building roads could invite a later dating, possibly during the reign of 'Abd al-Malik, who is known to have introduced new fiscal practices and seen to the building of roads.[20] Indeed, Edmund Beck, the text's most recent editor had already suggested that the text should be placed in the second half of the seventh century, since it refers to the existence of the *jizya*, the Islamic poll tax on non-Muslim subjects.[21] Suermann likewise has more recently proposed a date—for the interpolation regarding the "offspring of Hagar" at least—that mirrors Reinink's suggestion, pointing in this instance to the construction of roads as likely indication of a more recent composition sometime between 640 and 680.[22] Michael Penn too, presumably for similar reasons, favors a dating to generally sometime before 680.[23]

Despite these more recent waverings, the most likely date of this apocalypse in fact remains sometime during the early stages of the invasions by the sons of Hagar, and its composition around 640 still seems like a good approximation. As Kmosko and other early scholars noted, its chaotic account of their incursions suggests a time not long after the collapse of the Roman army and before the consolidation of authority and establishment of governance by the Believers. Indeed, only at the very end of this account do the invaders actually begin to take control of the region's cities: prior to this they are raging through the land, conquering and plundering. The supposed reference to the building of roads is clearly a misinterpretation of the Syriac, in my judgment. Although the words in question could legitimately be interpreted as a reference to road building, this is not their only possible or even most obvious meaning, and in fact, their immediate context strongly suggests that this is not their significance. The verb that others have rendered as "build," from the root *DRŠ*, is more properly translated here as "tread, open up." Moreover, the word that is interpreted as referring to actual roads, *urḥātā* is used not only for roads, but also with the meaning of "way" or "course," while the word for "paths," *šbile*, which also can mean simply "way," does not seem to designate actual roads. Indeed, such language does not seem to me indicative of actual road construction but something more akin to "make their way" in English.

Accordingly, this passage should be interpreted as stating that "they will make their way through the mountains and blaze paths across the plains," as translated also by Edmund Beck, for instance ("Sie werdern Wege in den Bergen bahnen").[24] Such an interpretation is further indicated by the opening of section four, which says that "the marauders will spread across the land, over plains and mountaintops." Surely this is a parallel expression. And again, the fact that in this account the invaders have yet to seize control of the cities makes it rather unlikely that road construction is in view. Instead, this line of the homily is presumably meant to indicate the haste and frenzy with which the marauders ran throughout the land. As for the imposition of tribute, while it is not entirely impossible that this could refer to the *jizya* poll tax, it is far more likely, I think, that this reference to tributes instead indicates payments on the part of cities and local authorities in acknowledgment of their submission to the invaders and in exchange for peace. Payment of such tribute by the defeated parties to the Believers was in fact quite common during the early stages of their conquest of the Near East.[25] And not only are the events of the Second Civil War absent, as Reinink notes, but so also are those of the First Civil War, which began in 656. Thus, a date of around 640 remains the most likely date of composition for this piece, despite these recent vacillations.

Like some of the other texts that we have already seen, this source again reports wanton death and destruction at the hands of Muhammad's followers. There is little indication of any tolerance for Christians or other inhabitants of the Near East, who were slaughtered and enslaved, according to this text. Other than that, the only thing that this apocalypse tells us about the faith and practice of Muhammad's followers is that they held fast "to the covenant of Abraham," which is rather vague. There seems to be little question that Muhammad's followers believed themselves to be the successors of Abraham, both in their lineage and in their religious practice. Yet this apocalypse is perhaps most important as an example of the tradition of imperial apocalypticism that had taken hold in the Mediterranean world during the years that witnessed the rise of Muhammad's new religious movement.[26] It demonstrates that this potent religious and political ideology extended across the tumultuous transitions of the early seventh century; thus, the Christians of this age began almost immediately to adapt their existing apocalyptic scripts to accommodate their new political circumstances.[27]

In Ps.-Ephrem's *Homily on the End-Times* we find the imperial eschatology of the pre-Islamic period reframed in order to understand the circumstances of Rome's defeat in the Near East and the new hegemony of Muhammad's followers in the region. As Ps.-Ephrem's apocalypse opens by describing the general conditions that portend the coming end of the world, nation will war against nation as wickedness proliferates throughout the world. Plague and famine will encompass the earth. Lawlessness will reign supreme, and the righteous will be beset by the wicked. The recent occurrence of such events offers clear signs that "the end times have arrived," as the author explains at the beginning of section two. Our visionary then "predicts" a coming war between the Romans and the Persians. After Rome's victory in this conflict, the descendants of Hagar, the Ishmaelites, will drive the Romans from the Holy Land. In this way, the apocalypse interprets the recent conquests by Rome (against the Persians) and the Ishmaelites as a single, connected apocalyptic harbinger of an imperial eschaton. Following these linked events, however, the author genuinely begins to predict the future, warning that the peoples of Gog and Magog will be unleashed, at which point our translation above leaves off. Nevertheless, the text continues to describe their ravages upon the earth, which will last for seven years, at which time the resurgent Roman Empire "will possess the earth and its boundaries, with no one existing who opposes it."[28] Rome's restoration then sets in motion the final events of the eschaton, with the rise of the Antichrist and his subsequent defeat, to be followed by divine judgment and the unending reign of God. Thus, this apocalyptic homily establishes important and immediate continuity between the imperial eschatology of late antiquity and its recurrence in the apocalyptic responses to the rise of Muhammad's new religious movement in the seventh and eight centuries.

9   *Letter 14C* (650s CE)

ISHOʿYAHB III OF ADIABENE

Ishoʿyahb of Adiabene is the first of our witnesses to write about
Muhammad's new religious movement from the perspective of having previously lived under Sasanian, rather than Roman, dominion.
He is also the first hierarch and major writer from the Syriac tradition
to provide information about the faith and practice of these invaders.
Ishoʿyahb was well positioned within the Christian communities of
Iran, and thus we may take his perspective as being knowledgeable
and well informed. Ishoʿyahb was born into an aristocratic family
from the region of Adiabene, an ancient center of Christianity in
northern Mesopotamia, whose main city, Arbela (modern Erbil in
Iraq), had a Christian presence probably as early as the beginning
of the second century. Ishoʿyahb belonged to the so-called "Nestorian" Church of the East, one of the two main Christian communities in the Sasanian Empire, and he quickly rose through the ranks
of its hierarchy, becoming bishop of Nineveh in the 620s, metropolitan bishop of Arbela by 640, and finally catholicos of Seleucia-
Ctesiphon, the highest-ranking position in the Church of the East,
which he held from 649 to his death in 659.[1]

It is from the helm of this Persian church that Isho'yahb offers some truly remarkable comments regarding the treatment of Mesopotamia's Christians by Muhammad's followers. Isho'yahb wrote over one hundred letters that survive, providing an unrivalled perspective on the administrative affairs of the Church of the East during the transition from Sasanian to the Believers' rule. The letter that particularly concerns us here is *Letter 14C*, which Isho'yahb wrote, while serving as catholicos, to Simeon, the metropolitan bishop of Rev Ardashir, a town at the northern end of the Persian Gulf. Rev Ardashir was the administrative center of the ecclesiastical province of Fars (Persia), which included northern Arabia as well as what is today southwestern Iran. At the beginning of Isho'yahb's reign, Metropolitan Simeon and the province of Fars were refusing to acknowledge the catholicos's authority, and the Christians of Qaṭar, which was part of the province of Fars, were seeking greater autonomy. *Letter 14C* forms part of a larger series of correspondence by Isho'yahb in which he sought, successfully in the end, to resolve the region's separatist aspirations, in part by creating a new metropolitan bishop for Qaṭar and India that was independent of Fars.[2]

Letter 14C[3]

And you alone [Metropolitan Simeon and the Christians of Fars] of all the peoples on earth have renounced all these things [i.e. the authority of bishops, metropolitans, and the catholicos]. And because of your estrangement from all these things, the influence of error has easily taken hold of you first, as it does now. For this one, this seducer of yours and the destroyer of your churches, also appeared before among us in the land of Radan, a land in which there is more paganism than Christianity. Yet because of the praiseworthy conduct of the Christians, not even the pagans were led astray by him. Rather, he was expelled from here as a reprobate. And not only did he fail to uproot the churches, but he was himself uprooted. But, your region of Persia received him, pagans and Christians, and he did with them as he wished, with the consent and obedience of the pagans and the stupor and silence of the Christians.

For these Nomads [ṭayyāyē], to whom God has given dominion over the world at this time, indeed are also among us, as you know. Not only are they not opponents of Christianity, but they even praise our faith and honor the priests and holy ones of our Lord and give assistance to the churches and monasteries. How then did your people of Mrwny' abandon their faith on this pretext of theirs? And this when, as even the people of Mrwny' admit, the Nomads did not force them to abandon their faith but only told them to give up half of their belongings and to hold on to their faith. But they abandoned the faith, which is eternal, and held on to half of their possessions, which is for a short time. And the faith that all peoples have bought and are buying with their lives, and through which they will inherit eternal life, your people of Mrwny' did not even buy with half of their belongings.

Commentary

In this particular letter, Ishoʻyahb upbraids the restive Simeon for his efforts to secede from the authority of the Catholicos. He chides Simeon for the fact that so many of his flock abandoned their Christian faith to join with Muhammad's followers. According to Ishoʻyahb, these apostates renounced their faith primarily in order to avoid forfeiting half of their belongings to these new rulers.[4] Ishoʻyahb specifically mentions a certain "seducer" and "destroyer of churches" who seems to have been instrumental in turning so many in Simeon's province away from the Christian faith. This same "seducer," Ishoʻyahb notes, had also been active "among us in the land of Radan," a region just to the north of the capital Seleucia-Ctesiphon in which "pagans" (presumably Zoroastrians) far outnumbered the Christians.[5] Nevertheless, he explains, on account of the excellence of the Christian minority there, not only were the Christians preserved from this seducer's deceptions but the area's "pagans" were as well. One imagines, judging from the context, that this "seducer" was one of Muhammad's followers, who encouraged the conquered Christians and Zoroastrians to join the new religious community of the Believers. Yet according to Isho'yahb, it was in fact God's will that these Nomads were given rule over the world. Moreover, he remarks, "they even praise our faith and honor the priests and holy ones of our Lord and give assistance to the churches and monasteries." Given such circumstances, Isho'yahb wonders, how it could be that in Simeon's jurisdiction "the people of Mrwny'" would abandon the Christian faith when the reigning Nomads not only did not force them to convert but even encouraged them to remain in their faith. Instead, as Isho'yahb explains, it was merely to avoid forfeiting half of their belongings to the invaders that so many from the people of Mrwny' embraced the faith of their new rulers.

Isho'yahb's brief comments here regarding the treatment of Iran's Christians following the victory of Muhammad's followers are revealing, especially for two points. First, according to Isho'yahb, as others have previously observed, Muhammad's followers were remarkably tolerant of their Christian subjects. Not only did they encourage them to remain in their faith, but they held the Christian community in high regard, showing reverence for its clergy and saints and supporting its institutions. This account certainly stands in sharp contrast to the frequent reports of widespread death and destruction in their wake that we have seen in most of the previous sources. Nevertheless, at the same time Isho'yahb reports that the new rulers demanded, in exchange for such tolerance, that their Christian subjects hand over half of their belongings. Only if they abandoned their Christian faith would they be allowed to retain all of their property, an option, according to Isho'yahb, that inspired many Christians to embrace the faith of their conquerors.

The question of just how much tolerance Muhammad's followers showed to their Christian and other subjects during the early decades of their rule is in fact a complicated issue, as the various sources in the present volume attest. Other contemporary voices seem to confirm Isho'yahb's account of the Believers as relatively tolerant of other faiths. Likewise, there is evidence to suggest that Christians and Christianity in particular were held in high favor by many Believers during the early years. Yet other witnesses, including many of those we have already seen, as well as Anastasius of Sinai, whom we will meet in the following chapter, paint a much less rosy picture and describe Muhammad's followers as actively persecuting Christians and showing utter disrespect for their faith. One should also note that the Qur'an itself reveals significant diversity of opinion regarding the treatment of members of other religious communities. As Reuven Firestone notes, no doubt correctly, on this topic, "The conflicting verses of revelation articulate the view of different factions existing simultaneously within the early Muslim community of Muhammad's day and, perhaps, continuing for a period after his death."[6] As for the seizure of half of one's property in exchange for religious tolerance, there is no other evidence for such an extortionate levy on non-Believers at any point in the early history of Muhammad's religious movement. Perhaps Isho'yahb is simply exaggerating what was actually a much lower imposition for rhetorical effect, although there is little reason to doubt the Christians in question were faced with paying some sort of significant tax.

One of the great mysteries of this passage, however, concerns the identity of the people of Mrwny', with whom Isho'yahb lays the primary blame for such widespread defections from the faith in Simeon's jurisdiction. Although Joseph Assemani originally suggested that this word refers to the inhabitants of Merv in modern

Turkmenistan, this does not seem possible given that these Mrwny'
were within Simeon's jurisdiction, which did not include central
Asia.[7] Accordingly, we should probably look somewhere along the
southern shores of the Persian Gulf, which was under Simeon's
supervision, to find the Mrwny'. Other scholars proposed that we
should read instead *Mzwny'*, a possibility given the peculiarities of
the Syriac script, which would give us "Mazonites": Mazon, a region
that corresponds roughly with the north of modern Oman and parts
of the United Arab Emirates, places us squarely in Simeon's territory.
Yet François Nau notes an instance in another context where both
Mrwny' and *Mzwny'* are used as distinct geographical identifiers,
leading him to look elsewhere. Instead Nau proposes that we have
in this instance a reference to the inhabitants Mahran, the "Maranites," a region corresponding with eastern parts of modern Yemen
and southern Oman, which also would have been within Simeon's
jurisdiction.[8]

Whether we decide to locate the people of Mrwny' in northern
or southern Oman ultimately does not matter very much for how we
understand this passage. It is enough to know that the Mrwny' were
almost certainly a sizable Christian population living somewhere in
the eastern part of the Arabian Peninsula at the time when Muhammad's followers seized control of most of western Asia. The likelihood that these Christians were dwelling in the Arabian Peninsula
could perhaps explain what may appear to be particularly severe
treatment from the Believers: either conversion or forfeiture of half
their belongings. Nowhere else do we find such a high price exacted
for tolerance, if in fact Isho'yahb has not greatly exaggerated it. Yet,
according to Muhammad's earliest biographies, "the last injunction
that the apostle [Muhammad] gave was in his words 'Let not two religions be left in the Arabian peninsula.'"[9] Of course, given the nature
of these biographies there is no guarantee that Muhammad actually
spoke such words from his deathbed.[10] Nevertheless, this tradition

is ascribed to the legendary early authority of Muhammad's life, Ibn Shihāb al-Zuhrī (d. 742), via two lines of transmission, establishing a probability that it came from him.[11] Accordingly, this report would appear to be one of the earlier collective memories of Muhammad, which began circulate among his followers around the beginning of the second Islamic century.

We should be careful about the conclusions that we might draw from this saying attributed to Muhammad. One should not assume, for instance, that there was any idea of an "Arabian" peninsula in the middle of the seventh century, given that Arab identity seems to have developed as a result of the process of Islamicization at the end of the seventh century and was not an operative idea for the early Believers.[12] Nevertheless, Muhammad's saying may indeed preserve at some historical distance a collective memory of more severe treatment of non-Believers in the eastern reaches of the Arabian Peninsula than they received in the more populous and religiously diverse contexts of Mesopotamia and the eastern Mediterranean. Perhaps this memory and such treatment were consequent to the complete lack of any Christian presence in the central Hijaz, in Mecca and Medina, during late antiquity: such, at least, remains the current state of our evidence.[13] One can imagine that differences in demographics may have conditioned the degree of tolerance that was extended. Indeed, Ishoʿyahb's report that the Believers showed great tolerance even reverence and support for Christians may be specific to his interactions with some of their leading authorities in the Sasanian heartland. Quite possibly things were rather different as the Believers extended their sovereignty over eastern Arabia. Perhaps, then, Ishoʿyahb's report that the invaders encouraged Christians to hold on to their faith (for a fee, of course) derives from his own context and was not in fact the circumstance faced by the Christians of Mrwny'. Insofar as Ishoʿyahb seemingly aims to belittle Simeon by portraying him as a poor shepherd of his flock, it may be that he has not bothered to consider such different circumstances and was only too willing to project the more favorable conditions of his milieu onto his rival's jurisdiction. Yet, regardless of how we understand this demand for excessive tribute or the location of the Mrwny', the tolerance and even reverence of the Believers for Christians described here by Isho'yahb is surely the most remarkable feature of his report.

Isho'yahb, one should also note, is seemingly the first Syriac writer to refer to Muhammad's followers using the term *mhaggrāyē*, albeit in a different letter from the one translated above.[14] Although many scholars would interpret this word as a reference to the Hagarene or Ishmaelite identity of these invading Nomads, more probably the word instead reflects their self-designation as "Muhājirūn," or "Emigrants." In addition to calling themselves the "Believers," Muhammad's early followers also seem to have adopted the name "Muhājirūn," understanding themselves as "Emigrants" who had undertaken the religious obligation of *hijra*. Although in later Islamic tradition *hijra* is of course used specifically to refer to Muhammad's migration from Mecca to Medina, beginning with Patricia Crone and now most recently with Ilkka Lindstedt and Peter Webb, scholars have demonstrated that in the first century *hijra* did not have this specific reference to Muhammad's flight to Medina. Rather, the *hijra* was an act to be undertaken by all of his followers, a "religiously motivated migration (*hijra*) during the conquests" to the lands recently seized from the Romans and Persians.[15] Thus, Muhammad's followers seem to have called themselves "Muhājirūn" in the early part of their history, a self-identification that is reflected in Isho'yahb as well as in the writings of Jacob of Edessa, who will be considered below.

10   *Edifying Tales* (ca. 660–90 CE)
      Homily on the Lord's Passion (?)
      The Hodegos (ca. 686–89)
      Questions and Answers (ca. 690)

ANASTASIUS OF SINAI

Anastasius of Sinai is easily one of the most important figures in Christian religious and monastic life during the seventh century, and yet both he and his corpus are very difficult to discern. Indeed, although his writings comprise "a key source for the history of the seventh-century east Mediterranean society and belief," one still requires something of a guide to navigate the various works attributed to him.[1] Most of what we know about Anastasius himself must be derived from these writings, and the resulting biography is frustratingly meager.[2] As best we can tell, Anastasius was born on Cyprus, probably sometime around 630 CE, and following the Believers' conquest of the island in 649, he left for the Holy Land. There, he entered the monastery of the Theotokos at Mount Sinai (today the monastery of St. Catherine), where, according to tradition, he came under the tutelage of perhaps Sinai's most famous monk, John Climacus. Nevertheless, Anastasius certainly did not remain cloistered, and he traveled widely among the Christians of the Near East throughout his life, serving as an itinerant polemicist in the cause of the council of Chalcedon's two-nature Christology against its Miaphysite and Monothelite opponents. Yet around 680 he retired, it would seem, to the monastery at Mount Sinai, where he spent the final decades of his life gathering together the wisdom that he had amassed and the stories that he had collected, remaining there until his death, probably around 700.

Anastasius wrote in a number of different genres, and only in the last few decades have his works begun to receive the attention that they deserve, including the production of critical editions. Anastasius's most well-known and widely circulated work is his *Hodegos*, or *Guide* to the true faith, compiled in the 680s, it would seem. The *Hodegos* is a bit of a hodgepodge, consisting of several treatises, part of a letter, alleged records of public discussions, and various other materials that Anastasius attached as appendixes. Between 686 and 689 he stitched together these varied works, adding in editorial scholia, or comments, as he worked.[3] Nevertheless, if the *Hodegos*'s contents vary in genre and occasion, their purpose is quite consistent—namely, vigorous defense of the Council of Chalcedon's two-natures Christology against its Miaphysite critics. Anastasius also compiled a collection of *Questions and Answers*, a popular genre in the early Middle Ages. In contrast to the *Hodegos*, this work takes a practical rather than a polemical focus, addressing matters of piety and practice directed toward the daily lives of ordinary Christian laypeople.[4] Although it is possible that this collection was compiled only after Anastasius's death by some of his followers, "in any case the material that it contains is authentic and goes back to the last third of the 7th century."[5]

In addition to these two main works, there are many other writings attributed to Anastasius, although their authenticity is not always certain. Scholars are largely agreed that Anastasius is also the author of a series of homilies on the creation of human-kind, as well as several homilies and sermons on a variety of other topics, ranging from the state of the dead to the Transfiguration to the apostle Thomas. Among the latter is an unedited *Homily on the Passion*, discussed briefly below, which includes information regarding building activity on the Temple Mount. A few anti-Miaphysite and anti-Monothelite treatises are also assigned to Anastasius with some confidence.[6] Yet particularly important for the present purposes is a collection of "stories" (*diēgēmata/Narrationes*) ascribed to Anastasius. These *Edifying Tales* stand very much in the same tradition as John Moschus's *Spiritual Meadow*, discussed in chapter 7, and Anastasius's compilation demonstrates the continuity of this monastic genre across the seventh century. There are, however, two different collections of *Edifying Tales* ascribed to Anastasius, only one of which is universally reckoned among his genuine works.[7]

Until rather recently, scholars were mostly agreed that the first of these two collections, sometimes also designated as collection "A," was compiled by Anastasius early in his career, most likely during the 660s, shortly after the death of John Climacus. Its stories concern primarily the exploits of the monks of Sinai, with little if any information about Muhammad's followers, and thus they are of little interest for the present purpose in any case.[8] Nevertheless, Karl-Heinz Uthemann has recently argued that this collection was produced much earlier, before 629 CE, and therefore cannot be the work of the author of the *Hodegos*. Accordingly, he maintains, this collection's passing notice of recent invaders who had profaned the holy summit of Sinai is a reference not to Muhammad's followers but rather to the Persians, who occupied the region from 614 to 628, while a single mention of Saracens in one story refers to the local pre-Islamic population.[9] It remains to be seen whether Uthemann's careful and detailed arguments will establish a new consensus.

The second collection, however, sometimes designated as "BC," is widely regarded as authentic and is of much greater interest for our purpose. Although most scholars have assumed that Anastasius made this collection sometime around 690, as we will see below, it may have been compiled as early as sometime in the 670s. Its stories have much to tell about relations between the Christians of the Near East and their new Arab (for so Anastasius occasionally names them) sovereigns.[10] Like Moschus before him, Anastasius gathered the stories in this second collection during his travels among the Christians of the eastern Mediterranean, and they relate various anecdotes that seem to date to the middle of the seventh century. Indeed, several of the stories translated in this chapter can be dated with high probability to between approximately 640 and 660.

At present, this second collection unfortunately lacks a proper edition, and only a handful of its stories have been published in piecemeal fashion. The complete text is available only in André Binggeli's Paris dissertation, copies of which are extremely rare and difficult to obtain. Nevertheless, a critical edition has long been promised by Binggeli, who remarks that "this collection is one of the early apologetic works entirely dedicated to the defense of Christian faith facing Islam. Its main interest lies in the insight it gives into many aspects of day-to-day Christian-Muslim relations in the first half-century after the Muslim conquests."[11] Not surprisingly, given the context in which Anastasius lived and wrote, his works occasionally refer to the recently arrived followers of Muhammad. Mostly the members of this religious community appear as wicked and blasphemous oppressors of the Christians, in contrast, perhaps, to some other contemporary sources that seem to describe more harmonious relations. Nevertheless, such divergent assessments of the Believers' rule are not entirely unexpected. One imagines that the new rulers were not always uniform in their treatment of Christians, and likewise, that different Christians may have perceived their collective treatment by Muhammad's followers differently.

Edifying Tales, Collection II (B/C)[12]

II.2 (B2)[13]   When the Saracens entered Constantia, immediately the tomb of Epiphanius gushed forth myrrh like a fountain, more than three hundred Megarian pots worth, so that the floor of the sanctuary was filled with this myrrh. And the Saracens drew from it due to its sweet fragrance—not because they believed in its holiness but out of delight for the myrrh. Behold with me the stupidity of the infidels, that even when seeing signs and wonders they did not believe [cf. John 4.48]. For this miracle happened not only in Constantia but also took place in Neapolis near Nemesos. Indeed, when the Saracens entered the church, immediately the sarcophagus of Tychicus, the disciple of the apostles, gushed forth so much that the feet of those who entered the sanctuary were submerged up to the ankles. And although the Arabs saw, they did not understand [cf. Mark 4.12]. They were not awestruck, and they did not believe. Instead, they considered the event a trifle, according to the saying, "the wisdom of God will not enter a foolish heart" [cf. Wis Sol 1.4–5], for "godliness is an abomination to sinners" [Sir 1.25]. For how, tell me, was Pharaoh served by such signs as those that Moses worked before him [cf. Ex 8–12]? Yet it is necessary to learn from such things. For I hear many people say: if signs and wonders had taken place, the infidels would have been able to believe. But let those who say this hear what the Jews said about Christ, concerning his miracles: "He casts out demons by Beelzebul, the ruler of the demons" [Luke 11.15]. And the Greeks also used to say these things about the signs of the holy martyrs, which were done by God as the holy ones were enduring their torments, just as the Jews also in no way believed in Christ, even though they beheld such signs in his Passion, but instead remained in their ungodliness.

And so that we may substantiate what has just been said, hear another story that reveals the stupidity of the infidel new Jews. Four[14] miles from Damascus, there is a town called Karsatas, where there is a sanctuary of the holy and victorious martyr Theodore. The Saracens entered this sanctuary and dwelled there, making it utterly filthy and unclean with women and children and animals. Then, one day, when most of them were sitting and talking, one of them shot an arrow at the icon of Saint Theodore, and it hit the right shoulder of the image. And immediately blood came forth and flowed down to the bottom of the image, as all the Saracens beheld the miracle that took place: the arrow stuck in the shoulder of the icon and the blood flowing down. And even having witnessed such a wonderous miracle, they did not come to their senses: the one who shot the arrow did not repent, not one of them cried out at him, they did not leave the sanctuary, and they did not cease their filthy ways. Yet they did pay the ultimate penalty, for there were twenty-four of them dwelling in the sanctuary, and a few days later all of them died a painful death, although no one else in the town died then, except only those who were dwelling in the sanctuary of Saint Theodore. But the icon that was struck with an arrow still remains and has the wound of the arrow and the mark of the blood. And there are many living people who beheld this and were there when this wonder took place, and inasmuch as I have beheld this icon and kissed it, I have written what I saw.

II.7 (C3)[15] Thirty years ago, I was dwelling in the Holy City, on the Mount of Olives, when the Capitolium [i.e., the Temple Mount] was being excavated by the multitude of the Egyptians. Then, one night I was awakened three hours before the wood [i.e., the semantron] was struck at the Holy Anastasis of Christ our God. And behold, I heard digging in that place like the sound of many people toiling and shouting and crying out and throwing lots of debris over the wall.

I was thinking then that it was the Egyptian people who were toiling, and as it were, I was distressed that they did not stop even at night. Then, as I was ruminating on such thoughts, the wood-striker of the Holy Anastasis cried out "Lord, bless" as he gave the signal with the wood. And as he was crying out, immediately the clamor that I heard fell silent and the voices ceased, and a great silence came upon that same place. Then I realized that this was the work of demons, who were rejoicing and collaborating in this excavation. For indeed, when I went down into the city in the morning and described this matter to some of those who were dwelling in Holy Gethsemane, I found that they had heard the same things at night, and they described them. I consider it necessary to mention these things on account of those who think and say that the Temple of God is being built now in Jerusalem. For how could the Temple of God be built in that place? A prohibition has been laid down for the Jews: "Behold, this house is left desolate" [cf. Matt 23.38]. "It is left," said Christ: that is to say, it will remain desolate forever. For this was "the final splendor of this house" [Hag 2.9] that was incinerated by Titus.[16] After the final glory, there is no other final glory, for nothing is more final than the final.

11.8 (C4)[17] Now, I thought it would be useful to make clear to readers the reason why I have set out to write these things down. Many and beyond number are the wonders and miracles of God that have presently come about in our days among the Christians in various places. The things that have been manifest and come to pass in various places on land and at sea are worthy of recording and remembering completely. Of these, I have sketched more than thirty in notes for recollection. But now, on account of the uncertainty of our life, I am eager to compile only those that strengthen the faith of Christians and provide great encouragement to our brothers who have been taken captive and for all those who hear and read them with faith. Among these is the one now about to be told.

When according to God's righteous judgment the nation of the Saracens went forth from their own land, they also came here to the Holy Mountain of Sinai, in order to take control of the place and to force those Saracens who were already there and were previously Christians to apostatize from faith in Christ. When those who had their dwelling place and tents near the fortress[18] and the Holy Bush heard this, they went up to the Holy Summit as if to a fortified place, in order to fight the approaching Saracens from above, which they did. Nevertheless, since they were unable to stand against the multitude of those who came, they surrendered to them and joined their faith.

Among them was an ardent lover of Christ. When he saw the apostasy and destruction of the souls of his kindred taking place, he started off for a certain treacherous, precipitous place, to throw himself off and escape, choosing a bodily death rather than to betray his faith in Christ and imperil his soul. Then, when his wife saw him turning to flee and about to throw himself down from that frightful and treacherous place, she rose up quickly. Forcefully taking hold of her husband's garment, with streams of tears she explained to him, saying in the Arabic language: "Where are you going, my good husband? Why are you abandoning me, the woman who has lived by your side since childhood? Why are you handing me over to destruction along with your orphan children, striving only to save yourself? Recall, with God as my witness in this moment, that I have never betrayed your marriage bed, so do not let me be defiled in body and soul. Recall that I am a woman, lest I lose my faith and my children. But if you have really decided to depart, save me and your children first, and then, having saved us, save your own soul. Beware lest on the day of judgment God will exact judgment on you for my soul and those of your children, because you strove only to save yourself. So, fear God and slay me and your children, and then go forth with honor. Do not let us, like orphaned sheep, fall into the hands of these wolves [cf. Matt 10.16], but imitate Abraham and offer us as a sacrifice to God in this holy place [cf. Gen 22.1–19]. And do not take pity on us, so that God will take pity on you. Sacrifice these your children to the one who gave them to you, so that through our blood, God may also save you. It is good for us to be offered to God by you, and not to be led astray by the lawless ones into destruction or to be viciously abused at the hands of the barbarians. Do not be led astray: I will not release you. Either you will remain with us, or you will slay both me and your children and then you will go forth."

By saying these things and other similar things, she persuaded her husband, and he drew his sword and slew both her and his children. And then, throwing himself down from the cliff on the southern side of the Holy Summit, he went forth and alone came away safe from the impending destruction, since all of the other Saracens surrendered and apostatized from faith in Christ. But while they went astray, he, like the prophet Elijah who saved himself from impious hands by fleeing to Horeb [3 Rgns 19.1–18)], "wandered in the deserts and in the mountains and in the caves and in the holes in the ground" [Heb 11.38]. By living among the beasts [cf. Mark 1.13], he escaped the wicked beasts. He became a wanderer who worshipped God, in order not to become a wanderer who worshipped idols, for thereafter he did not set foot in a house or a city or a village until he made his way to the Heavenly City. Instead, he was for many years, like Elijah, Elisha, and John, a hermit as well as a citizen of God.

Now, since what he dared to do to his wife and his children by his own sword is shocking, some may reasonably question whether God would actually accept such a sacrifice as his, the good God who loves humankind wants to give assurance to all, what did he do? Some days before, God revealed and foretold to his servant in the desert his departure from this life. And he went to the Holy Bush to pray and receive the holy mysteries. And when he became ill in what is called the guesthouse, some of the holy fathers came to his side. Most of them are still alive, being eyewitnesses to these things.

When the servant of God came to the very hour of his going forth to God, he saw coming toward him the holy fathers who had been slaughtered here by the barbarians as martyrs of God.[19] He greeted and embraced them as if he were seeing friends after a long time. And he received prayers from them and rejoiced and exulted with them as if in church. And some of them he greeted by name, and moving his lips, he kissed and embraced them. And as if he had been summoned to some feast and celebration by them all and was going forth with them, thus he went forth rejoicing merrily, having the holy fathers as fellow-travelers, as he himself related and described to those who were at his side.

For my part, I think that they were angelic powers appearing in the guise of the holy fathers who fought the good fight in this place and received the crown of victory [cf. 2 Tim 4.7–8]. They were honoring and escorting him well, this one who imitated their ways in their places, and who showed love and faith to God beyond the righteous ones of old.

II.11 (c7)[20]   Some men, true servants of Christ our God who had the Holy Spirit in them, told us that a few years ago a Christian man was present in the place where those who hold us in slavery have the stone and the object of their worship. He said: "When they had slaughtered their sacrifice, for they sacrificed there innumerable myriads of sheep and camels, we were sleeping in the place of sacrifice. Around midnight, one of us sat up and saw an ugly, misshapen old woman rising up from the earth. And immediately he nudged us and woke us up, and we all saw her take the heads and feet of the sheep that they had sacrificed and toss them into her lap, and then she descended into the netherworlds whence she had come. Then we said to one another: 'Behold, their sacrifices do not rise up to God, but go downward. And that old woman is the fraud of their faith.'" Those who saw these things are still alive in the flesh unto this very day.

II.13 (C8)[21] Above we spoke about Sartabias, who suffered because a demon spoke to him, and the demon called the Arabs his allies.[22] The story that we are about to tell confirms that story for our edification and benefit.

At Klysma[23] there was a certain man named Azarias, who was first among those who were called Doukatores[24] and was a friend and well-known to me. He had a son named Moses, who is still alive and living at In.[25] This Moses had been possessed since the age of childhood. Therefore, when his father, who was a good Christian, died five years ago, Moses found himself released, and he was led astray to renounce his faith in Christ. Then, after having been denounced by his fellow citizens, he became a Christian again. And after a little while, he again renounced our faith, and since he did this multiple times, he was denounced by his fellow citizens.

Therefore, when I came to In a year ago, I found this apostate, and since I had been an old friend of both him and his father, I denounced and chastised him for having renounced his faith in Christ many times. Then Moses groaned and said to me: "But what can I do, noble Abba, for each time when I turn back and become a Christian, the demon viciously assaults me, and when I again become an apostate, he doesn't attack me at all. But many times the spirit has appeared to me and warned me, saying, 'Do not venerate Christ, and I will not attack you! Do not confess him as God and the Son of God, and I will not come near you! Do not receive Communion, and I will not vex you! Do not make the sign of the Cross, and I will be content with you.'" I am not the only one who heard these things from Moses, but this miserable man found the courage to reveal these things in secret to some others of our brothers who are trustworthy.

Let the church of Christ hear and rejoice greatly! Let the children of Christians hear these things and let them dance and preserve them indelibly! Let the children of Jews and infidels hear these things and let them be ashamed! Let those who do not confess that

Christ is God hear and let them be put to shame! For since even demons acknowledge such things, they insult Christ even more than the demons. Demons fear the cross of Christ, but these demons in the flesh mock the cross. And the present story demonstrates that demons are frequently overcome by the sign of the cross, which is also confirmed by the one about to be told.

II.22 (C13)²⁶   The commemoration of the victorious martyr George the Black is still celebrated even now in Damascus. He was a slave of a Saracen in Damascus, and because he had been taken prisoner as a child, he renounced his faith when he was eight years old. Then, when he reached the age of adolescence and had grown in knowledge, he returned and became a steadfast Christian, disdaining all human fears. Then, one day when one of his fellow slaves, a Christ-hating apostate, was headed off for a beating, he slandered him, telling his master that so-and-so had become a Christian. And so when he summoned him there, he questioned him and urged him to pray with him. And even though he insisted and threatened him many times, he was not able to persuade him to apostatize from faith in Christ. Therefore, he ordered four of the Saracens who were gathered there to grab both of his hands and both of his feet and to hold him up with his belly toward the ground. And when this had been done, his master cut him in half with a sword by his own hands. But the inhabitants of Damascus took his remains and placed them with honor in a memorial tomb for him alone in front of the city, wherein no one lies except for the servant and martyr of Christ, George.

Commentary

Although we can only be certain that this collection was compiled by 690 at the latest, as noted above, many of its tales are significantly earlier, as evidenced particularly by the second story (II.7), which relates events from Jerusalem "thirty years ago." In this same anecdote, Anastasius explains that he wrote this story down in response to "those who think and say that the Temple of God is being built now in Jerusalem." There is general agreement that Anastasius refers here to the construction of the Dome of the Rock, which was completed in 691. Yet it seems unlikely that construction on the Dome of the Rock began only in 687 under ʿAbd al-Malik. Instead, it seems likely that construction must have begun significantly earlier, under the direction of the future caliph Muʿāwiya, who had served as governor of Syria and Palestine from 641 to 661, prior to reigning as Caliph from 661 to 680 after being crowned in Jerusalem.[27]

As Oleg Grabar notes of the circumstances surrounding the Dome of the Rock's construction, "The ten years that preceded the alleged completion of the Dome of the Rock, in fact the twelve years that followed Muʿāwiyah's death in 680 were years of almost unceasing internecine strife between various Arab factions, and it is not until the defeat of Ibn al-Zubayr by al-Hajjaj late in 692 that peace was restored within the half-urbanized factions of the Iraqi cities. By then the Dome of the Rock already had been completed."[28] Thus, Grabar concludes, we must presumably look to the reign of Muʿāwiya to find the planning, foundation, and design of the Dome of the Rock, a structure that likely was merely completed under ʿAbd al-Malik in 691 rather than initiated during his reign. Muʿāwiya, in contrast to ʿAbd al-Malik, had a demonstrable connection with Jerusalem, and accordingly he began construction there of a shrine "because Jerusalem alone was endowed with the kinds of associations with God and with kings that made an event there or a building reverberate throughout the world of Christians and of Jews as well as among the new Muslims." The Dome, then, was not built under ʿAbd al-Malik with the intent of diverting the pilgrimage, as alleged in some later anti-Umayyad polemics, but rather it was intended to commemorate the Jerusalem Temple, as attested by a number of sources in this volume, thereby laying claim to the Abrahamic legacy and the divine right of rulership.[29]

In such case we should perhaps rethink the dating of Anastasius's collection, which hinges primarily on his reference to those who thought that the Temple was being rebuilt as he was writing. Given the likelihood that construction on the Dome began prior to 680, the possibility that Anastasius compiled these pious tales sometime in the 680s seems quite possible. This dating would place his eye-witness account of workers clearing the Temple Mount thirty years prior, sometime in the 650s. Such a date comports with other sources collected in the present volume indicating that Muhammad's follow-ers first began their building activities at the Temple Mount shortly after capturing the city. Therefore, 690 must be understood simply as the latest possible date for this collection and its various stories, which are of course themselves older than the collection itself. But given the probability that work on the Dome of the Rock had begun well before 690, we must consider the strong possibility that both the collection and its components are earlier still.

II.2

This story from the collection has long been known, at least in its sec-ond part, from an earlier, incomplete edition of Anastasius's *Edifying Tales* made by François Nau over one-hundred years ago. Neverthe-less, this tale has never been translated into English and has likewise been largely ignored in the study of Islamic origins. Moreover, the version of the tale edited by Binggeli is about twice as long as Nau's, beginning with two parallel episodes that share the same themes as the final, previously published one: the disgraceful disrespect of the invading Saracens for Christian holy places and relics as well as their unfathomable disregard for divine signs and wonders that transpired before their very eyes. In the first story, from the longer version of this tale, Anastasius tells of events at the shrine of Saint Epiphanius in Constantia on Cyprus following the Saracens' invasion of the island, which took place in 649–50. When the Saracens enter Epiphanius's tomb, it miraculously fills with myrrh, yet the Saracens are not impressed; rather, they simply delight in the pleasure of the sweet-smelling myrrh. Likewise, on the same island in Neapolis, when the Saracens enter the church there, myrrh again gushes forth from the tomb of Tychicus, a companion of the apostle Paul. Once again, the Saracens show no regard for Christian holy sites and relics or for the miracles that they produced.

Their disrespect comes even more into focus in the final tale of the Saracen occupation of the shrine of the martyr Theodore, some four miles from Damascus in an otherwise unknown town named Karsatas. According to Anastasius, they took up residence in the shrine, which they defiled with every sort of debauchery. One of them even went so far as to shoot an arrow into an icon of the shrine's saint, Theodore, and immediately the wounded icon miraculously began to bleed. The Saracens, however, were completely unfazed by this wonder, and continued to pollute the shrine with their presence and their depravity. Then, one day, all twenty-four of the Saracens who were squatting in the sanctuary suddenly died a painful death, even though no one else living in the village at the time was affected. According to Anastasius, the miraculous icon still remained at the shrine, wounded by the arrow and with traces of the blood still visible, as he himself could attest, having seen the icon and venerated it himself.

No doubt, the most important point of these stories for Anastasius and his readers was the wonders that were worked at these shrines, a testament in their view to the truth of their faith and the spiritual ignorance of their conquerors. For the historian, however, these anecdotes are especially interesting for their reports of disrespect and even violence against Christian shrines and sacred objects by the Saracen invaders. Such actions are admittedly not entirely unexpected of conquering soldiers who adhered to a new, different religious movement. Nevertheless, such desecration of a Christian shrine, particularly in the final episode, stands sharply at odds with other reports from this period that describe the great respect that these invaders had for the Christians, their traditions, and their sanctuaries, some of which are included in this collection (for instance, Isho'yahb III in the previous chapter). As other scholars have noted, there is even some indication that the early Believers shared some sacred spaces with the Christians, especially in Jerusalem.[30] Yet Anastasius here alerts us that such reverence and condominium was not always in evidence, certainly, not in Cyprus and Syria. While it may be that many of the early Believers were open to Christian inclusion in their new religious movement, the experiences of Anastasius and the holy men and women that he knew clearly were otherwise.

II.7

The second anecdote above is among the most interesting. Here Anastasius relates events that he himself experienced some thirty years before committing them to writing, seemingly sometime before 657–60 at the latest, and perhaps even earlier in the 650s. In the anecdote, Anastasius reports that while he was living in Jerusalem thirty years ago, on the Mount of Olives across from the Temple Mount, he witnessed building activity at night on the Temple Mount, "excavating" the site—presumably clearing it in preparation for a new building. According to Anastasius, he mistakenly thought this work was being done by "Egyptians," only to discover that the laborers were in fact demons, who were assisting the Egyptians by continuing this work on their behalf at night. Of course,

Anastasius's report of demonic labor on the Temple Mount is not to be believed, and indeed, demonic collaboration with Muhammad's followers forms a frequent theme of these stories.[31] Nevertheless, his report that the Believers had begun construction work on the Temple Mount by the middle of the seventh century is another matter.

Presumably, Anastasius did in fact witness building activity on the Temple Mount at this time; his reference to Egyptians, as Bernard Flusin notes, possibly indicates conscript labor taken from Egypt during its conquest, which took place between 639 and 646.[32] Anastasius's eyewitness account thus offers important confirmation of similar reports seen already in the *Armenian Chronicle* attributed to Sebeos (chapter 6) and the appendix to the Georgian version of the *Spiritual Meadow* (chapter 7), as well as related accounts to follow from *The Secrets of Rabbai Shim'on* (chapter 12), Adomnán (chapter 15), and The Apocalypse of Ps.-Shenoute (chapter 16). Clearly the Believers had begun to build on the desolation of the Temple Mount well in advance of the Dome of the Rock's construction, apparently not long after they took control of Jerusalem. Collectively these witnesses attest, as Flusin concludes, to a program of building on the Temple Mount presumably under the direction of the future caliph Mu'āwiya, who served as governor of Syria and Palestine from 641 to 661.[33] The nature of this construction activity is not entirely clear, but there can be no doubt that soon after capturing Jerusalem, Muhammad's followers quickly constructed some sort of edifice and restored worship on the Temple Mount. Given the likelihood, then, that construction on the Temple Mount, and quite possibly the Dome of the Rock, began under Mu'āwiya and seems to have been an ongoing process, we certainly should not rule out that Anastasius here describes preliminary construction work on the Dome, particularly given his comments in this context rebutting those contemporaries who were claiming that the Temple was being rebuilt.[34]

The assault on Sinai that inspired this anecdote most likely took place in the middle of the seventh century, presumably sometime not long after the invasion of Egypt began in 640.[35] Its most shocking element is surely the protagonist's murder of his wife and children in order to protect them from either apostasy or physical abuse at the hands of the invaders—or possibly both. From the story's opening, we learn that the Saracens in the region of Mount Sinai had already been Christianized before Muhammad's followers seized control of the region. When the latter arrived, these Christian Saracens made a tactical retreat to the summit of Mount Sinai, hoping thereby to save themselves from the approaching enemies. They did not succeed, however, and ultimately, they surrendered, abandoning their Christian faith and joining instead the new faith of Muhammad's followers. The story's unnamed hero, however, refuses to submit. Instead, he decides to run for a precipice on the mountain and throw himself off, thereby saving himself from the perils of apostasy. Before he can escape, however, his wife grabs hold of him and insists that he must kill both her and their children before saving himself in this fashion. To take his own life without also first taking theirs would be a selfish act, she explains, for which he would be held accountable by God on the day of judgment.

Remarkably, the man is persuaded that it is God's will that he should sacrifice his family in order to save them, and he does just that before subsequently hurling himself down from the cliff. The man's fate thereafter is a bit perplexing, however. The tale prepares its readers to expect his death: his intent, so we are told, was to throw himself off the cliff, "choosing a bodily death rather than to betray his faith." Yet he seems to have survived his leap, remaining alive to wander in the deserts and live among the beasts for many years until he died in the monastery surrounded by the holy fathers, whom

Anastasius thinks were in fact angels. It is quite unexpected, I think, that our hero should escape with his life after having slain his own family. That he should slaughter them and yet himself survive to live a blessed life is even more outrageous than if he had simply perished alongside them—an outcome that would nevertheless be highly problematic in its own right.

Anastasius is well aware that many of his readers will question whether God would receive such a dreadful "sacrifice," the slaughter of one's wife and children to save them from the Saracens, yet his account of this man's wondrous departure from the world seems designed to assure us that his act was indeed righteous before God. The "moral" of the story, as it were, is astonishing: the implication is that it is better to murder one's own family rather than have them fall under the control and influence of these invaders, and, likewise, that one who did so would be reckoned as a holy man, beloved by God for such action. This position can only be characterized as extreme and exceptional, and to my knowledge one does not find anything similar advanced elsewhere in the literature responding to the emergence of Muhammad's new religious movement. That Anastasius would somehow see such actions as embodying an "edifying" tale that should be told to strengthen the faith of Christians in the face of this new religion seems truly bizarre even when judged within its own cultural setting.

Finally, in this story the invading Saracens certainly do not appear to be accommodating of Christianity, as other contemporary sources may seem to suggest. The Christian Saracens of Sinai are instead converted to the new faith of Muhammad's followers wholesale, with the implication that the only alternative to such apostasy was the death sought by the story's protagonist and his family. Of course, it is possible that in this instance it is Anastasius, rather than Muhammad's followers, who is determined to draw a firm religious boundary. It could be, for instance, that Muhammad's followers were simply welcoming these Christians into their community of the Believers even as they remained Christians, a practice suggested by some of our early sources, while Anastasius regarded any such association with this new religious community as tantamount to apostasy. At the same time, however, the story infers a compulsion to join this new community, which its hero sought to escape by the extreme means of death. On the whole, then, Anastasius's account of Muhammad's followers here does not portray them as particularly tolerant of Christianity, but to the contrary, only by death could one avoid forsaking one's faith in Christ through assimilation to the faith of the Saracen invaders. Yet perhaps special circumstances apply in this instance, much as we have proposed above for the Christians of Qatar and Oman. There is evidence from the early Islamic tradition of a policy that presented Christian Arabs with "the choice between conversion to Islam and great hardship, even death."[36] Although the notion of an "Arab" identity is, as we have noted previously, highly questionable at this early date, it certainly may have been the case that "Saracen" nomads who were Christians may have faced greater compulsion from the invaders to convert to their new faith.

II.11

According to this tale, Anastasius spoke with some Christians who had been to the place where the Believers offered their sacrifices—the place of "the stone and the object of their worship." There, we are told, they sacrifice "innumerable myriads of sheep and camels"; when or how often they do this is not made clear. The comments regarding the misshapen woman and the downward direction of their sacrifices are, of course, polemical and of little use for understanding the early history of this new religious movement. Nevertheless, this story provides one of the earliest references outside of the Qur'an to the Believers' practice of offering animal sacrifices at a particular, distinctive place of worship, presented here on the basis of Christian eyewitnesses. As we will see in chapter 11, the *Khuzistan Chronicle* also provides a roughly contemporary description of the Believers' desert shrine, the so-called "tent of Abraham," based on reports from tribal lore passed down among the Nomads [*ṭayyāyē*] themselves.

In both instances, however, the shrine's location is unfortunately not specified, and while the Meccan Kaʿba is certainly a strong candidate, one should not entirely exclude other possibilities at this early stage. Matters of sacred geography and sacred direction among the early Believers were complex, and there certainly may have been some sort of primitive, alternative shrine to the Meccan Kaʿba.[37] In favor of the Kaʿba, of course, is the reference here to a sacred stone, which, interestingly, is identified as "object of their worship" (*to sebas*). Yet at the same time, one wonders how this group of pious Christians would have found their way all the way down to Mecca, particularly given the startling lack of any evidence for a Christian presence in the Hijaz before or after the rise of Islam.[38] Perhaps it might be easier to envision these Christians witnessing the Believers' sacrifices at a shrine somewhere closer to the Mediterranean world? Or possibly these men had been taken there as slaves? The men do describe the Believers as "those who hold us in slavery," but the language seems more metaphorical and collective rather than indicating the specific status of these men. It certainly does not seem that they were slaves when Anastasius encountered them.

Binggeli, the text's editor, suggests that these men should be understood as sailors, since the previous two anecdotes in the collection concern sailors from the Roman port of Klysma on the Red Sea.[39] Yet, the anecdote itself makes no indication of this status, and presumably such an assumption is intended to identify this shrine with Mecca based on outdated notions regarding Mecca's importance in a network of international sea trade. As Patricia Crone has convincingly demonstrated, Mecca was in fact not a major center of international sea trade, as scholars once widely presumed.[40] Indeed, the fact that the Qur'an often makes reference to sailing and fishing stands among the primary reasons for questioning its genesis uniquely in the Hijazi context of Mecca and Medina, as the Islamic tradition (and scholarship deferential toward it) would have us believe. Maritime trade is something that is simply not in evidence for Mecca, nor is there any evidence for a culture of fishing and sailing (or agriculture for that matter): to the contrary, these things seem highly improbable in light of its inland desert location.[41] Therefore, while sailors from Klysma would certainly have traversed the Red Sea (if that is in fact what these men were!), one cannot simply assume on this basis that such travels would have somehow brought them to Mecca. Indeed, if the location of this shrine were Mecca, it still remains something of a mystery what these Christian men would have been doing there.

II.13

This anecdote concerns the son of one of Anastasius' friends, a young man named Moses who lived in the above-mentioned port city of Klysma, modern Suez, on the Red Sea. According to Anastasius, Moses changed his allegiance from Christianity to the faith of the Believers more than once, explaining that he left the Christian faith in each instance to silence demons that were tormenting him. In each case when he apostatized, the demons relinquished him, only to beset him again if he returned to faith in Christ. The anecdote's concluding polemics against the Jews and infidels are interesting in their own right for understanding how Christians articulated a response to the faith of their new rulers. Particularly noteworthy is the comment that these infidels insult Christ even more than the demons, since even the demons at least acknowledge that Christ is God. Clearly the issue of Christ's divinity was already emerging as a fault line between the two faiths. Yet the primary significance of this anecdote lies in its report that Moses passed multiple times between the faiths of the Christians and the Believers. One imagines that this was not an isolated incident of vacillating religious loyalties during this tumultuous era.

II.22

This anecdote is the first recorded martyrdom of a Christian at the hands of Muhammad's followers. Its hero, known as George the Black, was taken captive by the Believers when he was only eight years old and enslaved to a Saracen in Damascus. One would imagine that he was captured during the conquests of the Near East, sometime around 640, as Hoyland proposes. At this young age, he renounced his Christian faith for that of his master, only to reclaim his faith in Christ upon reaching adolescence. Assuming that George was approximately eighteen years old when he returned to the Christian fold, and also that he was exposed not long thereafter, he was martyred most likely around 650. Anastasius's opening remark that his victorious martyrdom was "celebrated even now in Damascus" likewise suggests that he was writing at some distance from the events themselves.[42] Of course, from his master's perspective George was not a Christian martyr but an apostate from the new faith preached by Muhammad.

Nevertheless, we may conclude two things from this tale. Firstly, that there were likely many young Christians who were taken captive during the conquests and effectively forced to convert by their masters. Such would seem to be the circumstances faced by the eight-year-old George. One should perhaps consider such possible compulsion alongside claims that Muhammad's followers did not force conversions to their new faith, even if, admittedly, it seems in the main they did not. Secondly, we learn that, at least in some quarters, apostasy from the community of the Believers was an act punishable by death. Certainly, George's martyrdom provides no evidence that Muhammad's followers martyred Christians simply for remaining in their faith. Nevertheless, it would appear to indicate that young Christians were at times taken captive during the conquests and forced to convert. Likewise, this story shows an early practice of capital punishment for apostasy from the faith of the Believers, at least in some instances, even for those who had presumably been converted under compulsion while they were still children. Of course, one should also allow that, as a slave, George's master could execute him more or less at will, and so perhaps it was simply for disobedience, rather than an official policy against apostasy, that George lost his life.

Homily on the Lord's Passion

Unfortunately, this text remains unpublished, although Karl-Heinz Uthemann is presently in the process of preparing a critical edition.[43] In this homily, Anastasius notes that the Temple remained in ruins, a clear sign that God had abandoned the Jews. Then he interjects the voice of an imagined Jew, who objects rhetorically, "But look, it [the Temple] is being built" (All' idou ktizetai, phēsin). Clearly this is a reference to the building activities by Muhammad's followers on the Temple Mount, which they—and seemingly many Jews as well—understood as a restoration of the Temple in some sense. Anastasius then answers, "Your Temple is being built in Jerusalem? Which Temple?" And he continued, listing various elements that were essential to the fallen Jewish Temple, such as its cohort of priests, the Ark of the Covenant, and so on. "Only when I see it all will I know that you have the Temple," he retorts, further declaring that "you will never rebuild the Temple, 'for your house will be left to you desolate' [Matt 23.38]."[44]

Commentary

Anastasius reports here that some Jews understood the building activities of Muhammad's followers to restore worship to the site of the Temple as in some way realizing the Temple's restoration. We have seen other reports to this effect already from other sources, and thus Anastasius adds further confirmation in this homily. One must imagine that there were Jews who identified the edifice that the Believers were building on the Temple Mount with the Temple itself, otherwise his rhetorical dialogue with an imagined Jewish opponent would make very little sense at all. From this we may conclude that some significant number of Jews took a positive view of the Believers' restoration of worship to the Temple Mount, as seen more directly below in the contemporary Jewish Apocalypse of Rabbi Shimʿōn b. Yoḥai (chapter 12). Furthermore, Anastasius's comments here appear to confirm that Muhammad's followers understood themselves as in some sense restoring the Jewish Temple, which is presumably the basis for the Jewish claim. Finally, this Jewish identification of the Believer's sanctuary on the Temple Mount as the restoration of the Temple also seems to indicate a close alliance and sympathy of these Jews with the Believers, if not their actual membership within the community of the Believers itself.

The Hodegos[45]

1.1   Before any sort of discussion, we must condemn all the false assumptions that our opponent presumes about us, such as when we are about to have a discussion with the Arabs, we must first condemn anyone who says that there are two gods, or anyone who says that

God has carnally begotten a son, or anyone who worships any sort of created thing, either in heaven or on earth, as God.

x.2, 4   And when [the followers of Severus] hear of "natures," they think that these are shameful and foul things, things related to the sexual intercourse of male and female bodies. Accordingly, they avoid such an expression as if they were disciples of the Saracens. For when the latter hear about the birth of God and the begetting of God, they immediately think of marriage and insemination and carnal union and blaspheme.

Commentary

This would appear to be the earliest text to refer to Muhammad's followers collectively as "Arabs," and its composition in the late 680s corresponds with the development of a distinctively Islamic confessional identity and Arab ethic identity by Muhammad's followers seemingly at the end of the seventh century.[46] Here Anastasius identifies certain points of theological disagreement between the Christians and their new Arab rulers. Apparently, the Christians found themselves having to explain to the Arab Believers that they do not in fact believe in two Gods, do not believe that God has begotten a son carnally, and do not worship a creature. Presumably, Muhammad's followers had begun to bring such accusations against the Christians on the basis of their worship of Jesus Christ the Son of God as God. Thus, we can see that by the end of the seventh century, the divinity of Christ had emerged as a theological boundary dividing Christians and those belonging to Muhammad's faith. The second passage here simply follows up on the second point from the first one. The Saracens seem to have been accusing Christians of believing that God had physically fathered a son through sexual intercourse since they believed that Christ was the Son of God.

Questions and Answers[47]

80   Question: Some wish to say that Satan fell because he did not bow down before Adam.

     Answer: 1. Such foolish myths belong to the pagans [*Ellēnōn*] and the Arabs, for one can learn from the prophets, and especially from Ezekiel [cf. Ezek 28.2–19; Isa 14.12–14], that Satan was cast out by God because of his pride before the creation of Adam. 2. When God was fashioning this visible creature, the devil thought that God would establish him as its master. Therefore, when he saw that God had made Adam and set him over the works of his hands and subjected all under his feet [Ps 8.7], he then took up arms against him and deceived him.

Commentary

In this collection, which is dated to around 690, Anastasius shows knowledge of a tradition that also appears in the Qur'an, namely that Satan's fall was a consequence of his refusal to bow before Adam after the latter's creation. In several places, the Qur'an relates that God "said to the angels, 'Bow yourselves to Adam'; so they bowed themselves, save Iblis; he refused, and waxed proud, and so he became one of the unbelievers."[48] Of course, one should not assume that Anastasius knew this tradition from reading the Qur'an, or indeed, even that the Qur'an in the form that we now have it had been compiled and was in circulation by this time.[49] This question and answer does, however, provide evidence that this tradition was circulating among Muhammad's early followers, and that it was known to certain Christians and rejected by them in favor of a different tradition from the Hebrew Bible.

11   *The Khuzistan Chronicle* (ca. 660)

The *Khuzistan Chronicle*, as this anonymous chronicle generally is known, has been dated to around 660 based on its contents, including most notably the fact that it makes no clear reference to any event after 652.[1] The chronicle's account of the appearance of Muhammad's followers is somewhat peculiar, given that it describes these events twice and in two very different contexts. Initially, the chronicle provides a rather general notice concerning the arrival of "the sons of Ishmael" and their invasion of Iran following a chronological sequence. Then, near its conclusion, the author again returns to the invasion of the Nomads outside of chronology and with more detail, giving special emphasis to the Believers' invasion of Khuzistan. Nevertheless, this doublet reflects a broader tendency of the chronicle's concluding section. For the most part, the chronicle strictly follows chronological sequence in its account of events, noting the time according to the Sasanian rulers and the leaders of the East Syrian (i.e., "Nestorian") church. Yet, as it draws to a close following reports for the reigns of Yazdgerd II (632–52) and Catholicos Maremmeh (646–49), the work suddenly alters its structure. The chronicle's final entries include, in order, "an account of the miraculous conversion of some Turks by Elias of Merv (d. after 659); a list of towns founded by Seleucus, Semiramis, and Ninus son of Belus; a portrayal of the Arab conquests (630s–40s); and a short survey of Arabian geography."[2]

The abrupt abandonment of chronological sequence at this point has led some scholars to posit that the chronicle's final sections are the work of another author, who has added this material, including the second description of the Nomads' invasion, to an older text that originally concluded with the death of Catholicos Maremmeh.[3] Most scholars are agreed, however, that this conclusion is in fact the work of the same author. As Hoyland proposes, "It may be, then, that the disjuncture is not an indication of a change in author, but of a change of focus and/or source."[4] Inasmuch as all of the events described in this appendix took place either before or within ten years of the ultimate date of the strictly chronological section, 652, there is no reason to suppose their addition by a later hand. One imagines, instead, that upon reaching the end of his historical narrative, the chronicler turned in conclusion to topics of special significance for mid-seventh-century Khuzistan and East Arabia. Such a shift in focus presumably reflects the author's concern with events from his own milieu; accordingly, there is a very real possibility that the information in this section derives from eyewitness reports or even the author's own personal knowledge.

The Khuzistan Chronicle[5]

And Yazdgerd, who was from the royal lineage, was crowned king in the city of Eṣṭak̲r, and under him the Persian Empire came to an end. And he went forth and came to Seleucia-Ctesiphon [Māḥōzē] and appointed one named Rustam as the leader of the army. Then God raised up against them the sons of Ishmael like sand on the seashore. And their leader was Muhammad, and neither city walls nor gates, neither armor nor shields stood before them. And they took control of the entire land of the Persians. Yazdgerd sent countless troops against them, but the Nomads [*ṭayyāyē*] destroyed them all and even killed Rustam. Yazdgerd shut himself within the walls of Seleucia-Ctesiphon and in the end made his escape through flight. He went to the lands of Khuzistan [Huzaye] and Merv,[6] and there he ended his life. And the Nomads took control of Seleucia-Ctesiphon and all the land. They also went to the land of the Romans, plundering and laying waste to the entire region of Syria. Heraclius, the Roman king, sent armies against them, but the Nomads killed more than one hundred thousand of them. But when the Catholicos Isho'yahb saw that Seleucia-Ctesiphon had been devastated by the Nomads and they had brought its gates to 'Aqulā [Kufa],[7] and that those who remained in it were wasting away from hunger, he left and took up residence in Beth Garmai in the town of Kirkuk. . . . And Mar Isho'yahb led the patriarchate for eighteen years. And his body was placed in the martyrium of the church of Kirkuk in Beth Garmai. And Maremeh was appointed as patriarch of the church. . . . And when he was appointed to the lampstand of the Catholicosate, he was held in honor by all the leaders of the Ishmaelites. . . .

. . . And at that time about which we spoke above, when the Nomads had conquered all the lands of the Persians and Romans, they spread out and also entered Khuzistan. They conquered all the fortified cities, namely, Beth Lapaṭ, Karka of Ledan, and the fortress of Shushan.[8] But Susa and Shushtar remained,[9] because they were well fortified, while no one from all the Persians remained to stand against the Nomads except King Yazdgerd and one of his generals, a Mede named Hormazdan, who assembled the troops and held Susa and Shushtar. And this Shushtar has a large population and is extremely well fortified, with mighty rivers and canals surrounding it on all sides like moats. One of the rivers is called Ardashira-gan, named for Ardashir,[10] who dug it. And another one that flows by it is called Semiramis, named for the queen,[11] and another one

Darayagan, named for Darius.[12] And the greatest of them all is a mighty torrent that flows down from the northern mountains.

Then a certain military leader of the Nomads, named Abū Mūsā, went up against Hormizdan the Mede. Abū Mūsā built Basra as a settlement for the Nomads, where the Tigris flows into the great sea, sitting between fertile land and the desert,[13] just as Saʿd ibn [Abī] Waqqāṣ built the city ʿAqulā as another settlement for the Nomads, which they call Kufa, after the name of the bend [*kpiputā*] in the Euphrates.[14] And when Abū Mūsā went up against Hormizdan, this Hormizdan devised a means to prevent them from attacking him while he assembled an army. And he sent a message to Abū Mūsā that he should refrain from taking captives and from destruction, and he would send him as much tribute as he demanded from him. And so they remained for two years. And because of Hormizdan's confidence in the walls, he broke the truce between them, and he killed those who were conveying messages between them, one of whom was George, the bishop of Ulay, and imprisoned Abraham the metropolitan of Prat [Basra].[15] And he sent many troops against the Nomads, and the Nomads destroyed them all. And the Nomads moved quickly and laid siege to Susa, and in a few days, they captured it and killed all the nobles there. And they seized the church there, which is called the church of Mar Daniel, and took the treasure that was kept there, which was protected by royal decree since the days of Darius and Cyrus. And they broke open the silver sarcophagus in which had been laid an embalmed body that many people said was Daniel's, and others, King Darius's, and they carried it off.[16]

And they also laid siege to Shushtar, and for two years they tried to capture it. Then, a certain man from Qatar among the foreigners there became friends with another man whose house was on the wall. And the two of them conspired, and they went out to the Nomads and said to them, "If you give us a third of the spoils from the city, we will let you into the city."[17] And they made an agreement among themselves. And they dug tunnels from inside under the wall and let the Nomads in. And they captured Shushtar and poured forth blood in it like water. They killed the city's interpreter and the bishop of Hormizd-Ardashir,[18] along with the rest of the students, priests, and deacons, whose blood they shed in the sanctuary. But they captured Hormizdan alive.

Afterward, a certain man came forth from among the Nomads named Khālid, and he went to the west and seized lands and cities as far as Arabah.[19] And Heraclius, the king of the Romans, heard about this, and he sent a great army against them, whose leader was named Sacellarius.[20] The Nomads vanquished them, and they destroyed more than one hundred thousand Romans and killed their leader. They also killed Isho'dad, the bishop of Ḥira,[21] who was there with 'Abdmeshih, who served as an emissary between the Nomads and the Romans. The Nomads took control of all the lands of Syria and Palestine, and they wanted to invade Egypt as well. Nevertheless, they were not able, because the border was guarded by the patriarch of Alexandria with a great and mighty army, and he had closed off the entries and exits of the land and had built walls along the banks of the Nile throughout the land.[22] On account of their height, the Nomads could only enter with great difficulty, and they captured the land of Egypt, Thebes, and Africa.

And King Heraclius, on account of distress that came upon him because of the Romans' defeat, went up to his royal city, became ill, and died. And he reigned with his son for twenty-eight years. But the triumph of the sons of Ishmael, who subdued and subjugated these two mighty kingdoms, was from God. Yet God has not yet granted them rule over Constantinople, because victory belongs to him.

And regarding the tent of Abraham,[23] we could not find out what it is, except for the following. Because blessed Abraham was rich in possessions and also wanted to be far away from the jealousy of the Canaanites, he chose to dwell in the remote and vast places of the desert. And since he was dwelling in tents, he built this place for worship of God and offering sacrifices. And because the memory of this place was also preserved with the descendants of this tribe, it received this name also presently, on account of what it was. And it is not new for the Nomads to worship there, but from long ago and from their early days, as they bestow honor on the forefather of their people.

And Hazor,[24] which scripture names "head of the kingdoms" [cf. Josh 11.10], also belongs to the Nomads, and Medina, named for Midian, the fourth son of Abraham by Keturah [cf. 1 Chr 1.32], which is also called Yathrib, and Dumat Jandal,[25] and the land of the Hajarites,[26] which is rich in water, date palms, and fortified buildings, in the similarly abundant land of Hatta,[27] which is on the sea near the islands of Qatar and also is dense with all sorts of vegetation, as is also the land of Mazun,[28] which is also located on the sea, and the land encompasses more than one hundred parasangs, and the land of Yamama,[29] which is located in the middle of the desert, and the land of Ṭawf[30] and the city of Ḥira, which was established by King Mundhir (III, 503/5–54 CE), who was called the warrior and was the sixth in the line of the Ishmaelite kings.[31]

Commentary

The chronicle's initial notice of the Believers' invasion, which appears according to chronological sequence, describes the initial assaults against both Iran and the Romans in Syro-Palestine. According to this account, Muhammad was the leader of sons of Ishmael at the time of their invasion, seemingly in parallel fashion to Rustam's leadership of the Sasanian army. Taking the passage at face value, and without knowledge of the much later Islamic historical tradition, one would certainly assume that the report identifies Muhammad as still alive at the time of the invasion and leading his followers against Rustam and the Sasanian forces. Muhammad's positioning alongside of these other leaders in the conflict, including Yazdgerd III, Rustam, and Heraclius, strongly suggests that we should read this passage as reporting Muhammad's continued leadership of the community into the initial phases of the Near Eastern conquest. Here again, then, we have one of many witnesses from the first Islamic century suggesting that Muhammad was still alive and leading the Believers as they entered the Roman and Sasanian Empires. The Sasanians were massacred in this initial encounter with Muhammad's forces, including their leader Rustam. Muhammad's army then came against the Sasanian capital, Seleucia-Ctesiphon. According to the chronicle, the resulting devastation was severe, so that its citizens were starving. Yazdegerd III then fled the city, first to Khuzistan and then seemingly to Merv in modern Turkmenistan, where he died in exile, while the Catholicos Isho'yahb II (628–45) also left the ruined capital city for Kirkuk in northern Mesopotamia, where he lived until his death. Isho'yahb II's successor, we are told, was the Catholicos Maremmeh (646–49), who "was held in honor by all the leaders of the Ishmaelites." One should certainly note, incidentally, the stark contrast between this account of violent destruction under Isho'yahb II and the report of Isho'yahb III (649–59), who, as seen above (chapter 9), described the great respect that Believers showed toward Christians and Christianity.

The chronicle's second account of the conquests by Muhammad's followers, in its concluding section, narrates the Nomads' invasion of northern Khuzistan, focusing especially on the capture of the cities Susa and Shushtar. The account is so rich in detail that, again, it may very well derive from eyewitness reports and, as Howard-Johnston notes, its quality is deserving of "considerable confidence in the modern reader."[32] After retreating from the capital, Yazdgerd had holed up Khuzistan with one of his generals, an otherwise unknown Hormizdan the Mede. Muhammad's followers soon arrived and took control of the region and most of its cities, excepting only the fortified cities of Susa and Shushtar. Hormizdan initially secured a truce with the leaders of the Believers' army, figures who are known as well from the later Islamic historical tradition, by agreeing to pay tribute in exchange for peace. Hormizdan used the time, however, to build an army, and after two years, he decided that he was in a strong enough position to end the truce. He was wrong. Muhammad's followers quickly took Susa, slaughtering its prominent citizens and stealing the relics of the prophet Daniel from its church, both of which are also reported in the Islamic historical tradition. Then, they laid siege to Shushtar, a well-fortified city. After two years, two men within the city made an agreement with the Nomads, offering to get them into the city by digging tunnels in exchange for one-third of the spoils. The Believers agreed, and with their assistance, they entered the city and massacred many of its inhabitants. The chronicle then shifts theaters, moving to Syria and Palestine, noting that one of Muhammad's generals went west to Arabah, the Wādī ʿAraba, where he engaged the Romans and defeated them, extending the Believers' rule to "all the territories of Syria and Palestine." They wanted to hurry on to Egypt but were temporarily prevented by a large army and fortifications, both of which had been raised by the patriarch of Alexandria. Eventually, with some difficulty, they would seize Egypt as well, all according to the will of God, who nevertheless prevented them from taking Constantinople.

As the chronicle draws to a close, the author reports what he had been able to learn about the "tent of Abraham," an important cultic site for the Believers. This shrine's location, unfortunately, once again is not specified, and while it is quite possible that this "tent" could refer to the Meccan Kaʿba, as with the reference in the previous section from Anastasius, one should not entirely exclude other possibilities at this stage.[33] The main concern in this account of the

Believers' shrine is not so much the animal sacrifices that took place there, but rather that it seeks to explain the shrine's origins as related in the tribal lore of the Believers themselves. Since Abraham, the author relates, was wealthy and was known for wanting to distance himself from the Canaanites, he settled in the desert. There, because he lived in tents, he also set up a tent in which to offer sacrifices to God. These "remote and vast places of the desert" in which the shrine was to be found certainly do not sound like Mecca, at least as it is described by the later Islamic tradition (which is, unfortunately, our only source of information concerning Mecca at this time).

Finally, the chronicle concludes with a list of the territories that had come under the Believers' control by the middle of the seventh century, describing an expanse reaching from northern Galilee to Medina/Yathrib, across northern and central Arabia to the southern coast of the Persian Gulf, all the way to Oman, also including southern Mesopotamia, whose new settlements of Kufa and Basra are mentioned in this text. One should note that the reference to Medina/Yathrib here is the first mention of this city in a source other than the Qur'an. Then, in its final sentence, the chronicle identifies King Mundhir (III, 503/5-54 CE) as "the sixth in the line of the Ishmaelite kings." Al-Mundhir III ibn al-Nuʿman was in fact one of the most famous and longest reigning of the Lakhmid kings, to whom the Sasanian authorities had given authority over all the Saracens in the Persian lands. Judging from this statement, then, it would appear that this Christian author from mid-seventh-century Khuzistan understood the present rulers of these invading "sons of Ishmael" as a continuation of the Lakhmid line, rather than as a new dynasty.[34]

The chronicle, we should note, relates substantial death and destruction as a result of the Believers' invasion, echoing similar reports in many of the other sources that we have already seen. Nevertheless, these invaders were seeimingly willing to forego violence so long as they were paid an adequate tribute, as the truce with

Susa and Shushtar would seem to indicate. When they captured Susa the chronicle says that they stole the relics of the prophet Daniel from a church there, actions which on the one hand would seem to show their disregard for the sanctity of Christian holy places, yet on the other hand the theft perhaps shows the Believers' shared reverence for the bodily relics of this prophet from the Hebrew Bible/Old Testament. In the account of the capture of Shushtar, similar disregard for the Christians and their holy places is on display, as the Believers are said to have executed the bishop there "along with the rest of the students, priests, and deacons, whose blood they shed in the sanctuary." Such violence certainly does not bespeak an interconfessional community of the Believers in this instance. Yet perhaps such bloodshed against the Christians may have been conditioned by the attack the Persians brought against the Believers. It certainly would seem that not all Jews and Christians were seen as the same in the eyes of Muhammad's early followers. Indeed, the chronicler's remark that the successor of Isho'yahb II, the Catholicos Maremmeh (646–49), "was held in honor by all the leaders of the Ishmaelites," seems to indicate in this instance a more positive and engaging attitude toward the Christians of the Near East and their leaders, as do the comments of Maremmeh's successor, Isho'yahb III, seen above.

12 The Apocalypse of Rabbi Shim'ōn b. Yoḥai *(ca. 660?)*
The Secrets of Rabbi Shim'ōn b. Yoḥai

A complex of closely related early medieval Jewish visionary texts ascribed to Rabbi Shim'ōn b. Yoḥai seems to bear witness to an early apocalyptic tradition that understood Muhammad as a messianic deliverer divinely chosen to liberate the Jews and their Promised Land from Rome's oppressive yoke. The various texts all relate Rabbi Shim'ōn's visions of the Ishmaelite invasion, with each giving a slightly different version of events that seems to depend on an earlier common source.[1] The oldest of these works, however, and also the most important, is *The Secrets of Rabbi Shim'ōn b. Yoḥai*, an apocalypse written sometime around the middle of the eighth century whose visions cover the period between the first invasions by Muhammad's followers and the Abbasid revolution. Here we translate only the beginning of this text, which seems to best preserve the oldest traditions of this apocalyptic cluster. Based on the content of the seer's initial visions, and particularly their remarkably positive assessment of Muhammad and his followers, one imagines that the early apocalyptic tradition that has been adopted and adapted by this more recent text was originally produced sometime in the middle of the seventh century.

The Apocalypse of Rabbi Shim'ōn b. Yoḥai[2]

These are the secrets that were revealed to Rabbai Shim'ōn b. Yoḥai while he was hiding in a cave on account of Caesar king of Edom [Rome]. And he stood in prayer for forty days and forty nights and he began thus: "Lord God, how long will you spurn the prayer of your servant?" Immediately the secrets and hiddden things of the eschaton were revealed to him.

And he began to sit and to interpret [the passage] "Then he looked on the Kenite . . ." [Num 24.21]. When he understood that the kingdom of Ishmael would come upon [Israel], he began to say, "Is it not enough, what the wicked kingdom of Edom has done to us that [we must also endure] the kingdom of Ishmael?" And immediately Metatron the prince of the Presence answered him and said: "Do not be afraid, mortal, for the Holy One, blessed be He, is bringing about the kingdom of Ishmael only for the purpose of delivering you from that wicked one [i.e., Edom/Rome]. He shall raise up over them a prophet in accordance with His will, and he will subdue the land for them; and they shall come and restore it with grandeur. Great enmity will exist between them and the children of Esau."

Rabbi Shim'ōn answered him and said: "How will they be our salvation?" He said to him, "Did not the prophet Isaiah say: 'When he sees riders, horsemen in pairs, . . .' [Isa 21.7]? Why does the one riding a donkey come before the one riding a camel? Should he not have said instead, 'the one riding a camel, the one riding the donkey'? No, but rather when the one who rides on the camel comes [i.e., Muhammad], through him the kingdom of the one who rides on a donkey [Zech 9.9] has emerged." Another interpretation of the rider on the donkey is that when he comes he is [also] riding on a donkey. Therefore, they will be the salvation of Israel like the salvation of the one riding on a donkey.

And Rabbi Shim'ōn said that he learned from Rabbi Ishmael that when he learned that the kingdom of Ishmael was coming to measure the land with ropes, as it is said, "and he shall distribute the land for a price" [Dan 11.39], they will make cemeteries into pastureland for flocks, and when one of them dies, they will bury him in any place they please. And they will return and plow over the grave and sow it, as it is said, "Thus shall the people of Israel eat their bread, unclean" [Ezek 4.13]. Why? Because the corrupted field will be unknown. Again, "Then he looked on the Kenite . . ." And what was the parable that the wicked one [Balaam] brought? When he saw that his [the Kenite's] descendants were going to rise up and subjugate Israel, he began to rejoice and say: "'Enduring [*Ethan*] is your dwelling place' [Num 24.21]. I see people who eat only according to the commands of Ethan the Ezrahite."[3]

The second king who will arise from Ishmael will be a friend to Israel.[4] And he will repair their breaches and the breaches of the Temple. And he will shape Mount Moriah and make it completely level. And he will build for himself there a place for worship over the Foundation Stone [*Even Shtiyya*], as it is said, "and your nest is set in the rock" [Num 24.21]. And he will make war with the sons of Esau, and he will slaughter their troops and take a great many of them captive. And he will die in peace and with great honor.

And there will arise a great king from Hazarmavet [Gen 10.26], but he will reign for only a short while and the sons of Kedar will rise up against him and kill him. And they will bring to power another king, and his name will be MRY'W.[5] And they will take him from following after flocks and mule herds and elevate him to the kingship. And there will arise from him four arms, and they will build a wall around the Temple.

Commentary

The Secrets of Rabbi Shim'ōn opens with Rabbi Shim'ōn reflecting on the "Kenite" of Numbers 24.21, which is soon revealed to him as a prophecy about the Ishmaelites and their coming dominion over the land of Israel.[6] Rabbi Shimʿōn cries out in distress, wondering if the Jews had not already suffered enough oppression at the hands of Edom (i.e., Rome). Then, the angel Metatron appears to him and reassures him that, quite to the contrary, God will use the Ishmaelites to free the Jews from Byzantine oppression. As the revelation continues, Metatron responds to Rabbi Shimʿōn's questions by foretelling Israel's liberation through this Ishmaelite prophet and his followers as the fulfillment of the messianic deliverance foretold in Isaiah's vision of the two riders (Isa 21.6–7) and also in Zechariah (Zechariah 9.9).[7] Such direct identification of Muhammad as the fulfillment of Jewish messianic hopes as expressed in these biblical traditions is extraordinary, and it would seem to confirm the report from the *Teaching of Jacob* that this Saracen prophet was "preaching the arrival of the anointed one who is to come, the Messiah." Whether or not Muhammad was actually proclaiming the messiah's advent, this apocalypse certainly affords evidence that there were in fact Jews who understood the appearance of Muhammad and the rise of his new religious movement as realizing this eschatological promise.

Metatron then makes predictions regarding various Umayyad rulers, including a prophecy that Muhammad's successor, apparently in this case the caliph ʿUmar, would restore worship to the Temple Mount. This "prediction" corroborates, it is worth noting, the evidence from other early sources, much of which we have already seen, indicating that Muhammad's followers established a place of worship on the Temple Mount soon after taking control of Jerusalem. The apocalypse then continues with a forecast of the Abbasid revolution, which augurs the beginnings of a final eschatological conflict between Israel and Rome. This ultimate war will usher in a two-thousand-year messianic reign, followed by the final judgment. These final prophesies are not included in the translation above, since they appear to reflect a later redaction of the earlier apocalyptic tradition, although a complete translation of this apocalypse is readily available in English for those who are interested.[8]

Inasmuch as the opening section of this apocalypse provides a positive assessment of both Muhammad's prophetic mission and the early years of Islamic rule, there is widespread agreement that *The Secrets of Rabbi Shim'ōn b. Yoḥai* must depend on a much earlier source for its description of these events.[9] Otherwise, it is difficult to imagine that a Jewish author of the mid-eighth century, when the now extant version of this apocalyptic tradition was redacted, would portray the arrival of this new religious tradition in such favorable terms, identifying Muhammad and his followers as messianic saviors of the Jewish people. By the middle of the eighth century, Islam had developed into a new, distinctive religious confession that drew a sharp boundary between itself and Judaism, which it viewed as erroneous and inferior. Thus, it would have been only too clear to most Jews of this era that the rise of Islam had not, in fact, brought about messianic deliverance. Moreover, as Crone and Cook rightly observe, "the messiah belongs at the end of an apocalypse and not in the middle," which is where the messiah appears in the present version of *The Secrets*. It is yet another anomaly that seems to indicate the text's incorporation of an older messianic tradition into its mid-eighth-century apocalyptic narrative.[10]

Accordingly, the opening section of this apocalypse appears to have incorporated very lightly edited traditions from an older Jewish apocalypse that must have been produced not long after Muhammad's followers arrived in Syro-Palestine, most likely within a decade or so of their conquests. One imagines that the matrix for this Jewish messianic embrace of Muhammad's followers and their success was a group of contemporary Jews either within or closely allied with this new religious movement. As we have noted before, there is significant evidence that Muhammad's earliest followers welcomed Jews into their community of the Believers, while allowing them to remain Jews in their faith and practice. Presumably, the messianic convictions echoed in this more recent apocalypse took their origin within a group of Jewish Believers aligned with Muhammad's early followers. Otherwise, it is extremely difficult to understand the seer's conviction that Muhammad and his community were divinely appointed "messianic" deliverers who would restore worship to the Temple Mount. *The Secrets of Rabbi Shim'ōn b. Yoḥai* thus seems to preserve the perspective of those contemporary Jews who joined Muhammad's followers and believed them to be divine agents that were realizing God's messianic promise to Israel. It is a Jewish perspective on the formation of Muhammad's new religious community that likely is also behind much of the *Teaching of Jacob's* early account of the arrival of Muhammad's followers in the Near East (chapter 1).

One should also note that, like the *Teaching of Jacob*, the *The Secrets of Rabbi Shim'ōn b. Yoḥai* appears to envision that the Ishmaelite messiah, obviously Muhammad, was the one who led the conquest of the Holy Land and its liberation from the Romans, a tradition that, as we have seen, is reported by numerous early sources. Presumably this memory of Muhammad as the one who would subdue the Land also derives from the older apocalyptic source used by *The Secrets*. Likewise, *The Secrets of Rabbi Shim'ōn b. Yoḥai* reports that Muhammad's early followers took a keen interest in restoring worship to the Temple Mount after conquering Jerusalem. The singular importance of the Temple site and its exceptional holiness for the early Believers are attested in a number of early sources that we have already seen, and it will be also in others that follow. Again, it seems that the sanctity of the Jewish Temple and the return of divine worship to its precincts were central tenets of the apocalyptic faith held by the early Believers.

13   *Pirqe de-Rabbi Eliezer* 30 (665–70?)

This short apocalyptic text survives in an early medieval rabbinic collection known as the *Pirqe de-Rabbi Eliezer*, a sort of rabbinic "apocryphon" that interprets the early traditions of the Hebrew Bible from the Creation to Esther by expounding them in new extended renarrations. In this regard it is often compared to the Syriac Christian *Cave of Treasures*, which is a similar collection of expansions on the early biblical tradition.[1] This collection is attributed, falsely, to a well-known second-century rabbi, Eliezer ben Hyrcanus, yet it appears to have been collected during the early Islamic period in Palestine, most likely in the eighth or ninth century. There is no question, however, that it includes many older traditions, including, it would seem, this brief apocalypse.[2] The apocalypse occurs at the end of a section (30) describing Abraham's visit to Ishmael, who was living in "the desert of Paran" (Gen 21.21), which, as we have seen already above, was identified in late antiquity with Arabia Deserta, the desert region between Nabataea and Mesopotamia. It is of course possible that this tradition has been influenced by later Islamic traditions about Ishmael from the time when *Pirqe de-Rabbi Eliezer* was being collected. Nevertheless, one should not rule out the possibility that the Islamic tradition itself owes the roots of its traditions about Abraham and Ishmael to earlier rabbinic speculations about their relationship that survive in this collection and other rabbinic sources.[3]

In any case, finding the source of these Abraham and Ishmael traditions is of little consequence for the part of the text that interests us. This short apocalypse is clearly a separate tradition that was included at the end of this section because it predicts the role of Ishmael's descendants in the events of the eschaton: it has no mention of Abraham or Ishmael himself and is largely disconnected from the rest of the section. Moreover, the date of this apocalypse does not depend on when the *Pirqe de-Rabbi Eliezer* was collected, which can only assure us that the tradition was in circulation already before the eighth or ninth century. Instead, by following a practice frequently used with apocalyptic texts, we can determine a date of composition by identifying the historical events named by the seer as signs of the approaching End. Fortunately, this apocalypse offers several such chronological anchors. The only question is what are the events to which it refers? Several possibilities have been proposed, yielding a range of dates from 639 CE to 830 CE.[4] Nevertheless, sometime in the 660s CE seems to be the most likely date, for reasons that I will explain in the commentary.

Pirqe de-Rabbi Eliezer, 30[5]

R. Ishmael said: The sons of Ishmael will do fifteen things in the future at the End of Days in the Land [of Israel], and these are:

They will measure the Land with ropes;
And they will make cemeteries [places for] pasturage of flocks
   and for garbage;
They will measure from them and by them on the mountains;
And deceit will increase;
And truth will be hidden;

And law will be removed from Israel;

And afflictions will abound in Israel;

And they will mix the scarlet dye of the worm with wool;

And paper and pen will decay;

And the ruling kingdom will withdraw coinage;

And they will repair the destroyed cities and clear the roads;

And they will plant gardens and orchards;

And they will repair the breaches of the walls of the Temple
   [*Beit HaMikdash*];

And they will build a building on the [site of] the Temple [*Hekhal*];

And two brothers will rise as rulers over them.

In their days the son of David will arise, as it says, "And in the days of those kings the God of heaven will set up a kingdom . . ." [Dan 2.44].[6]

R. Ishmael also said: The sons of Ishmael will fight three great battles on the earth at the End of Days, as it says, "For they have fled from swords" [Isa 21.15], and there are no "swords" without battles. One in the woods—"from the drawn sword" [Isa 21.15]; and one at sea—"from the bent bow" [Isa 21.15]; and one at the great city of Rome, and it will be more severe than the other two, as it says, "and from the stress of battle" [Isa 21.15]. And from there [Rome] the son of David will sprout forth, and he will come to the Land of Israel and will look upon the destruction of these and those, as it says, "Who is this that comes from Edom [i.e., Rome], from Bozrah in garments stained crimson?" [Isa 63.1].

Commentary

In terms of what this text has to offer regarding the religious beliefs and practices of Muhammad's early followers, we find yet another confirmation that they took a keen interest in restoring worship to the site of the Temple and set to work building a structure there soon after taking Jerusalem. On this matter it echoes the previous apocalypse from the *The Secrets of Rabbi Shim'ōn b. Yoḥai* (chapter 12), as well as many other texts in this volume. Both of these Jewish apocalypses forecast that these sons of Ishmael will repair "breaches of the Temple" and build a sanctuary on the site of the former Temple. Likewise, they share the belief that the arrival of the sons of Ishmael and their rule are signs that the Messiah and the End of Days would soon arrive. In this sense both apocalypses share in the broader phenomenon of widespread messianic expectation within Judaism during the later sixth and early seventh centuries, an apocalyptic impulse that was shared by the Christian and Zoroastrian communities as well. The tradition that the Messiah would arise from Constantinople (Rome) is a well-attested trope in the Jewish apocalypticism of this period.[7] Nevertheless, unlike *The Secrets of Rabbi Shim'ōn*, the *Pirqe de-Rabbi Eliezer* does not view Muhammad or his followers in an especially positive light, let alone as having a messianic role. Rather, their appearance seems to yield mixed results: there will be destruction and war, yet they will restore some order by rebuilding the cities and clearing the roads. Following the chaos and disruption of the Persian invasion and occupation, the Persians' expulsion by the Romans, and then the conquest by Muhammad's followers, surely there was a fair amount of such maintenance to be done.

As for the dating this apocalypse, three of its predictions seem to hold the key: (1) building a sanctuary at the site of the Temple; (2) rule of the Ishmaelites by two brothers; and (3) the series of three battles that they will fight just before the Messiah's appearance, particularly an assault on Rome—that is, Constantinople. Not surprisingly, mention of building a shrine at the location of the former Temple has led some scholars to the conclusion that the reign of ʿAbd al-Malik (685–705), who oversaw the Dome of the Rock's completion, is likely in view here. In that case the two ruling brothers would be

'Abd al-Malik and his brother 'Abd al-'Azīz, who served as governor of Egypt. 'Abd al-Malik also made improvements to infrastructure and introduced new coinage, yet it is not entirely clear to me what should be identified with the attack on Rome, since there is no major campaign against Constantinople during 'Abd al-Malik's reign.

Hoyland proposes dating the apocalypse to this period, albeit with some hesitancy, and ultimately he comes to the more general conclusion that it was composed most likely sometime before 700 CE.[8] Reeves similarly dates this apocalypse to the final decades of the seventh century or the early decades of the eighth (which did see a major campaign against Constantinople), as does Uri Rubin, making for a consensus in these recent studies that it is a work belonging to the first Islamic century.[9] Nevertheless, Bernard Lewis has proposed that the two brothers in question are to be identified with Abu al-Abbas al-Saffāh (750–54) and his brother Abu Ja'far, or al-Manṣūr (754–75), making for a date in the second half of the eighth century, a period when there was also considerable messianic expectation among the Jews.[10] Yet as Hoyland notes, in the apocalypse, the two brothers seem to rule simultaneously,[11] and furthermore, this date seems fairly remote in relation to the construction of a sanctuary on the site of the Temple and major changes in currency, and again it is not clear what to make of the attack on Rome in this case.

While composition under 'Abd al-Malik is certainly a possibility, it seems that the reign of Mu'āwiya (661–80 CE) affords a much more likely context, an interpretation first advanced by Abba Hillel Silver.[12] As we have noted already, more than once, it is clear that construction of the site of the former Temple had begun long before 'Abd al-Malik came to power and, moreover, that it was Mu'āwiya who probably undertook the initial construction of the Dome of the Rock, while 'Abd al-Malik merely brought it to completion. Likewise, inasmuch as Mu'āwiya made Damascus the capital of his caliphate and held special favor for Jerusalem and its holy places, it makes sense to find mention in this Palestinian source of repairs to infrastructure under his rule. As for the withdrawal of coinage, this fits particularly well with Muʿāwiya. As we will see in the following source, *The Maronite Chronicle* (chapter 14), Muʿāwiya famously introduced coinage lacking the customary image of a cross, which was a significant visual change from most earlier, especially Roman, issues. The absence of this conventional element led many of Muʿāwiya's subjects to question the legitimacy of this new currency, so he was forced to withdraw it and issue new currency with the expected imagery. Likewise, Muʿāwiya's reign saw the first major military campaign by the Believers against Constantinople (Rome).[13] Finally, Muʿāwiya ruled in close conjunction with his brother Ziyād ibn Abī Sufyān (d. 673). Ziyād was a bastard son of Muʿāwiya's father, Abū Sufyān, yet Muʿāwiya acknowledged him as his true brother and placed him in a position of highest authority during his reign. Initially he appointed Ziyād as governor of Basra (665), but before long he was given authority over Iraq and Iran and made viceroy over the eastern half of his brother's caliphate.[14] Thus two brothers were ruling over the Believers.

Muʿāwiya's reign matches the historical references of this apocalypse almost perfectly, making for a high probability that this messianic vision was composed sometime in the later 660s. The fit could hardly be any better. In any case, there seems to be relative consensus in recent scholarship that it belongs to the first Islamic century. As such, it offers a parallel witness to the Jewish apocalypticism of the mid-seventh century that presumably gave rise to the slightly different vision of the Believers evident in the contemporary apocalypse underlying *The Secrets of Rabbi Shimʿōn* in its current form.

14   *The Maronite Chronicle* (ca. 665)

This Syriac chronicle was originally a history covering events from Alexander the Great up to the early 660s, although today it survives only in a dozen or so folios that report on various intervals within this span. The section covering the period from the late fourth century through the beginning of the seventh is missing, for instance. Likewise, we do not have the opening section of the chronicle, and so we do not know what it may have been called in late antiquity. Nevertheless, the chronicle suggests an affiliation with a seventh-century Christian group known as the Maronites, the early medieval ancestors of the contemporary Christian group by this name, located primarily in Lebanon. In the seventh century, the Maronites were distinguished from other Christian groups in the Near East by their adherence to a doctrine known as Monothelitism, a belief that after the incarnation Christ had only a single divine will and no human will. Although many contemporary Maronites vigorously deny this element of the group's formative history, the evidence for this confessional identity in the early Middle Ages is unmistakable.[1]

The final entry in the chronicle is for the year 664, although here again the chronicle is missing its conclusion. Accordingly, it is not entirely certain whether the chronicle may have continued beyond this point. The chronicle's manuscript dates to the eighth or ninth century, and so it must have been composed sometime before then. Theodor Nöldeke, who was the first to study the text, noted this copy is almost certainly not the original, "since the text has suffered significantly in places at the hands of copyists."[2] It seems, then, that we are dealing with a fairly old chronicle, but the question remains as to just how old. Current consensus holds that the chronicle was in fact written very close to the final events that it relates. The author is clearly well informed concerning this period, and as Sebastian Brock and Andrew Palmer note, his notice of accurate dates and days of the week for certain events in this period indicates composition near to the period in question. Likewise, the chronicle's account of its final event, an Arab raid in southern Asia Minor in 664, presents these events in a manner suggestive that they took place not very long ago. Finally, inasmuch as the chronicle reflects a pro-Byzantine bias, it seems unaware of the divide and conflicts between the Maronites and the Byzantine church that would begin in the early 680s. As Palmer further notes, the presence of many Greek and Latin loan words in the text is likely a sign of the close relations between the Maronites and Byzantines before 681.[3]

All of this points, with perhaps some hesitancy, to a likely date of the *Maronite Chronicle*'s composition sometime in the later 660s and not long after the events that it relates in the section translated below concerning Muhammad's early followers. In general, the chronicler seems well-informed about developments within the community of the Believers, even as he gets some details wrong. Perhaps most significantly, the chronicle provides an intriguing account of Muʿāwiya's coronation, after which, according to the chronicle, he prayed at Christian shrines in Jerusalem. Nevertheless, the accuracy of these details is not entirely certain.

The Maronite Chronicle[4]

... Mu'āwiya, his nephew Ḥudhayfa.[5] And Mu'āwiya gave an order concerning him and he was killed. And also 'Alī was threatening to rise up again against Mu'āwiya. And they struck him while he was praying in Ḥira and killed him. And Mu'āwiya went down to Ḥira, and there the entire army of the Nomads [ṭayyāyē] acknowledged his authority. And he returned to Damascus.

In the year 970 [659/60 CE], and the 17th of Constans, in the month of June, on a Friday at the second hour, there was a severe earthquake in the land of Palestine, and it caused many places there to collapse.

In the same month, the Jacobite bishops Theodore and Sabuk came to Damascus, and in the presence of Mu'āwiya they had a debate with those of Mar Maron [i.e., Maronite bishops] concerning the faith. And when the Jacobites were defeated, Mu'āwiya ordered them to give 20,000 denarii, and he ordered them to be silent. And it became a custom for the Jacobite bishops to give this gold to Mu'āwiya every year, so that he would not withdraw his protection of them and they would be persecuted by the clergy. The one who is called Patriarch by they Jacobites established for all the monasteries of monks and nuns what share of the gold they would contribute each year. And he established likewise for all the members of his faith. And he made Mu'āwiya the heir to his estate, so that out of fear of him [Mu'āwiya] the Jacobites would submit to him. And in the same month in which the debate with the Jacobites took place, on the ninth day, a Sunday, at the 8th hour there was an earthquake.

In the same year King Constans gave an order and his brother Theodosius was put to death—unjustly, for he had done nothing wrong, as many said. And many were distressed by his murder, and they say that the people of the city made an outcry against the king and were calling him a second Cain, a murderer of his brother. And greatly enraged, he left his son Constantine on his throne and taking the queen and the entire Roman fighting force, he went forth to the north, against foreign peoples.

And in the year 971 [660/61 CE], the 18th of Constans, many Nomads gathered in Jerusalem and made Muʿāwiya king. And he went up and sat at Golgotha and prayed there. And he went to Gethsemane and went down to the tomb of the blessed Mary and prayed there. And in those days, when the Nomads were assembling there with Muʿāwiya, there was a tremor and a severe earthquake. Most of Jericho collapsed in it, and all of its churches. The Church of St. John on the Jordan, where our Savior was baptized, was uprooted from its foundations, along with the entire monastery. And the Monastery of Abba Euthymius with many cells of monks and solitaries and many other places collapsed in it.

In the same year, in the month of July, the emirs and many of the Nomads assembled, and they pledged their allegiance to Muʿāwiya. And an order went forth that he should be proclaimed king in all the villages and cities of his dominion, and that they should make acclamations and ovations to him. And he also struck gold and silver coinage, but it was not accepted, because there was no cross on it. Muʿāwiya also did not wear a crown like the other kings of the world. And he set his throne in Damascus and refused to go to the throne of Muhammad.

In the following year [661/62 CE], ice fell on the morning of Wednesday the 13th of April, and the white vines withered in it.

And when Muʿāwiya became king, as he wanted, and had a break from the civil wars, he broke the truce with the Romans and no longer accepted a truce with them. Rather, he said, "If the Romans seek a truce, let them hand over their weapons and pay the tax (*gzita*). . . . [A folio is missing in the manuscript.][6]

Commentary

This section of the fragmentary chronicle opens abruptly with a notice concerning the First Civil War, or *Fitna*, in which Muhammad's followers fought with one another over the leadership of their religious polity. The war was set in motion when the third caliph, Uthmān, was murdered in 656 CE, and 'Alī, Muhammad's cousin and son-in-law, was proclaimed caliph after him. Mu'āwiya had been governor of the important province of Syria since the reign of the second caliph, 'Umar, who appointed him in 639, and he was a cousin of the murdered caliph Uthmān.[7] When 'Alī came to power, a conflict soon developed between him and Mu'āwiya for leadership of the Believers, in which Mu'āwiya emerged victorious following 'Alī's assassination in January 661 in Kufa by one of his own disaffected followers.

Although the beginning of this section is missing, the *Maronite Chronicle* appears to locate this event mistakenly in 658/59, but such errors in chronology are not uncommon in the historical writings of this era.[8] Nevertheless, the *Maronite Chronicle* accurately reports that 'Alī was murdered while praying in a mosque, and although it locates this mosque in Ḥira rather than Kufa, this is actually not incorrect. Kufa was a new military encampment established by the Believers in 639 adjacent to Ḥira, which had been the capital of the Lakhmids, the Christian Arab allies of the Sasanians mentioned in chapter 11 in relation to the *Khuzistan Chronicle*. Accordingly, it was not uncommon for medieval writers, and for Christians in particular, to use the names Ḥira and Kufa interchangeably.[9] Given Ḥira's importance for the Christians of the pre-Islamic Near East, it is no surprise to find that this text names the location of 'Alī's assassination Ḥira rather than Kufa.

As for Ḥudhayfa, or Muḥammad b. Abi Ḥudhayfa, he was one of the chief conspirators against Uthmān, although he was put to death shortly thereafter in 656.[10] The *Maronite Chronicle* seems to place the death of 'Alī' and Ḥudhayfa mistakenly in the same year, 658/59 judging from what follows, an error in both instances. Yet despite these lapses in chronology, which again are endemic in the historical writing of this period, the author of this chronicle does indeed seem well informed about political developments among the Believers during the First Civil War and the establishment of the new Umayyad caliphate under Muʿāwiya.

The section that follows offers a window into relations between the different Christian groups of the early medieval Near East, particularly as they sought to compete with one another for favor with their new sovereigns. Here the chronicle reports a debate between the Jacobites, that is, the Miaphysites, and the Maronites, a Monothelite and Diophysite group aligned with the Roman imperial church at this time, with which the author of the chronicle seems to be aligned. This debate allegedly took place in the presence of the recently triumphant Muʿāwiya, with the Maronites emerging victorious in the dispute. There is much to ponder here. Did Christian leaders actually debate with one another about the content of their faith before the leader of the Believers? Moreover, are we to believe that the latter played some role in the debate? The text is not entirely clear here, but it seems to suggest that Muʿāwiya served as judge in the debate, as suggested by his imposition of a fine on the Jacobites and ordering them to be silent. Michael Penn maintains that the author of the *Maronite Chronicler* expresses dismay at the outcome, since the Miaphysite Patriarch "soon used this to his advantage and continued to pay 20,000 denarii each year to persuade the caliph to protect the Miaphysites from the Maronites."[11] Nevertheless, I understand the passage differently; it seems to me that, instead, the caliph has effectively forced the Miaphysites to continue paying him protection money so that he will not allow the Maronites to persecute them. In any case, the episode portrays the leader of the Believers playing a surprisingly influential role in deciding theological issues within the broader Christian community of his dominion. Did such a thing happen? Was it common?

Penn, for his part, hesitates at times to draw such a conclusion, although in other instances he seems to assume that these debates took place. Jack Tannous, however, takes the report at face value, locating it within the broader context of a number of christological debates said to have been held in the presence of Christian leaders and even, in two instances, before the Sasanian leaders. The adjudication of intra-Christian debates by Muslim leaders continued to be a motif in later Syriac literature, and it seems plausible that such debates may have taken place, in this case no less than the others.[12] Another near contemporary source, for instance, *On the Holy Places* by the English monk Adomnán (discussed in the following chapter), relates a very fanciful account in which Mu'āwiya mediates a dispute between Jews and Christians.[13] While the story itself is highly implausible, its circulation nonetheless indicates that the idea of Mu'āwiya arbitrating a religious dispute certainly was not foreign among his readers. I suspect that the *Maronite Chronicle* reports accurately here regarding the occurrence of the event itself. It knows the names of the two Miaphysite bishops involved, and it seems an odd thing for the chronicler to have invented out of whole cloth.

Nevertheless, the significance of Mu'āwiya's involvement is not clear, and different conclusions could be drawn from this report, if it is indeed accurate. Perhaps Mu'āwiya intervenes here to settle a dispute among the Christians of Syria in order to put an end to what was a disruptive rivalry between the Christian factions among the peoples of his domain.[14] After all, Christians would have made up the overwhelming majority of the population in Syria and Palestine at this point. Alternatively, perhaps we should understand Mu'āwiya's role in this debate as evidence for the persisting inter-confessional nature of the Believer's new religious movement. In such a case, an intervention by Mu'āwiya in the doctrinal disputes of the Christians would not simply reflect a concern for greater social stability among the various religious communities of his dominion. Rather, such action may have been necessitated by the inclusion of Christians—at least some Christians—within the still emergent community of the Believers.[15] As leader of the Believers, it would thus fall to Muʿāwiya to adjudicte this dispute between different Christian members of the community. Since Chalcedonian Diophytism was ascendent in and around Damascus, in Palestine, and in Jordan, in either case the reported outcome of the contest, in favor of the Chalcedonian Maronites, is not surprising.[16]

The second interpretation, that Muʿāwiya here arbitrates a dispute among Christians because it affects members of the nascent community of the Believers, is in fact consistent with a number of other reports concerning Muʿāwiya and his personal involvement with Christianity, including especially the account of his coronation that follows in this very chronicle. Other Christian sources from this period, as we will see, similarly describe Muʿāwiya, almost reverently, for his tolerance of Christianity and his respect for the Christian faith and its churches. Moreover, the later Islamic historical tradition is often hostile to Muʿāwiya (and indeed, the Umayyads in general), accusing him of, among other things, being indifferent to the practice of true Islam while demonstrating what the later Islamic tradition considered inappropriate pro-Christian sympathies.[17] One could attribute this memory of Muʿāwiya in the Islamic historical tradition as a result of its well-known anti-Umayyad bias.[18] Yet, in light of a farily consistent pro-Christian portrait of Muʿāwiya that emerges from the contemporary Christian sources,[19] maybe we should consider the possibility that the estimation of the Islamic historians concering Muʿāwiya may in this case be based in some historical realities.

If we follow Donner's hypothesis regarding the interconfessional nature of the community of the Believers for the first several decades of its existence, these reports about Mu'āwiya from both Christian and Islamic sources converge to suggest a very different understanding of his actions and religious faith of the community that he led. From such a vantage, Mu'āwiya appears not as the Muslim caliph of an Islamic polity, but instead as the leader of an alliance of Abrahamic monotheists that included Christians. His preferred title, it would seem, was not caliph but *amīr al-mu'minīn*, "the leader of the Believers," judging from the coinage, inscriptions, and papyri of his age. Moreover, his marriage to a Christian, the fact that the core of his army, not to mention his navy, consisted primarily of Christian troops, and his appointment of Christians to high-level positions in government certainly would all be consistent with his leadership of such an interconfessional community.[20]

Indeed, perhaps nowhere in any of the relevant sources is such an interpretation of Mu'āwiya and the community that he led more strongly suggested than in this chronicle's initial notice for the next year, 660/61. The chronicle reports that Mu'āwiya had his coronation in Jerusalem: presumably, the choice of this location was deliberate. Mu'āwiya chose to become the new leader of the Believers in the city of King David and of Christ the King. One imagines that these Jewish and Christian associations were not insignificant in his decision to be proclaimed ruler there. And there can be little question that Jerusalem was a locus of the highest sanctity for Muhammad's followers in this age. Jersualem and the biblical Holy Land seem to have been the primary focus of the Believers' sacred geography, holding far greater significance than Mecca and Medina in the Hijaz. These two Arabian cities would emerge as the foci of a new distinctively Islamic holy land only somewhat later in the history of the religious movement, as it sought greater distinction from the biblical religions that were its matrix.[21]

There is reason enough, then, on this basis for Mu'āwiya to have chosen Jerusalem for his coronation. Yet the sanctity of Jerusalem and the Holy Land for Muhammad's earliest followers is inextricably bound up with the matter of apparent proximity and overlap between the early Believers and the Jewish and Christian communities of the seventh-century Near East. The paramount sanctity of Jerusalem and the biblical Holy Land for Muhammad's followers is itself an important sign that his new religious movement was much more deeply intertwined with the faith of the Jews and Christians than one would conclude from collective memory of the later Islamic tradition, as it began to assume its "classical" form at the turn of the eighth century. Thus, the decision to have his enthronement in Jerusalem was no doubt a purposeful choice that linked his authority as leader of the Believers directly to the biblical tradition and to the faith of the Jews and Christians. It is a move, as James Howard-Johnston notes, that affords "evidence for the inclusiveness of Islam in its earliest phase, as a religion which embraced the two established monotheist faiths."[22]

What Mu'āwiya is said to have done next is nothing short of astonishing, and if the report is accurate, his actions provide some of the strongest evidence for the interconfessional nature of the community that he was leading and the faith that it practiced. According to the chronicle, immediately after his enthronement, Mu'āwiya went and sat at Golgotha, the site of Christ's crucifixion, where he prayed, and then went down to Gethsemane, to the Tomb of the Virgin Mary, and prayed there as well. These acts portray the new leader of the Believers worshipping in two of Jerusalem's oldest and most important Christian shrines, showing his devotion to Jesus and Mary in the context of their Christian veneration. One could hardly ask for better evidence that the community of the Believers was confessionally open in its earliest history.[23] According to this chronicle, Mu'āwiya's first act as the community's leader was to pray not in a mosque or on the Temple Mount, but in the two holiest Christian shrines dedicated to the two most imporant figures of the Christian tradition.

If the leader of the Believers worshipped in these two churches on such a momentous occasion, surely the confessional lines between Christians and the Believers were not yet firmly established, as they would later come to be.

The main question, however, is: did this really happen? It is hard to say with complete certainly. Penn again hesitates slightly, although he notes that there is certainly nothing implausible in the account, while Andrew Marsham concludes that "there are good reasons to believe that . . . the account of Muʿawiya's actions is based in fact," and Tannous judges the report as being "historically likely." Tannous notes that the chronicle seems to have recorded these events only a few years after they happened, and as we have seen above, the *Maronite Chronicle* otherwise shows evidence of being well informed regarding developments in the leadership of the Believers, a judgment shared also by James Howard-Johnston.[24] There is certainly ample testimony that in the early history of the Believers movement, members of the community used Christian churches for their worship, either cooperatively or through co-option. Perhaps the most well-known example is the Believers' use of the Church of St. John the Baptist in Damascus, which they ultimately appropriated in the construction of the Umayyad Mosque.[25] Yet reports of interconfessional sharing of sacred space are especially prominent in regard to Jerusalem during the early years of the community of the Believers. For instance, although the relevant sources are understandably complex, particularly in light of their tension with later Islamic confessional identity, it appears that the early Believers in Jerusalem initially joined the Christians in the Holy Sepulcher for their worship. After capturing the Holy City on Palm Sunday, as Heribert Busse argues, the Believers joined in the Christian celebrations of Holy Week. It did not take very long, however, before they abandoned this practice and turned their attention to the Temple Mount, where they would begin building not long after the conquest, a project that would finally culminate in the Dome of the Rock and the al-Aqsā Mosque.[26]

Suliman Bashear has collected numerous other reports of Muhammad's early followers praying in Jerusalem's churches, including not only this report of Muʿāwiya praying at Golgotha and the Tomb of the Virgin, but also reports of ʿUmar also having gone to pray in the Tomb of the Virgin.[27] This phenomenon was of course not unique to Jerusalem, and Bashear notes additional examples of prominent early Believers praying in Christian churches in other early Islamic centers such as Edessa, Kufa, and Damascus.[28] The practice apparently continued into the second Islamic century in some locations, proving one of the most lasting vestiges of Islam's inter-confessional origins.[29] Most significant for our purposes, however, are the testimonies from the Islamic historical tradition that Bashear cites for this phenomenon. Although there is no specific confirmation of Muʿāwiya's prayers at Golgotha and the Tomb of the Virgin in these sources, the use of early Christian churches for worship by members of the early community of the Believers is well attested. These testimonies provide a solid basis on which to stand the *Maronite Chronicle*'s report that Muʿāwiya prayed in these holiest Christian shrines following his enthronement. There is no obvious reason to imagine why the chronicler or a source would have fabricated this information: it does not fit any sort of clear tendency or agenda, other than showing Muʿāwiya's deep sympathy for Christianity, which is well attested independently by other sources. Indeed, most modern scholars have assumed that the chronicle here relates reliable information concerning Muʿāwiya's worship in these churches on this momentous occasion, and I see little reason to doubt it. Accordingly, we have in this chronicle, it would seem, substantial evidence that still at the time of Muʿāwiya's enthronement, the community of the Believers remained an interconfessional religious movement that embraced

Christian faith and practice in significant ways, as demonstrated here by its leader's actions.

Finally, the *Maronite Chronicle* reports that in the same year of his coronation, Mu'āwiya issued new coins, both gold and silver, "but it was not accepted, because there was no cross on it." There has been some debate about this passage, which is particularly important for understanding the history of early Islamic coinage.[30] Of course, it is interesting that Mu'āwiya of all people would have removed the cross from his official coinage, inasmuch as he seems to have merged his political authority with Christianity so dramatically at his enthronement. Perhaps he wanted to distinguish his own currency from that of the Byzantines, whose coins frequently had a cross on their reverse. If that was the case, clearly it backfired, since the coinage was rejected, presumably since there was concern as to whether it was genuine or not without this feature, and all the more so given that the population of Syria and Palestine would have been overwhelmingly Christian at this time. So the cross was retained until the currency reform of 'Abd al-Malik, in which, as part of a broader program of Islamicizing the state, he established a distinctively Islamic coinage without a cross and eventually without any figures at all, only text.[31]

Questions have been raised about the accuracy of this passage, causing some numismatic scholars even to propose a later date for the chronicle on this basis. The main issue concerns the minting of silver coinage, for which there is no clear evidence in Syria prior to 'Abd al-Malik. Nevertheless, gold coins have been discovered from Mu'āwiya's reign near Antioch with the cross on the reverse altered or removed, which can confirm the report that he introduced this change. Moreover, these coins show evidence that "the obverse die had seen heavy use and was beginning to deteriorate badly when this coin was struck,"[32] meaning that these coins were produced in large numbers, yet this coin type is extremely rare. As Clive Foss explains,

this evidence seems to indicate a situation in which a large number of coins were produced but failed to be accepted in circulation,
precisely the circumstance that the *Maronite Chronicle* describes.
Likewise, this would also explain the absence of any silver coinage.
Although we know that Muʿāwiya minted silver in other regions,
presumably no exemplars have been discovered from Syria because
these crossless verions were rejected by the populus.[33]

15   *On the Holy Places* (ca. 680)

ADOMNÁN / ARCULF

Adomnán of Iona (ca. 628–704) was the abbot of one of the oldest and most influential British monasteries, the Iona Abbey, established by the famous Irish missionary Columba in 563 on an island just off the coast of western Scotland. Among his most important works is a pilgrimage guide to the Holy Lands, *On the Holy Places*, which is the first description of the holy sites of Jerusalem and Palestine written after their conquest and occupation by Muhammad's followers. Adomnán did not himself, however, visit the Holy Lands, and he wrote his account based on information supplied by a Frankish bishop from Gaul, Arculf, who had traveled in the eastern Mediterranean lands and visited the many sacred places there. Shortly after completing his pilgrimage, Arculf allegedly visited Adomnán at Iona and recounted his journey and the sites he had visited in great detail for the latter, who wrote them down.

The circumstances of Arculf's visit to the Iona monastery are not made entirely clear, and while Bede reports that Arculf became shipwrecked on Iona as he was returning from his pilgrimage, this seems a little far-fetched.[1] Indeed, some scholars have recently questioned

whether or not Arculf actually even existed, proposing that Adomnán has simply made him up, along with much that he reportedly
had to say.[2] This goes too far, I think, and while there may not have
been an actual person Arculf who was his informant, clearly Adomnán relies on oral reports from someone and has not simply made the
account up out of thin air. It is true that Adomnán's account of early
building activity on the Temple Mount, which is translated below,
may show some polemical nuance. Nevertheless, it seems highly
implausible to suppose that he invented out of whole cloth the existence of a structure on the Temple Mount that the early Believers
used for worship, particularly since, as we have seen, other sources
attest to building activity on the Temple Mount much earlier than
Arculf's alleged visit.

We do know that Adomnán presented a copy of *On the Holy Places*
to King Aldfrith of Northumbria, and his last visit to Aldfrith was
in 688. Thus, the work must have been composed sometime before
688 CE. Moreover, according to Adomnán, Arculf told a pious tale
involving the Caliph Muʿāwiya (661–80), which he said described
events that took place just three years ago. Thus, Arculf's visit
must have taken place sometime before 683 at the very latest, and
we may date the account approximately to 680 CE on the basis of
this remark.[3] The pilgrimage account attributed to Arculf provides
detailed descriptions of many other holy sites and includes plans
of a number of important churches that Adomnán copied and that
have come down to us in the manuscript tradition. Among these is
a plan of the Holy Sepulcher, for instance, but unfortunately there
is no drawing of the structure that the "Saracens" had built on the
Temple Mount to serve as a locus for their worship. The description
of this building appears at the beginning of Arculf's account, in a
general description of the layout of Jerusalem, which is recorded by
Adomnán as follows.

On the Holy Places[4]

Also in that famous place, where once the Temple had been magnificently constructed, located near the wall on the east, now the Saracens have built a quadrangular house of prayer, which they constructed poorly by standing boards and great beams over some of the remains of its ruins. They visit it frequently, and it is said that the building can hold at least three-thousand people at once.

Commentary

Here Adomnán's source, whatever name we want to give him, clearly bears witness to early building activity and worship by the Believers on the Temple Mount, and indeed, at the location of the Temple's ruins, according to his account. What he describes certainly does not sound like the Dome of the Rock, to be sure, although as we have already seen, it would appear that work on this structure had already begun by the time of his visit, most likely during the caliphate of Muʿāwiya (661–80). What exactly this "house of prayer" (*orationis domus*) was is not entirely clear. Some scholars have suggested that Arculf's account here describes an early mosque on the Temple Mount, to be understood as a building distinct from the Dome of the Rock and perhaps as a sort of precusor for the al-Aqsā mosque.[5] The rectangular shape of the building as well as the designation "house of prayer" would seem to favor this interpretation, particularly since the Arabic word for mosque, *masjid*, literally means a place of prostration. Based on recent archaeological study as well as the indication that the structure stood on the eastern wall, Beatrice St. Laurent and Isam Awwad have proposed instead to identify Arculf's "mosque" with the building today known as the Stables of Solomon, which stands in the southeast corner of the Haram al-Sharif.[6]

Nevertheless, I would propose that we should not completely rule out the possibility that there may be some sort of a relation between this early structure and the Dome of the Rock. And even if mention of a rectangular shape admittedly could potentially suggest otherwise, the report that this place of worship had been erected over the site of the destroyed Jewish Temple certainly suggests a link with the Dome, which eventually rose up in this very location. The site of the Temple is, again, not consistent with the location of the al-Aqsā mosque, which seems to exclude this identification, whereas the large rock on the Temple Mount was known in collective memory to have stood within the Temple's Holy of Holies.[7] Moreover, scholars have often noted that Adomnán's description of the actual building itself seems polemical,[8] and accordingly, we should not place too much stock in his mention of its rectangular shape and wooden construction. If the account is polemical, then no doubt these qualities are also introduced in order to belittle the building's crude simplicity, as Hoyland and Sarah Waidler also note: it was made of the simplest materials and in the simplest shape.[9] Wooden, rectangular buildings would also have been the type of religious structures most familiar to Adomnán, perhaps further coloring his account in this instance. We must, after all, remember that he did not himself see the building that stood over the remains of the Temple and should consider that perhaps his source had visited Jerusalem as early as the 660s.

As we have already seen from other witnesses in this volume, the Dome of the Rock was seemingly not, at least in its present form, the first structure that the Believers built on the Temple Mount. Both Sebeos (chapter 6) and the Georgian fragment from John Moscos (chapter 7) describe construction of a building at the site of the destroyed Temple soon after the Believers came into possession of Jerusalem, while other sources refer to building activities there

(Anastasius, chapter 10) or a restoration of the Temple (Rabbi Shim'ōn and the *Pirqe de-Rabbi Eliezer* chapters 12 and 13). One imagines that these early structures were much simpler than the magnificent Dome that would eventually follow them, and it is possible that Adomnán's source here describes such an early precursor to the Dome. Indeed, by the time of his visit, one imagines that some sort of construction on the Dome had likely already begun, although it would only be finished a decade or so later by 'Abd al-Malik. Perhaps the remark that the construction was poor reflects the fact that when his source visited Jerusalem the building was still incomplete and under construction, although again, as others have noted, this estimation of the building's condition may reflect Adomnán's own prejudices.

Morover, even though the Dome today is not a mosque, it was seemingly used as a place for twice-weekly prayers in its early history by the Believers, who understood the structure as a monument built in place of the Jerusalem Temple. As we noted already in the introduction, a number of early Islamic traditions, particularly eschatological traditions and traditions about the holy sites in Jerusalem, identify the Dome of the Rock's significance as a sort of place-holder for the destroyed Temple. According to certain accounts, the Dome was attended by a large staff numbering in the hundreds, who supervised the veneration of the shrine's sacred rock. Following Jewish tradition, the early Believers revered the Dome's rock as the "Foundation Stone" of divine Creation, which was at the center of the Holy of Holies when the Temple still stood. The Believers' Dome, it would seem, had been constructed as a temporary, earthly stand-in for the destroyed Temple as they awaited its divine resortation in the events of the eschaton. It certainly was not a simple restoration of the Temple, particularly since the sacrifices were not resumed. Yet the Dome appears to have served as a kind of ersatz Temple, constructed to restore honor to the site of the Temple, which had lain in a state of humiliating devastation for almost six hundred years.[10]

In these early years, when the Dome was a stand-in for the Temple, the public was allowed to worship in the Dome only on Mondays and Thursdays, when they came to venerate its sacred stone.[11] The rituals for these days, as we noted already in the introduction, commenced in the evening, with the Dome's attendants preparing an opulent perfume that sat overnight. In the morning, the attendants purified themselves with ritual washing and donned ritual garments. They commenced the ceremonies by anointing the Dome's sacred rock with the fragrant perfume while burning incense all around it. Then they lowered the curtains that surrounded the rock, "so that the incense encircles the Ṣakhra [the Rock] entirely and the odour [of the incense] clings to it."[12] Then the curtains were lifted, and a crier went out to the market calling the faithful to come to the rock for prayer. The public was allowed in only for a short time, however, allowing for the prostrations of only two prayer cycles, or maybe four if one was quick.

The location of the Believers' house of prayer over the ruins of the Temple in this account thus invites us to envision this structure as somehow connected to the Dome of the Rock. If we place any stock at all in the various reports that we have already seen of the Believers building on the Temple Mount and at the site of the Temple well in advance of the Dome of the Rock's completion, we should imagine that the Dome was likely preceded by earlier and probably simpler structures. Perhaps Adomnán describes just such a structure. Recall, for instance, Sebeos's report that immediately following the conquest of Jerusalem, the Jews initially built a house of prayer on what they determined to be the site of the Holy of Holies, doing this in collaboration with the "Hagarenes," who then appropriated the building for themselves, forcing the Jews to build another structure elsewhere.

One suspects that some sort of work on what would become the Dome of the Rock had already begun by the time of Arculf's alleged visit, but almost certainly it would not have been completed, whether or not we should identify Arculf's house of prayer as its direct precursor. Possibly the Believers were using a more temporary structure to worship near the site of the Temple as they awaited the Dome's completion, perhaps even a hastily constructed large wooden quadrangle. But from this account alone we cannot know with any certainty the significance that this building held for the early Believers or what their acts of prayer and worship within it may have meant. Accordingly, we should not blithely assume that this account describes a mosque, in the sense that such a building would come to be identified as the offically sanctioned venue for daily Islamic prayers: this building on the Temple Mount may have functioned in slightly different ways for the Believers as their faith was rapidly developing during this phase. In any case, this report confirms other earlier accounts of the Believers building on the Temple Mount, and the placement of this building over the Temple's ruins indicates their reverence for the sanctity of the fallen Temple and its location. Ultimately, this final point perhaps holds the greatest significance for our purposes: Adomnán's terse report again corroborates other sources regarding the importance of the Jerusalem Temple in the religious worldview of the early Believers and their eagerness to restore some sort of worship to its sacred precincts.

16   *The Apocalypse of Ps.-Shenoute* (650–90)

Shenoute of Atripe (ca. 348?–465) was an early monastic leader in Egypt and is to this day one of the most revered saints of the Coptic Church. Not only was Shenoute influential in defining the patterns of Egyptian monasticism, but he was also a prolific writer, whose oeuvre was highly influential in establishing the standards for writing in Coptic during the early middle ages. A lengthy *Life of Shenoute* survives, attributed to his disciple and successor Besa, although current consensus holds that this biography of Shenoute is a later collection of traditions about this patriarch of Coptic culture that formed gradually over time and was only later ascribed to Besa to invest it with authority.[1] Fragments of the *Life of Shenoute* survive in Sahidic Coptic, the original language of composition, while complete versions of the text are known only through translations into Bohairic Coptic, Arabic, and Ethiopic (Ge'ez), as well as a shorter version in Syriac.

For many years, scholars were confident that the version surviving in Bohairic Coptic was more or less equivalent to the original version of Shenoute's biography, while the longer Arabic and Ethiopic versions were understood as subsequent expansions. Nevertheless, Nino Lubomierski has now persuasively argued, on the basis of similarities between the Arabic version and the extant Sahidic fragments, that the Arabic version preserves this collection of pious tales about Shenoute in its oldest and most complete form, a view that, one should note, was initially proposed by the *Life*'s first editor, Émile Amélineau. Accordingly, we now understand the Arabic version (along with the Sahidic fragments) as a reliable witness to the *Life of Shenoute* as it had taken shape by the seventh century, while the Bohairic, Ethiopic, and Syriac versions all represent subsequent efforts to abridge this late ancient compendium of pious memories about Shenoute.[2] The particular tradition from this *Life* that concerns us is an extended apocalyptic vision of the end-times ascribed to Shenoute, which survives complete only in the Arabic and Ethiopic versions, as well as in small part in a Sahidic fragment.[3] There is agreement that this episode was a part of the late seventh-century *Life of Shenoute* in Coptic that was the model for the Arabic translation, dating to approximately 685–90, although there is a strong possibility that it may have been composed even earlier, much closer to the events of the conquest of Egypt by Muhammad's followers.[4]

The Apocalypse begins as Shenoute's monks spot him coming out of his cave one day with a scowl on his face. They ask him what is wrong, and in response he tells them of a vision that he received from Christ. One day the devil appeared to Shenoute in the form of a man, and the two began to struggle. Shenoute gained the upper hand, and as he was smashing the Devil's head against a rock so much that the rock was stained with his blood, Christ suddenly appeared to him and commanded Shenoute to stop, telling him that "His time has not come." Shenoute then asked for an explanation, and in response Christ revealed to him the events of the end-times, and the Devil's role therein. The forecast begins with a prediction of the Persian conquest and occupation of Egypt, followed by a Roman restoration, and then finally the rise of "the sons of Ishmael and the sons of Esau," whose triumph will inaugurate the appearance of the Antichrist. This first part of Shenoute's vision is what concerns us, and accordingly it is translated below. But Christ continues to foretell the tribulations of the Antichrist's reign and his eventual defeat, concluding with the resurrection and the final judgment. When Shenoute has finished his account of Christ's revelation, he completes this episode with a discourse to his followers urging them to live righteously in preparation for the Lord's return and the final judgment.

Although it has been proposed that the Apocalypse of Shenoute "was strongly influenced by the third-century Egyptian *Apocalypse of Elijah*," there is little evidence that I can see where this text has directly influenced the Apocalypse of Shenoute.[5] Rather, the Apocalypse of Shenoute shares some similarities with this earlier apocalypse because both participate in a broad trend of late ancient apocalypticism, for which the *Apocalypse of Elijah* is one of the earliest witnesses, namely, "imperial eschatology." This was an apocalyptic worldview that viewed the demise and triumph of successive empires as the means by which the final eschatological kingdom would ultimately arrive, as we find also on display in the Apocalypse of Shenoute.[6]

The Apocalypse of Ps.-Shenoute[7]

[Christ is speaking] . . . And I will tell you what will happen before it happens. The Persians will go against the people of Mosul, and they will come down to Egypt, and with them there will be much killing. And they will plunder the wealth of Egypt and sell their children for gold: so severe is the persecution and cruelty of the Persians. And many masters will become slaves, and many slaves will become masters. Woe to Egypt because of the Persians, for they will take the church vessels and drink wine from them before the altar without fear or concern. Likewise, they will rape women in front of their husbands. And there will be great adversity and distress, and of those who survive, one-third of them will die from grief and sorrow.

Then after a little while, the Persians will leave Egypt. Then the Antichrist will arise, and he will enter upon the king of Rome and will be put in charge by him as leader of both the authorities and the bishops. And he will enter Egypt and do many things. And he will take possession of Egypt and its provinces and will build moats and fortresses and order that the walls of towns in the deserts and wastelands be built, and he will destroy the east and the west. Then he will attack the shepherd, the archbishop of Alexandria, who has authority over the Christians living in the land of Egypt. And they will expel him, and he will flee to the land of the south until he arrives at your monastery, sad and sorrowful. And when he arrives here, I will return him and place him on his throne another time.

And after that the sons of Ishmael and the sons of Esau will arise, and they will pursue the Christians. And the rest of them will want to rule over the entire world and dominate it, and they will build the Temple in Jerusalem. When that happens, know that the end of time approaches and has drawn near. And the Jews will expect the Antichrist and will be ahead of the peoples at his arrival. Then when you see the desolation rising up in the holy place, as was spoken of by the prophet Daniel [Dan 11.31; cf. Matt 24.15], they are those who reject the pains that I received on the cross, and those managing affairs[8] within my church fear nothing and dread nothing. Then those who crucified me will agree with the Antichrist and will reject my holy resurrection. Let the one who reads understand . . . . [Shenoute continues after this point to describe the tribulations of the Antichrist's reign].

Commentary

To discuss the content of this text, we must also revisit the question of its dating, since the two issues are intertwined. At present, there is consensus that this Apocalypse of Shenoute was part of the Sahidic Coptic *Life of Shenoute* as it had taken shape by the end of the seventh century, and moreover that this version is transmitted, with relative faithfulness, in the Arabic version of Shenoute's *Life*. Accordingly, the Apocalypse of Shenoute cannot be later than the last part of the seventh century. Likewise, the same consensus holds that the various episodes that comprise this *Life of Shenoute*, including the Apocalypse, were originally individual traditions about Shenoute derived from the collective memory of the monks of his monasteries.[9] Therefore, the Apocalypse of Shenoute must be older than the collection itself and should presumably be dated somewhat earlier than the end of the seventh century: yet the question is, once again, just how much earlier?

Amélineau's original dating of the Apocalypse, which continues to hold sway, hinges on its notice that "they will build the Temple in Jerusalem." Amélineau identifies this prediction with 'Abd al-Malik's construction of the Dome of the Rock, in light of which he dates the tradition to sometime after 685. Nevertheless, in reaching this conclusion, Amélineau operates within an outdated understanding of the Dome's construction and its alleged relation to the events of the Second Civil War. Amélineau follows certain reports from the Islamic historical tradition alleging that 'Abd al-Malik had the Dome of the Rock built to divert pilgrimage from Mecca to Jerusalem. He did this, so we are told, not only because the Umayyads seem to have favored the lands of Syria and Palestine over the Hijaz, but also because for a time during his reign pilgrimage to Mecca was not possible, since it was under the control of the rival caliph 'Abd Allāh ibn al-Zubayr during the Second Civil War. As a result, many scholars in the nineteenth and early twentieth centuries, including most notably Ignác Goldziher, took these reports at face value, with the result that the Believers' construction on the Temple Mount was understood to have begun as a specific response to the events of the Second Civil War.[10] In such case, any reference to Muhammad's followers building on the site of the Temple would be understood as subsequent to these events—that is, after Ibn al-Zubayr proclaimed himself caliph in 683, with effective sovereignty over the Hijaz and its sanctuaries, to which ʿAbd al-Malik responded, so the theory goes, by beginning work on his replacement shrine on the Temple Mount. Yet, while according to Amélineau the Apocalypse of Shenoute knows that ʿAbd al-Malik was building a new sanctuary, its author did not know the outcome of the Second Civil War, and so he dates the tradition's composition to the period between 685 and 690.

Nevertheless, these accusations against ʿAbd al-Malik of trying to divert the pilgrimage are almost certainly the product of clear tendencies at work within the early Islamic historical tradition and not indicative of the historical realities in the later seventh century. As we have already mentioned, the early Islamic historical tradition has a well-known and pronounced anti-Umayyad bias; likewise, it exhibits a clear trend of seeking to diminish Jerusalem's sacred status in favor of a distinctively Islamic, alternative sacred geography that centered on the Hijaz. The Islamic historical tradition as we now have it was written under the Abbasids, and so it is hardly surprising that it is overtly hostile to their predecessors the Umayyads, whom it regularly accuses of impiety and un-Islamic behavior.[11] Among the Umayyads' greatest sins, according to these historians, was an illegitimate propaganda campaign to elevate the sanctity of Jerusalem and the Holy Land to parity with the Hijaz.[12]

This traditional Islamic perspective about Jerusalem and the Umayyads, the Dome, and ʿAbd al-Malik, continued to determine the views of Western scholarship until the middle of the last century. At that time, S. D. Goitein radically altered our understanding of Jerusalem's role in early Islamic history through a series of articles that drew attention to the anti-Umayyad bias underlying such reports. Likewise, Goitein exhumed substantial evidence for the sanctity of Jerusalem and Palestine in Muhammad's new religious movement, showing that it was not a product of Umayyad political machinations but instead had its basis in the genuine religious beliefs of the early Believers.[13] As Goitein rightly observes, it is extremely improbable that ʿAbd al-Malik would have attempted something as outrageous and potentially inflammatory as diverting the pilgrimage to Jerusalem when he was in such a politically tenuous situation: if in fact the hajj to Mecca were already established as a standard practice (which is itself questionable), such actions would have unmistakably branded him as a *kāfir*, a heretic, and only strengthened the cause of his Meccan rival, Ibn al-Zubayr.[14] Moreover, there is considerable evidence from the early Islamic tradition itself, in addition to the non-Islamic texts that we have considered, that indicate a high regard for the sanctity of Jerusalem and the Holy Land in the primitive traditions of the Believers. Therefore, neither the sanctity of Jerusalem nor the construction of a sanctuary on the Temple Mount can be imputed to the events of the Second Civil War. Both are clearly much earlier developments in the faith and practice of the Believers.[15]

Furthermore, as we have already seen from other texts included in this volume, there is significant and persuasive evidence that Muhammad's followers began constructing a sanctuary on the Temple Mount long before Ibn al-Zubayr and ʿAbd al-Malik came to power. There can be little mistaking the impressive convergence of this evidence to reveal that the Believers revered the site of the Jerusalem Temple and the sanctity of the former Temple itself from very early on, and likewise that they set about building a shrine to represent the Temple shortly after taking possession of Jerusalem during the middle of the seventh century. Furthermore, on the basis of these contemporary sources, there is every reason to suppose that the Believers had constructed a sanctuary on the Temple Mount, in the place of the Temple, well before ʿAbd al-Malik, a project that they began not long after taking control of Jerusalem. In similar fashion, the Apocalypse of Shenoute refers to the construction of a sanctuary on the Temple Mount, additionally warning that the "standing up" in this holy place will be a sign that the end of the world has arrived. The Apocalypse clearly echoes here the wording of Matthew's gospel with its reference to the "standing up," and thus in its immediate historical context, this gospel's description of the "abomination of desolation" as being made to "stand up" (*hestos / hestēkota* in Greek, *qāʾima* in Arabic) in the holy place must have found new and specific meaning as the Believers erected a new sanctuary on the site of the Holy of Holies.

This finding has obvious importance, then, for how we should date the Apocalypse of Shenoute. The Apocalypse's knowledge of the Believers building a Temple does not anchor it to the time of the Second Civil War. Rather, based on the collective witness of other sources that we have already seen in this volume, we learn that several contemporary Christian and Jewish writers were aware that the Believers were constructing just such a "Temple" seemingly as early as the 640s. On this basis, the Apocalypse of Shenoute could very likely date to around the same time, potentially being composed not long after the expansion of the Believers movement into Syro-Palestine and Egypt and their dominance over these regions. Indeed, Robert Hoyland proposes just such a dating for the Apocalypse, noting that in it "no mention is made of any aspect of their occupation, not even heavy taxation, the most ubiquitous complaint of the apocalypses of the early Islamic era." The reference to their desire "to rule over the entire world and dominate it" presumably refers to the astonishing velocity with which they assumed control of so much of the known world, and likewise reference to the rebuilding of the Temple would only indicate, as Hoyland further notes, that "the author was provoked to write by news about Arab construction on the site of the former Jewish temple, a task which would seem to have been initiated ca. 638."[16] Hoyland's proposal is quite reasonable in light of the evidence, and it demands that we give serious consideration to the likelihood that this Apocalypse of Shenoute was in fact composed sometime in the middle of the seventh century, fairly soon after the Believers invaded and took control of Egypt.

The main objection to such re-dating would be the Apocalypse's mention of "those who reject the pains that I received on the cross," which, as Jos van Lent suggests, could be an "allusion to the Muslims' denial of Christ's crucifixion, which testifies to some knowledge of Islamic tenets, [and] makes such an early date of composition rather doubtful."[17] Nevertheless, the most recent scholarship on this particular issue both as described in the Qur'an and in the faith of the early Believers complicates this hypothesis. Scholars of early Islam have long followed the Islamic exegetical tradition in understanding the Qur'an's reference to Jesus's crucifixion in 4.157 as a denial of the reality of his crucifixion. While this is indeed how the later Islamic tradition interprets the passage in question, this is not what it actually says, as Sidney Griffith, among others, has noted. In this verse, the Qur'an says of Jesus the Messiah that "They did not kill him, and they did not crucify him, but it was made to seem so to them. Those who differ about it are certainly in doubt of it; they have no knowledge of it except the following of opinion. They certainly did not kill him. Rather, God raised him up to Himself; God is mightily wise."[18]

Taken out of context, this passage certainly could be interpreted as indicating the Qur'an's denial of the reality of Jesus's crucifixion and death, as, again, the Islamic commentary tradition has indeed understood it. Yet as Griffith explains, to understand this statement as it stands within the Qur'an itself, we must look to its broader context there. In so doing, we find that this comment on the crucifixion occurs as part of a broader polemic leveled against the Jews that "can be seen to be echoing the language of contemporary Christian controversy."[19] When read within this immediate Qur'anic context, then, the passage does not deny the reality of Christ's death and crucifixion, but rather it rebukes the Jews for foolishly believing that they were the ones responsible for Jesus's death. They did not kill him, despite their implied boasting to this effect. Rather, God was in complete control of these events, so that the Jews did not kill Jesus, and ultimately God raised him up. This more careful reading further comports with the clear references to the death of Jesus as a reality elsewhere in the Qur'an, in three separate passages.[20] The belief of Muhammad's earliest followers, then, if we take the Qur'an as our best witness to their religious convictions, did not deny the reality of the crucifixion and mortality of Jesus, but rather emulated contemporary Christians in turning these events into occasions for anti-Jewish polemic.

Therefore, this brief reference to rejecting the sufferings of Christ in the Apocalypse certainly does not exclude the possibility of an earlier dating, since we have no evidence that Muhammad's followers held such a belief until later in the eighth century. Accordingly, if the Apocalypse is from the seventh century, we must find a different understanding of this polemic. Rather than referring to docetic ideas about the crucifixion, the passage instead likely rebukes those who reject Christ's sufferings on the cross by refusing to acknowledge soteriological efficacy of these sufferings—presumably, the Jews. Such an understanding is seemingly confirmed by the passage that follows, which likewise rebukes those who refuse to confess the divine economy of salvation through his resurrection, explicitly identifying these people as Christ's crucifiers, that it, the Jews. Thus, it would seem that in the previous statement it is also the Jews, and not Muhammad's followers, who reject his sufferings on the cross. The Jews are the subject of both the sentence that precedes the accusation of rejecting the sufferings on the cross and the one immediately following, which very strongly suggests such an interpretation. Moreover, the link between these infidels who reject Christ's pains on the cross and the rebuilding the Temple is also consistent with Jewish support for the Believers' restoration of worship to the site of the Temple, as we have seen reported in several other sources in this volume, including Sebeos (chapter 6), Anastasius (chapter 10), and the Apocalypse of Rabbi Shimʿōn (chapter 12).

Nevertheless, the mention here of those "managing affairs in my church" alongside those who reject Christ's sufferings is somewhat perplexing. I must confess, I am not entirely sure what this passage means, but I suspect it almost certainly does not refer to the Jews. Perhaps it is meant to refer to Muhammad's followers, yet it is not clear in what sense they would be managing affairs in the church. Most likely, I think, the passage is instead voicing objection to those bishops and other Christian leaders who have joined or aligned themselves with the Believers or were collaborating with their rule. Nevertheless, at the same time, we should note that this apocalypse certainly does not represent the Believers as especially tolerant of Christians, like some of the other texts in this volume, inasmuch as from the moment of their introduction the sons of Ishmael are described as "pursuing" the Christians, or even "hunting" them (*yaṭradūna*). Unfortunately, the Ethiopic version of the *Life of Shenoute*, which translates a different Arabic version, offers no help in clarifying the identity of "those managing affairs in my church," since this passage is absent from the Ethiopic. Nevertheless, in the Ethiopic version those who reject the pains on the cross are directly identified with those who crucified Christ and deny his resurrection, as well as his faith more generally, thus seeming to confirm our interpretation of these passages in the Arabic version as referring to the Jews as well.[21] One wonders, however, if a proper critical edition of the Arabic, which we presently lack, would possibly resolve all of these issues with much greater clarity.

Finally, there is the peculiar equation of the sons of Ishmael with the sons of Esau, so that both are pursuing the "Christians." Amélineau did not know what to make of these sons of Esau, whom he thought were "probably first cousins of the sons of Ishmael."[22]

Hoyland concludes that "both terms refer to the Arabs," citing for reference a passage from a tenth-century apocalypse attributed to the seventh-century Pisentius of Qift which predicts that "the king of the Greeks will arise . . . and go up to Egypt to fight the sons of Esau."[23] Nevertheless, in late ancient Jewish and Christian apocalyptic literature, the sons of Esau is a title regularly given to the Romans, and so one would imagine that this is also its significance in this instance.[24] As John Reeves notes, in Jewish apocalypticism especially, Esau "functioned as an emblem for the 'evil empire' of Rome and triumphalist Christianity."[25] Indeed, it is hard to imagine in an apocalyptic text of this era that "the sons of Esau" is anything other than a stand-in for Rome and the Romans: I find no precedent for identifying them in such a context with Arabs. In such case, then, how should we understand the Apocalypse's forecast that "the sons of Ishmael and the sons of Esau will arise, and they will pursue the Christians," particularly when the text elsewhere specifically refers to the Romans as Rome?

One possible reading would be to understand the sons of Esau as indeed some sort of reference to Christian Rome, which one would generally expect. In this case, we would understand the Apocalypse of Shenoute as indicating here some sort of alliance between Muhammad's "Ishamelite" followers and Christians who were loyal to the Roman Empire and its church, making them "sons of Esau," in the early decades of the Believers movement. The warning that these sons of Esau will "pursue the Christians" does not contradict this reading, inasmuch as we should accordingly understand "the Christians" in this apocalypse as a reference to the "true" Christians—that is, the Miaphysite Christians, who remained loyal to Cyril and the Third Council, in contrast to the wicked Diophysite heretics loyal to the Roman imperial church. The majority of Egypt's Christians rejected the two-natures Christology of the Council of Chalcedon that was officially sanctioned by the Roman imperial church, and for this "disloyalty" they had been severely persecuted by the Roman authorities in the later sixth and early seventh centuries. Indeed, we find specific reference to these events at the beginning of Shenoute's Apocalypse, as the Antichrist and Rome together tyrannized Egypt between the departure of the Persians and the arrival of the Ishmaelites.

Such a reading of the "sons of Esau" comports with and likewise supports the hypothesis that there were in fact many Christians within Muhammad's early community of the Believers, even as they remained in their Christian faith. This interpretation also infers that these Christians would be of a Chalcedonian persuasion, or, at least, they would have been largely perceived as such by the local Christian populace of Egypt. It is not presently clear whether we may conclude that Chalcedonian, Roman Christians were the clear majority of those who aligned themselves with Muhammad's followers as they assumed sovereignty over Syro-Palestine and Egypt. More research would be needed to determine whether such a conclusion is warranted. Yet insofar as the early Believers seem to have enlisted authorities from the Roman provincial administrations, many of whom would have been Chalcedonian Christians, to assist them in governing their new territories, it is easy to imagine how in Egyptian eyes the sons of Ishmael and Esau had together formed an alliance against them. For instance, Arietta Papaconstaninou notes in her analysis of the passage from the *Maronite Chronicle* that we considered in a previous chapter (14), that the Christian communities allied with the Roman imperial church seem to have enjoyed special favor under Muʿāwiya, as reflected also in his appointment of a Chalcedonian, Sarjūn ibn Manṣūr (the father of John of Damascus), as his chief tax-collector, not to mention his decision in favor of the pro-Roman, Chalcedonian Maronites in that very chronicle and the fact that John later followed his father, Sarjūn, in the same position. There is some indication, Papaconstaninou proposes, that during this time these "Roman" Christians "had in a sense 'joined' the umma"—that is, the community of the Believers.[26] Likewise, the predominance of Chalcedonian Christianity in Damascus and Palestine, the main centers of the Believers' polity under the Umayyads, which we noted in the previous chapter, could also have created the impression that Muhammad's followers and the Roman Christians of the Near East were allied against them. Indeed, given these two circumstances, it is tempting to suppose that the majority of Christians aligned with the Believers in Syro-Palestine and Egypt may have come from the Roman, Chalcedonian church, thus explaining the persecution of the (true) Christians by the sons of Ishmael and the sons of Esau. This interpretation would then also correlate with our proposed understanding of "those managing affairs" in the church: both would stand as parallel polemics against Roman Christian leaders exercising ecclesiastical authority in conjunction with the Believers' polity.

17 *The Book of Main Points* (ca. 687)

JOHN BAR PENKAYE

John bar Penkaye, or John of Fenek as he also is known, was an East Syrian Christian (i.e., "Nestorian") who lived in northern Mesopotamia at the end of the seventh century. John was a monk at the monastery of John of Kamul in the city of Gazarta or Jazira, today the modern town of Cizre in Turkey, which sits on the western bank of the Tigris just north of the Syrian border and just under fifty kilometers northwest of Iraq. There John wrote a chronicle of world history, focusing his attention on what he perceived to be the "main points," from the Creation up through the events of the later seventh century, the time when he was writing. The last event recorded in the chronicle is the death of al-Mukhtār, an anti-Umayyad insurgent who died in 687 while fighting in the Second Civil War for the cause of Alī's son, Muḥammad ibn al-Ḥanafiyyah.[1] Thus, scholars are largely agreed in dating this text to sometime not long after 687.

John's chronicle is divided into fifteen books, and the very end of book fourteen and all of book fifteen are dedicated to the period following the emergence of Muhammad's religious polity and its occupation of the Near East. The overarching themes of the chronicle are theodicy and divine Providence, as John seeks to explain for his readers how God has been continuously at work in the world's history, directing the course of events up until the present age, when turmoil and affliction have been set loose. John is confident that he is writing on the cusp of the eschaton, the end of the world, which he seems to expect will be inaugurated by the devastation and misery that had come upon the world in recent years. An apocalyptic tenor thus pervades the work. Nevertheless, the chronicle relates much important information concerning the religious and political history of the middle and later seventh century that adds considerably to our knowledge of the Believers' religious movement and polity and their relation to the Christians and other religious groups of the early medieval Near East.

The Book of Main Points[2]

And when the kingdom of the Persians reached its end, in the days of their king Khosrau, immediately the kingdom of the sons of Hagar seized control of almost the entire world, for they seized the entire kingdom of the Persians and overthrew all of their warriors, who were extremely boastful in the arts of war. For indeed, we should not consider their coming as something ordinary, for it was a divine act. And before calling them, he prepared them in advance to hold Christians in honor. Thus a specific order also deliberately came to them from God concerning our monastic order, so that they would hold it in honor. And when these people came by God's command, they seized, as it were, both kingdoms without any war or combat. Thus in contemptible fashion, like a brand rescued from a fire, without weapons or human cunning, God gave victory into their hands, so that what is written about them was fulfilled: "One pursues a thousand, and two put to flight ten thousand" [Deut 32.30]. How else could naked men, riding without armor or shields, have been victorious without divine help? He called them from the ends of the earth to destroy, through them, the sinful kingdom, and to bring low, by them, the arrogance of the Persians.

It was not long before the whole world was handed over to the Nomads [*ṭayyāyē*]. They captured all the fortified cities and ruled from sea to sea and from east to west: Egypt and all of the Nile;[3] from Crete to Cappadocia; from Yāhēlmān[4] to the Gate of Alans;[5] Armenians, Syrians, Persians, Romans, Egyptians, and all the regions in between. It was "his hand against all," as the prophet said [Gen 16.12]. And only half of the Roman Empire was left by them. Indeed, who can relate the carnage that they wrought against the Greeks, and in Kush [Nubia] and Spain and other distant places, taking captive their sons and daughters and subjecting them to slavery and servitude! And against those who in peace and prosperity did not cease from fighting against their Creator was sent a barbarian people who had no mercy on them. But since we have reached this point in the account, let us end this book here and give praise to the Father, the Son, and the Holy Spirit forever, Amen [the end of Book Fourteen].

BOOK FIFTEEN [John describes the troubled condition of the Christian communities in Rome and Persia before the arrival of Muhammad's followers] . . . Therefore, when God saw that there was no reform, he summoned the barbaric kingdom against us, a people who knew no persuasion, had no treaty or covenant, and would not receive flattery or blandishment. Bloodshed without reason was their comfort, rule over all was their pleasure, plunder and captives were their desire, and anger and rage were their food. They were not appeased by anything that was offered to them.

And when they were successful and had done the will of the one who summoned them, they reigned and ruled over all the kingdoms of the world. And they subjected all the peoples to ruthless subjugation and took their sons and daughters into harsh servitude. And they took vengence against them for their insult against God the Word and for the blood of the martyrs of Christ that was shed in innocence. Then our Lord was comforted, satisfied, and content to act with mercy upon his people. And because it also was just for the sons of Hagar to be repaid for the course of action that they had taken, for that reason from the beginning of their kingdom he made it have two leaders and divided it into two parts, so that we might understand what was said by our Savior. For they had unity until they conquered the whole world. But when they turned to themselves and had rested from war, then they quarelled with one another. Those in the west were saying, "Greatness is rightfully ours, and the king should be from us." But those in the east were contending that this was rightfully theirs. And from this dispute they were stirred up to war with one another.

And when this dispute came to an end, after much bloodshed among them, the westerners, whom they call the sons of ʾAmmāyē [the Umayyads] were victorious. And from them a man named Muʿāwiya became king and took control of both kingdoms, that of the Persians and that of the Romans. Justice flourished in his days, and there was great peace in the regions that he controlled. And he allowed everyone to live as they wanted. For as I mentioned above, they upheld an order from the one who was their guide [*mhaddyānā*] concerning the Christian people and concerning the monastic order. And through this one's guidance [*mhaddyānūtā*], they also upheld the worship of the one God, according to the custom of ancient law. And at their beginning they upheld the tradition [*mašlmānūtā*] of Muhammad, who was their teacher [*tārʾā*], so that they would confer a death sentence on anyone who was seen to be audacious against his laws.

And every year their raiders went to distant regions and to the islands, bringing back captives from every people under heaven.

And from everyone they demanded only tribute and allowed them to remain in whatever faith they wished, for among them were also Christians in no small numbers, some from the heretics, and some from us. And when Muʿāwiya reigned, there was peace throughout the world the like of which we have never heard nor seen, neither from our fathers, nor from our fathers' fathers, so that our Lord said, "I will tempt them with this, as it is written, 'In grace and truth iniquity is forgiven'" [Prov 16.6].

[John describes the conflicts that resume among the Christians in this time of peace. As Sebastian Brock summarizes: "John now goes on to enumerate in general terms the moral degradation and malpractices of bishops, clergy, rulers, judges and ordinary people during this time of peace, at a time when crops were bountiful and trade 'doubled.'"[6] God then gives signs indicating the need to repent, but the people do not respond]

...And when Muʿāwiya ended his days and went forth from the world, his son Yazid reigned after him. And he did not walk in the ways of his father, but he was fond of childish games and vain pleasures. The strength of men came to an end in his feckless tyranny, for Satan brought the discipline of men to an end through useless toils. But God took him quickly. And when he too went forth from the world, there was one of them named Zubayr who made his voice to be heard from a distance. And he was professing about himself that he had come out of zeal for the house of God, and he was accusing the westerners of being transgressors of the law. He came to their sanctuary somewhere in the south and lived there. And they prepared for war against him, and they defeated him. Thus, they also set fire to their sanctuary and shed much blood there. From that time on the kingdom of the Nomads was no longer stable. And when Zubayr died, they set up his son after him in the emirate [ʾamīrūtā].

The westerners had a general, ʿAbd al-Raḥmān bar Zāyāt [ʿUbayd Allāh ibn Ziyād],[7] and the easterners had another one named

Mukhtār. Now at that time, the westerners held Nisibis, and an emir named bar ʿUtmān[8] was ruling in it. And another emir from the easterners, named bar Niṭrōn,[9] went forth into battle against him. The westerners were saying, "Nisibis was under the authority of Rome, and so it was rightfully ours." But the easterners were maintaining, "It was under the authority of Persia, and so it is ours." On account of this, there was great turmoil in Mesopotamia.

And the westerners were victorious, and the easterners were driven away from there. But in the following year, bar Niṭrōn[10] made ready many troops, and horsemen like sand in number were prepared with him. He was armed with great pride and was determined to go down to battle against the ʿAqūlāyē [the Kufans], taking with him also John, who at the time was metropolitan of Nisibis. For because Mār Giwargis, the patriarch of the east of the church of Christ, had already gone forth to the blessed life, and Mār Ḥnānishoʿ the exegete had been appointed to the patriarchal throne, bar Zāyāṭ promised John, "If you come with me, I will remove him and establish you to the patriarchate in his place." And thus he was already thinking that victory was his, for he had many generals with him.

Now Mukhtār, because he was angry with the ʿAqūlāyē since they were useless in battle, issued an order that all their slaves should be set free and go into battle in their place. And when this order went forth, many thousands of captive slaves gathered to him. And he appointed a general for them named Abraham [Ibrāhīm ibn al-Ashtar] and sent him to meet bar Zāyāṭ with thirteen thousand men, all of them foot-soldiers with no armor or preparation, and no horses or tents, but each one of them was holding in his hand either a sword or a spear or a staff, and they set off. And when they met one another at a river called Ḥāzar [Khazir], there was a fierce battle between them, and all of the westerners' soldiers were killed. Their boasting turned to deep shame, for they were defeated not by men but by weaklings. And the man who was prepared for the patriarchate was barely able to save his cloak. The westerners were severely crushed, and their general also was killed. Their enemies took all the provisions that they had assembled, their wealth, possessions, weapons, and money, and in defeat they retreated until they crossed the Euphrates.

Those former captives, who were called *Shurṭē*, a name indicating their zeal for justice, entered Nisibis and held it, and they ruled over all of Mesopotamia. And wherever their enemies showed themselves, there was a *Shurṭē* victory. When they entered Nisibis, Abraham appointed his brother over them as general, and he went down to ʿAqūlā [Kufa]. But, because they wanted someone from among themselves to be general over them—since Abraham and his brother were from the Nomads—they rose up against him and killed him and all of his associates. And they appointed an emir from among themselves, whose name was Abuqarab.

The ʿAqūlāyē regretted what they had done, for they saw that their slaves had rebelled against them, and they rose up against Mukhtār and went to war against him. Although he had defeated them many times, in the end he was defeated by them, and they killed him and many soldiers from the former captives that were with him. But others from the former captives assembled and joined those who were in the city of Nisibis. And every day more were gathering from every direction, and they joined them. They captured many fortresses, and fear of them fell on all of the Nomads. Everywhere they went, they were victorious.

From then on God began to afflict the earth. [John continues to describe sufferings and catastrophes that befell the world on account of its wickedness, including a plague and a famine in the year "67 of the Nomads rule" (686/87 CE), and the lack of repentance in response to these divine signs, for which he chastises the current generation.]

For the coming of these *Shurṭē* and their victory is from God. And I believe that they will be the cause of the destruction of the sons of Ishamael. And the prophecy of Moses will be fulfilled that says, "his hand against all, and the hand of all against him" [Gen 16.12], for the hand of the Nomads rules over all peoples. And all peoples under heaven are among these *Shurṭē*. Therefore it seems to me that through these people their kingdom will come to an end. But it is clear that they also will not last. They will mix together with the other kingdoms, with those from which they were taken captive, and will be awakeners for them. And it seems likely that those who survive the sword, famine, and plague of today are being kept for even more bitter afflictions than these. For a distant people has been summoned against them, one whose actions the prophets also made known [cf. Deut 28.49], and they will destroy them, because they are also seeking to destroy the kingdom of the Romans and are determined to rule over all. It is a greedy people that has been summoned to do something that is unseemly and unknown.

And when this people is released from its chain, arm yourself against the things that are within: the senses will be a clear sign. . . . [John forecasts the eschatological events that will occur when this people is set loose. The text concludes with a final exordium to the addressee of the *Book of Main Points*, Sabrīshō, presumably the abbot of the monasetry of John of Kamul, which, according to Brock, "adds nothing of substance."][11]

Commentary

John bar Penkaye's chronicle is replete with valuable information about the early history of the community of the Believers during the middle of the seventh century. In general, John writes positively about Muhammad's followers, even as he also indulges in numerous stock aspersions against them, such as were de riguer among Christian writers of the era: for instance, he describes them as irrational "barbarians," who were filled with rage and thirsty for bloodshed and plunder. Yet at the same time, he notes the remarkable tolerance that the Believers had for the Christians and especially their monks, and he believed that they had arisen through the Providence of God, who specifically prepared them to hold Christians in high honor. Indeed, what besides the hand of God can explain, he asks, the ease and haste with which these primitive and disorganized Nomads were able to overcome both the Persian and Roman Empires. John also confirms in very strong terms much of what we have already seen concerning the high regard for Muʿāwiya in contemporary Christian sources, and likewise he provides one of the clearest indications that Christians were included as members of the community of the Believers, seemingly even still in his day. He is remarkably well informed about political developments among the Believers, and he gives a fairly detailed account of campaigns in Mesopotamia during the Second Civil War, some of which may derive from firsthand knowledge, given his domicile.

Even though the success of the Believers was ordained by divine will, John observes that they too were made to suffer God's punishment, presumably for their violent actions in the conquests. For this reason, he explains, at "the beginning of their kingdom he made it have two leaders and divided it into two parts," as rival factions within the community sought to have a leader chosen from their group. It is worth noting that John does not seem to know much about the history of the Believers before the events of this First Civil War: as far as his account is concerned, this is when their "kingdom" began. Quite possibly this perspective tells us something significant about the precise nature of the religous polity formed by Muhammad's followers in its early history. Indeed, there is much discussion as to precisely when we should begin to talk about the actual establishment and function of state apparatus among the early Believers.

Under the first four caliphs and up through the conclusion of the First Civil War in 661, it seems unlikely that there was much in the way of a strong, centralized state apparatus governing the Believers and their territories. Their movement was expanding rapidly across the globe, with relatively small numbers in relation to the populous regions of Syria, Persia, and Egypt that they absorbed so quickly. As they were constantly on the move and growing the expanse of their polity with such velocity, there would have been little opportunity or even motive to begin the hard work of setting up structures of government. We should envision, then, during the leadership of these first caliphs a continuation of a "'*jihād* state,' a politico-religious entity comprising fighting men of different religious affiliations whose overriding aim was the expansion of the state in the name of God and who shared a belief in the One God and the Last. Day." This early, expansionist *jihād* state, then, seems to have included peoples of different, monotheist religious traditions who fought together on behalf of their community of the Believers, while remaining in their own religious faith.[12]

Things began to change, it would seem, in the reign of Muʿāwiya. Although some scholars would insist that we only see a well-developed, centralized state emerge from the Believers' movement during the reign of ʿAbd al-Malik, it would seem at least that the first significant steps toward the emergence of a functioning state apparatus in fact took place under Muʿāwiya. Presumably, Muʿāwiya would have begun the process of building the necessary structures for governance during his decades as governor of Syria and Palestine. Since 639 he ruled the province from Damascus, and when he was proclaimed the commander of the Believers in 661, he continued to rule from Damascus, in contrast to the caliphs before him, who according to tradition, ruled from Medina. In Damascus he surely would have drawn on the existing remnants of the Roman administration for governing this complex, wealthy, and populous territory. With Muʿāwiya we get the first clear signs of a state with an army and a navy (the latter of which he founded while governor of Syria), a police force, taxation and coinage, official state media bearing his name, and so on.[13] It is no wonder, then, that for John, and presumably many other citizens of the seventh-century Near East as well, it was only at this point that it became clear that they were indeed now living under a new state government, rather than facing bands of roving marauders.

What John does tell us about the earliest history of the community of the Believers is noteworthy, however. For instance, like many other seventh-century Christian writers, particularly in Syriac, John does not identify Muhammad as a prophet. Although other texts more commonly describe him instead the "king of the Arabs,"[14] John refers to Muhammad as the community's "guide" (*mhaddyānā*), who gave it "guidance (*mhaddyānūtā*)," rather than naming him either a prophet or apostle. He was their teacher (*tārʾā*), and his followers "upheld the tradition [*mašlmānūtā*] of Muhammad." There is no sense in John's report of Muhammad as a prophet who was charged with revealing a dispensation from God, nor is there any hint of a sacred scripture with authority among his followers. This is persistent across all of the contemporary Christian witnesses: none describes him in terms other than as a teacher or a political leader, nor is there any reference to a sacred writing. This pattern is consistent, moreover, with a trend also observable in the early Islamic tradition, where we find evidence indicating that Muhammad's status as prophetic revealer was not initially a defining marker of the Believers' faith but was something that developed much later among his followers. And to the extent that members of the early community of the Believers would have seen him as prophetic, his prophetic status was not understood as unique in the manner that it would be later. Insofar as Muhammad was viewed as a prophet, he was merely the last in a long line of monotheist prophets, including Moses and Jesus, whose revelations from the one true God were in their essentials identical with Muhammad's message, as certain passages from the Qur'an itself indicate.[15]

It is presumably in such a context that we should understand John's remark that the Believers "demanded only tribute and allowed them to remain in whatever faith they wished, for amongst them were also Christians in no small numbers, some from the heretics, and some from us." Here John indicates that there were large numbers of Christians within the early community of the Believers, with the implication that so long as these Christians paid their dues, as it were, they were allowed to maintain their faith while being counted among the Believers.[16] No doubt, this policy applied only to other monotheists, such as the Christians and Jews, who would have been easily drawn into this community of the Believers if they were not required to renounce their faith. In addition to monotheism, the message of the Believers was to emphasize regular prayer, fasting, charity, and purity, all hallmarks of the common piety of late ancient Judaism and Christianity, and the Believers' conviction that the eschaton, the end of the world, was at hand would have been welcomed by many of the Jews and Christians of this era.[17]

Indeed, John's report of Christians in significant numbers among the Believers seems to witness to the interconfessional nature of the early community prior to the reign of ʿAbd al-Malik. In this era, as Robert Hoyland explains, "The religiously pluralist character of the community would explain why no Islamic pretensions were advanced and why the leader was designated by such confessionally neutral terms as 'servant of God' and 'commander of the believers.' The latter would have replaced Muhammad as the arbiter for all parties, and the Quran would at this time have been of significance only for the Muslim members, just as the Torah and Gospel were only binding for the Jews and Christians."[18] This portrait of the early community is consistent with Muʿāwiya's alleged fondness for Christianity as well as the glowing terms in which contemporary Christian sources describe him. John's report that the Believers held the Christians in general and their monastics especially in honor seems to confirm what we have already seen in Ishoʻyahb's letter, written during the 650s in Adiabene, also in northern Mesopotamia. Muʻāwiya's administration likewise included a number of prominent Damascene Christians, as we have noted before, including the father of John of Damascus, a pattern that the Umayyads would continue as late as John of Damascus himself (d. ca. 750). Muʻāwiya married a woman from the powerful Christian Kalb tribe, who was the mother of his successor, the caliph Yazīd, who also was married to a woman from the Kalb tribe. Muʻāwiya's armed forces also had a significant number of Christians, and, during the Second Civil War, Muʻāwiya's son Yazīd marched into battle—in the Hijaz of all places!—with soldiers from the Christian Kalb and Taghlib tribes bearing the cross and an image of their patron, St. George, as their military standards.[19]

As for the Second Civil War, John bar Penkaye has much to say about that. Although many details in John's account can be corroborated from the much later Islamic sources, John's testimony has tremendous value in its own right, since he writes as a contemporary of the events in question and was perhaps even an eyewitness to some of what he reports. He begins with the short reign of Yazīd (680–83), whom he describes as unpopular and ill-suited to rule. Although John locates the beginning of the Second Civil War after the death of Yazīd, the conflict in fact began almost immediately after Yazīd's accession to the throne. In effect, as Donner notes, the various competing interests that had caused the First Civil War were not really resolved, but only put on hold by Muʻāwiya's reign, after which they quickly resurfaced, becoming particularly acute after the death of Yazīd.[20] Yet John omits some of the initial events of this conflict, particularly since he begins his account only after Yazīd's death. We learn nothing, for instance of the revolt in Kufa on behalf of Ḥusayn ibn ʻAlī just after Yazīd's accession, which Yazīd's army put down while also killing Ḥusayn at the Battle of Karbala in 680.

The rebellion of ʿAbd Allāh ibn al-Zubayr also began before Yazīd's death, including most of what John has to say about him. When Ibn al-Zubayr refused to recognize Yazīd in 680, he fled from Medina to Mecca, which John here refers to as the location of the Believers' "sanctuary" in the south. Yazīd's forces invaded the Hijaz to deal with Ibn al-Zubayr's disloyalty, capturing Medina in late August 683 and then laying siege to Mecca in September, during which time the sanctuary there caught fire, as John says. The siege came to an end when Yazīd suddenly died toward the end of November and, as a result, Ibn al-Zubayr proclaimed himself the new caliph and secured the loyalty of the general of Yazīd's army, as well as recognition in Egypt and Iraq. No doubt, this is why Ibn al-Zubayr enters John's narrative after Yazīd's death: that is when he proclaimed himself caliph, with considerable support throughout the Believers' domain, even in parts of Syria. The powerful Christian Kalb tribe in Syria remained the most important holdout, however, seeking to put one of their Umayyad allies back in power.

John's report that Ibn al-Zubayr "was professing about himself that he had come out of zeal for the house of God, and he was accusing the westerners of being transgressors of the law" also finds broader confirmation in the early Islamic tradition. Ibn al-Zubayr's resistance to the Umayyads (i.e., "the westerners") was not just political but was grounded in religious differences. In particular, Ibn al-Zubayr was a partisan of the sanctity of the Hijaz and its holy sites, and the Meccan sanctuary especially, as John here relates, in opposition to the Jerusalem-centered piety of the Umayyads that valued holy places whose original significance derived from Jewish and Christian traditions. When ʿAbd al-Malik rose up against Ibn al-Zubayr, their struggle was not just for political control, but at the same time "ideas about the pilgrimage and the sanctuary were involved in the conflict."[21] Ibn al-Zubayr's revolt against the Umayyads was in large part a response to the Israelite and Jerusalemite piety of the Umayyads, against which he championed a distinctively Arabian and "Islamic" holy land in the Hijaz centered on the Meccan sanctuary.[22] Oddly, however, John has nothing to say about either 'Abd al-Malik or his father Marwān, failing to mention, for instance, that Ibn al-Zubayr's death came at the hands of 'Abd al-Malik's troops while attempting to defend Mecca. Instead, John merely notes that after Ibn al-Zubayr's death, his followers established his son as "emir" after him. Nevertheless, there is no evidence for one of Ibn al-Zubayr's sons succeeding him, and as Brock notes, John seems to be confused here.[23]

If John is missing some details in regard to the struggle between the Umayyads and the Zubayrids, which was the main engagement of this civil war, he is much better informed regarding another front in this conflict, namely, that between the Umayyads (the "westerners") and the Alids (the "easterners"), the supporters of 'Alī and his sons. Since Ḥusayn was killed early in Yazīd's reign, the Alids placed their support primarily behind 'Alī's son Muḥammad b. al-Ḥanafīyya, who was his son not by Muhammad's daugher Fatima, but from another of 'Alī's wives. The leader of this faction was not al-Ḥanafīyya himself, who did not lay claim to the caliphate. Rather, al-Mukhtār took up the struggle on al-Ḥanafīyya's behalf, whether or not the latter was in fact actively seeking the caliphate, and for a time al-Mukhtār achieved significant power for himself in Iraq in al-Ḥanafīyya's name. As John continues his narrative of this conflict, he comes closer to home, turning to Nisibis, approximately one hundred kilometers to the west of his monastery. Nisibis was originally held by the Umayyads, under the governance of an otherwise unknown emir named bar 'Uthmān. John identifies the Umayyad general in this region as 'Abd al-Raḥmān bar Zāyāt, although as Brock rightly observes, this must be a mistake for 'Ubayd Allāh ibn Ziyād, who was the actual leader of the Umayyad forces in this area: 'Abd al-Raḥmān was his brother and the governor of Khorasan.[24]

The easterners, that is, the Alids, made an attempt to capture Nisibis under the leadership of another emir, also otherwise unknown, named bar Niṭrōn, but the Umayyads drove them back. As John reports, the two sides in this territorial dispute were arguing for ownership on the basis of whether Nisibis had previously been Roman or Persian territory, as if that should decide whether the Umayyads or Alids should have jurisdiction.

In what follows, John's narrative becomes a little confusing, as he says that bar Niṭrōn, the eastern/Alid emir, gathered an enormous army with countless horsemen and marched down to attack Kufa, "taking with him also John, who at the time was metropolitan of Nisibis." John bar Penkaye continues to explain that this was because bar Zāyāt, the western/Umayyad general, had promised to give him the patriarchal throne after his victory. Yet this does not make much sense. Bar Niṭrōn and bar Zāyāt were on opposing sides in this conflict, and accordingly it does not seem possible that Bar Niṭrōn would take Metropolitan John with him on a campaign against Kufa because bar Zāyāt had promised John the patriarchate. Nor is it clear why bar Niṭrōn, an "easterner," would march against Kufa which was in Alid hands. Although no one else seems to have noticed this problem, perhaps we should understand the second appearance of bar Niṭrōn as a mistake for bar Zāyāt. It makes perfect sense for bar Zāyāt, the Umayyad general, to attack Kufa and to bring with him Metropolitan John, to whom he had promised the patriarchate following his victory. Perhaps, once again, a critical edition of the text, which we presently lack, would help to clarify the issue.

Meanwhile, Mukhtār had taken control of Kufa in al-Ḥanafīyya's name and was looking to assemble an army to enage bar Zāyāt's Umayyad army. When the local notables were not receptive to his call, he offered freedom for any of the non-Arab captives who had been enslaved, the *mawālī*, that would join his army. The offer was apparently well received, and he amassed a force of thirteen thousand former slaves who set off with only minimal armaments under the leadership of the general Ibrāhīm ibn al-Ashtar to meet the Umayyad army. The two forces clashed in the Battle of Khazir in 686, and Mukhtār's army won a dramatic victory. This Alid army of freed slaves was indeed known as the *shurṭat Allāh*, "the enforcers of God," as we know from other sources.[25] The remainder of John's account, however, relates information that is not otherwise known from the Islamic tradition, and here he probably draws on his own local knowledge of recent events. Mukhtār's *Shurṭē* continued on to Nisibis after their victory and took control of the city. Their general, Ibrāhīm, returned to Kufa, leaving his brother in charge.

The *Shurṭē*, however, rose up against Ibrāhīm's brother and killed him, because he was one of the Nomads [*ṭayyāyē*] and they wanted to be led by one of their own, Abuqarab, who also is otherwise unknown. As for the situation in Kufa, the citizens there were angry with Mukhtār for causing their slaves to rebel, and so they turned on him and killed him, along with many of his associates. The freed *mawālī* that remained in Kufa went to join the others in Nisibis, and at the time that John was completing his chronicle, it seems, they were only strengthening their hold on the city and the region: "Every day more were gathering from every direction, and they joined them. They captured many fortresses, and fear of them fell on all of the Nomads. Everywhere they went, they were victorious." In view of this, John concludes his history with the conviction that this slave army, the *Shurṭē*, has also been summoned by God, who gave them their victories. They are harbingers of the eschaton's near approach, who will defeat the sons of Ishmael, after which the end of the world will arrive, in the very near future, according to John's estimation.

18 *Fourth Letter to John the Stylite* (ca. 684–708)

JACOB OF EDESSA

Jacob of Edessa was a prolific author of the later seventh century, whose stature in Syriac Christian culture has been compared to that of Jerome in Western Christendom.[1] Jacob's contributions to the Syrian Miaphysite tradition are extensive. In his day he was particularly renowned, or perhaps more accurately, notorious, for his work in canon law: in addition to compiling a number of important volumes on the subject, he famously burned a copy of church regulations while bishop of Edessa in order to protest the laxity of their observance, after which he (perhaps wisely) withdrew to a monastery. He also authored a number of liturgical texts, and his extensive correspondence with people throughout Syria survives. Jacob played a fundamental role in standardizing various aspects of Syriac grammar, including the West Syrian tradition of vocalization, which was his invention. Also like Jerome, he labored to produce a more accurate version of the biblical text, and he wrote numerous biblical commentaries in addition to his various theological and philosophical works. In his youth Jacob had gone to Alexandria to undertake advanced study of Greek, which enabled him to translate, among other things, the works of Severus of Antioch from Greek into Syriac and the *Categories* of Aristotle.[2] Yet it is Jacob's personal observance of the religious practices of Muhammad's follower during his time in Egypt, as well as thereafter, that concerns us in the following excerpt from one of his letters. This letter offers responses to thirteen questions that had been sent to Jacob by a certain John the Stylite, one of which concerns the direction of prayer observed by Muhammad's followers.

From *Fourth Letter to John the Stylite*[3]

"Why do the Jews pray toward the south?" Behold, I say to you that this question is in error, and what has been asked is simply not true. For the Jews do not worship toward the south, nor do the Muhājirūn [*mhaggrāyē*; "the emigrants"].[4] For as I saw with my own eyes and write to you now, the Jews who live in Egypt and in fact the Muhājirūn there also prayed toward the east, and both peoples still do: the Jews toward Jerusalem and the Muhājirūn toward the Kaʿba. And those Jews who are south of Jerusalem pray to the north, and those in the land of Babel and in Ḥira [Kufa] and Basra pray to the west. And the Muhājirūn there also pray to the west toward the Kaʿba,[5] while those who are south of the Kaʿba pray to the north toward that place. So, in fact, from all that has been said it is clear that the Jews and Muhājirūn here in the regions of Syria do not pray toward the south but toward Jerusalem and toward the Kaʿba, these ancestral places of their peoples.

Commentary

The significance of Jacob's response to John's query concerning the direction of prayer observed by the Jews is fairly obvious. According to Jacob, the Jews, like Muhammad's followers as well, did not pray toward a specific direction on the compass but rather toward a specific place: Jerusalem (and the Temple) for the Jews and the Kaʿba for Muhammad's followers. Praying toward the Jerusalem Temple is an ancient practice in Judaism, while prayer in the direction of the Meccan Kaʿba is a standard practice of Islam, observed to the present day. The issue here, however, is that the Kaʿba of Jacob's contemporaries was not, according to his own eyewitness observances, located in Mecca or even in the Hijaz. Rather, the Kaʿba that he saw Muhammad's followers turn to face in his time was seemingly located somewhere in Palestine, presumably not too far from Jerusalem. In each instance, Jacob describes the Muhājirūn as orienting their prayers in the same direction as Jews, depending on the region that they were in. And while we might forgive some slight variations from the precise direction of Mecca, according to these reports, it does not appear that Muhammad's followers were even aiming for the Hijaz.

As noted above, in his youth Jacob studied in Alexandria, and there he saw Muhammad's followers regularly praying, like the Jews, toward the east in order to face the Kaʿba. What Jacob says he saw simply is not compatible with the location of the Kaʿba in Mecca or the Hijaz: from Alexandria, one would have to turn sharply to the south to face Mecca, in a markedly different direction from the Jews. Directly to the east was instead Palestine and Jerusalem, toward which the Jews, he says, like the Muhājirūn, prayed. Lest one should think that Jacob's remarks about the direction that Muhammad's followers in Egypt turned to face in prayer are simply confused, we should note that he very deliberately identifies the location of Kaʿba, the focus of the Muhājirūn's prayers, somewhere to the east of Alexandria. He continues to explain for John that in Mesopotamia Muhammad's followers, like the Jews, turn to the west to face their shrine. Again, there is no way that this can be made consistent with a Meccan Kaʿba. From Basra and Kufa one would turn even more sharply south than from Alexandria. And while minor astronomical inaccuracies might be understandable, here we are dealing with major divergences from the supposedly "correct" direction, and the rising and setting of the sun would make relative east, west, and south quite apparent to all.

If Jacob's report is accurate, then, and there is every reason to suppose that it is, since he relates his own eyewitness testimony based on his experiences living in Egypt and Mesopotamia, we must conclude that the Ka'ba revered by Muhammad's Near Eastern followers was not yet identified with Mecca but seems to have been located instead somewhere in Palestine. Moreover, Jacob's account cannot be dismissed as a mere blip, as some sort of idiosyncratic anomaly from one befuddled individual. There is a good deal of evidence that can corroborate Jacob's report, and in fact it is anything but clear that Muhammad's early followers regularly turned to face a shrine in Mecca as they observed their daily prayers. Above we noted in the discussion of Anastasius's anecdote about Christians who visited the shrine of the Saracens (chapter 10) that it seems relatively unlikely that Christians would have traveled to Mecca in the middle of the seventh century, even if such a journey is not, admittedly, entirely out of the question. The *Khuzistan Chronicle* (chapter 11) mentions the "tent of Abraham," revered by the Nomads in some unidentified desert location, while only John Bar Penkaye (chapter 17) says that the Believers had a sanctuary in the south, which would be the correct direction given his geographic position.

Nevertheless, there is substantial evidence from a number of sources indicating that prayer in the direction of a Meccan shrine was not a standard practice among Muhammad's early followers, but this shrine and its veneration instead emerged only gradually as a central focus of Islamic faith and practice. As I have noted elsewhere, there can be little question that the original direction of prayer for Muhammad's followers was indeed Jerusalem.[6] The Qur'an itself mentions a change in the direction of prayer, the *qibla*, but its notice is frustratingly vague: neither the occasion nor the original direction is named, and the new direction is identified only as "toward the sacred place of worship" (*al-masjid al-ḥarām*).[7] Yet Muhammad's earliest biographies are quite clear in identifying Jerusalem as the original focus of worship for Muhammad himself and his early followers.[8] Although these biographies are late and generally unreliable, as we have noted, it seems hard to imagine that the later Islamic tradition would invent such practice and ascribe it to Muhammad and the early community if it had not been so. Indeed, the fact that this memory survives in the traditional accounts of Islamic origins, despite its clear contradiction to the established practice of the times when these biographies were composed, strongly vouches for its authenticity. And while the Islamic historical tradition offers a variety of explanations for why Muhammad did this, it seems clear that these rationalizations were designed to minimize the "embarrassment" that Mecca was not originally the focus of the Believers' or even Muhammad's prayers.[9]

One should note, however, that Jerusalem and Mecca were not the only two options for sacred direction in nascent Islam. There is scattered evidence of other early trajectories, leading Suliman Bashear to conclude, "As far as the first century is concerned, one cannot speak of 'one original *qibla* of Islam,' but rather of several currents in the search for one."[10] As Bashear notes, for instance, there is significant evidence for an early eastern *qibla*,[11] and before him, Tor Andrae, Frants Buhl, and Vasily (or Wilhelm) Barthold all argued that Muhammad's original *qibla* had been toward the east, a practice that he adopted from Christianity.[12] Nevertheless, such reasoning bypasses the difficult question of whether Christianity had any significant presence at all in the seventh-century Hijaz, when this remains rather doubtful in light of the current state of our evidence. Although Christianity had literally encircled the Hijaz by

Muhammad's lifetime, there is simply no evidence of a significant Christian community in either Mecca or Medina.[13] Consequently, any Christian influence on the *qibla* would likely have come not in Mecca or Medina, but only after the Believers had entered the confessional diversity of the Roman and Sassanian Empires, as Moshe Sharon more plausibly speculates.[14]

Moreover, Sharon has drawn attention to possible archaeological evidence for an eastern *qibla* in what appears to be the remains of an early mosque at Be'er Orah in the southern Negev. Sharon describes this rectangular building as "an open mosque with two miḥrābs, one facing east and one facing south. The one facing south was clearly a later addition made after ʿAbd al-Malik's reforms came into effect."[15] Although some have suggested the possibility that this structure may be a converted church, whose eastern niche was simply the church's apse, the archaeology of the site confirms its original construction as a mosque with an eastward *miḥrāb*.[16] Two early Iraqi mosques have also been found with deviant *miḥrāb*s, the mosques of al-Ḥajjāj in Wāsiṭ and of Uskaf bani Junayd near Baghdad, both of which are oriented approximately thirty degrees too far to the north, pointing almost due southwest to somewhere in northwestern Arabia. While it is difficult to assess the significance of these deviant *miḥrāb*s, they certainly add support to Bashear's proposal of different currents searching for the appropriate direction of prayer for Muhammad's followers.

According to various reports in the Islamic tradition, the mosque of ʿAmr b. al-ʿĀs at Fusṭāṭ in Egypt originally had an eastward *qibla*: the sources relate that it was "very much turned toward the east."[17] This would seem to directly confirm Jacob's observations. Likewise, accounts of the construction of Kufa's mosque in 638 clearly indicate that the direction of the *qibla* was to the west, seemingly due west, exactly the direction of Jerusalem, leading Hoyland to conclude that the original direction of prayer in Kufa was indeed westward.[18]

When paired with Jacob's report of western prayer in Ḥira [Kufa] and Basra, it seems highly likely that the early Believers of Mesopotamia were praying toward the west, and those in Egypt to the east, in the direction of Palestine rather than the Hijaz. Yet the *miḥrāb*s of the early mosques at Wāsiṭ and Uskaf bani Junayd are truly aberrant, pointing neither toward the Holy Land nor the Hijaz but somewhere in between. Largely on this basis, Crone, Cook, Hawting, and others have argued for the existence of an early sanctuary revered by Muhammad's followers somewhere in northwest Arabia, whose traditions (including possibly the title "Kaʿba") were only later conferred on the Meccan shrine.[19]

Jacob's report that in his day Muhammad's followers prayed not toward Mecca but instead somewhere in the direction of Palestine, is not anomalous in the least, then, but rather, it is consistent with a wide range of evidence from the Islamic tradition itself as well as archaeology. It seems increasingly clear that prayer toward Mecca and the location of the Believers' sacred shrine there were not primitive elements of Muhammad's new religious movement. Indeed, it is rather certain that Jerusalem was the original focus of the Believers'—and Muhammad's—prayers, a practice that undoubtedly corresponds with their devotion to the Jerusalem Temple, as we have already seen in a number of other texts, and their fervent interest in restoring worship to the "abomination of desolation" of its state at the beginning of the seventh century. Indeed, Jerusalem and the biblical Promised Land were almost certainly the original "Holy Land" for Muhammad and his early followers. Only over the course of the first Islamic century, it would seem, did Mecca, Medina, and the Hijaz slowly replace the biblical Holy Land as a new distinctively Islamic Holy Land, a development that coincided with the broader program of Islamicization and Arabization inaugurated at the end of the seventh century by ʿAbd al-Malik.

19   *The Passion of Peter of Capitolias* (ca. 720)

According to its title in the manuscript, the *Passion of Peter of Cap-itolias* was written by "our holy and blessed father John, monk and priest of Damascus," an attribution, it would seem, to the most important Eastern Christian intellectual of the eighth century, John of Damascus. Although it is difficult to be certain whether John of Damascus is in fact the author of this text, it is worth noting that Theophanes the Confessor also identifies John of Damascus as the author of a martyrdom of Peter of Capitolias in his *Chronicle*, which Theophanes composed during the early years of the ninth century.[1] Nevertheless, there are some important differences between the Georgian text and Theophanes's account of Peter's martyrdom, and so the relationship between this *Passion* and the text that The-ophanes attributes to John of Damascus remains a little uncertain. So far, only the text's original editor, Kekeliże, has voiced a clear opinion regarding the attribution's authenticity, and Kekeliże con-cludes with conviction that "it is impossible in this case to doubt the Damascene's authorship." John, he notes, according to his own *Life* had retired to the monastery of Mar Saba at this time, where he devoted himself to composing hagiographies of great men. Peter's martyrdom, he maintains, thus occurred while John himself was living in Palestine, so that "Peter suffered, so to speak, in front of John of Damascus." The high literary style, he additionally notes, seems worthy of John of Damascus.[2]

While it is tempting to assign this martyrdom to John, it seems more prudent to wait until more eyes have had a chance to examine the text before reaching any judgment. There may have been more than one John who was a monk and priest of Damascus, or some medieval copyist may have wanted to ascribe this text to the greatest theologian of the period in question. Nevertheless, the circumstances of John's life invite a real possibility that he was its author. The chronology of John's personal history as well as the history of his renowned family have long been problematic: much confusion exists as to whether or not John is to be identified with the Mansur ibn Sarjun known especially from Islamic sources who was a high court official in the Umayyad administration in Damascus. Nevertheless, in a recent article, Sean Anthony has argued, persuasively in my opinion, on the basis of the Christian and Islamic sources, that John of Damascus is in fact the son of this Mansur. This would mean, among other things, that John of Damascus lived one generation later than much scholarship has assumed.[3] Unfortunately, reliable dates in the life of John are very hard to come by, but his Arabic biography reports that not long after assuming his father's administrative position in Damascus, John was forced to flee to the monastery of Mar Saba when the iconoclast emperor Leo III (r. 717–41) forged a treasonous letter in John's name, turning the Islamic leaders against him.[4]

If this chronology is correct, it would mean that John was likely serving as a high-ranking administrative official in the Umayyad court at the time when Peter was brought to Damascus to appear before the caliph Walid and his son ʿUmar (and so was not in Palestine, *pace* Kekeliże). Then, only a few years later, he fled to Mar Saba, where, as Kekeliże notes, John's *vita* says that he began to write hagiography. Such circumstances certainly comport favorably with the

Passion's attribution to John. One should note, however, that Marie-France Auzépy has argued that John never was at Mar Saba, and her arguments have convinced some scholars to abandon the tradition that he was a monk there.[5] Nevertheless, her arguments are not particularly persuasive, in my opinion, and there is no good reason to remove John from the monastery on their basis. Her main contention is that John of Damascus is not mentioned in a list of Mar Saba's past luminaries in the late eighth-century *Life of Stephen the Sabaite*, nor is he mentioned in the *Twenty Martyrs of Mar Saba*. Yet, as Andrew Louth was quick to respond, the key foundation of her argument, the list, identifies Mar Saba's wonderworkers and martyrs, whose miracles brought the monastery fame, while "no one pretends that John was such."[6] Learning and scholarship, John's métiers, do not appear to have been similarly valued by the list's compiler. And as for the *Twenty Martyrs*, the events of this text took place in 797, well after John had died: I am not sure why we should expect his mention there. In any case, Auzépy's argument is one from absence, and as the dictum goes, absence of evidence (particularly in one list) cannot be evidence of absence, especially when reasons for the absence can be supplied.

There are in fact several different accounts of Peter's martyrdom in addition to this *Passion*, and the variations among these literary remains have so far been the primary focus of scholarship on this Christian neo-martyr. I have little interest in repeating such efforts to recover the "historical Peter of Capitolias" who underlies these diverse accounts, and so far I am not persuaded that we can understand exactly how all the complex data that we are given should relate. Robert Hoyland favors giving precedence to Theophanes's brief account of Peter's martyrdom (which, again affirms John of Damascus's authorship),[7] but the passage in question is quite confused and seems to reflect an amalgamation of various different Peters, including someone named Peter of Maiouma, which, one should note, is also the name of the famous Palestinian monk from the later fifth century, and Peter the Iberian, who was an early leader in the anti-Chalcedonian movement.[8] Moreover, I do not think that Peter's Georgian *Passion* has yet been given the full consideration that it merits, in large part because it has only recently been translated. I suspect that this *Passion* probably provides our best information about Peter and his martyrdom, although it is clear that this is not a straightforward "history" of actual events by any measure. It is true that the text survives only in a fairly recent Georgian manuscript, and such late attestation invites a measure of skepticism. Nevertheless, the text often seems quite knowledgeable about contemporary events and local geography, qualities that suggest its author had good information at his disposal and was working in relatively close historical proximity to Peter's martyrdom. Its authorship by John of Damascus should not yet be completely excluded, but even if he is not the actual author, it is quite likely that we have here a work of the early eighth century written not long after the events in question.

The Passion of Peter of Capitolias[9]

[The martyrdom begins with a brief biography of Peter prior to his martyrdom, as well as a description of his personal encouragement of others who had borne witness as martyrs before him. The account of his own martyrdom then begins.]

5.... For then [Peter] saw that the cloud of godlessness and the fog of seduction were widespread and that truth was violently oppressed by falsehood, when many who had vacillating thoughts were captivated by the ease of pleasures, by apostasy from the truth, and by falling willingly into falsehood. And some were attracted and won over through flattery, while others were stolen away by the promise of gifts. And once it happened that they broke some people through coercion by torture and beat them into exchanging light for darkness and made them renounce the name of our Lord Jesus Christ. Because of this he was enraged and distressed and forsaking life. He considered life unlivable and longed for death. And from that time on because of the dissolution he was stricken by the apostasies[10] as if by stones. When he saw the world besieged by such evils, just like one who is in smoky and foul air longs to breathe pure air, so he too, truly of eternal memory, was longing to remove himself from this earthly life in order to depart the stinking evil of blasphemy by going forth to the pure place. He lamented even more, weeping dolorously, when he heard the servant and creature speaking blasphemy against the creator of all things, although no one dared to expose this blasphemous treachery, because of the wormwood's concealment with honey. For these seducers of the people maintained—explaining this all with false fairytales—that they served a single sovereign, brutishly saying that only the Father is God, and they professed that his Son and Word is a servant and a creature. And by dishonoring the Son, they dishonor the Father, for truly the one who does not honor the Son does not honor the Father who sent him.

6. When he heard this foolishness, this blessed and pious man whom he [God] foreknew in his mind through foreknowledge and from calling nonexistence into existence, and whom he "predestined to become the image of his Son" [Rom 8.29], was furiously torn to pieces and laid to waste and brought to death. Thus when he had spent much time with his thoughts in turmoil, by some predetermination of God, who knows the workings of the will of those who fear him, he fell into illness of the flesh so that he would become healthier in spirit. So then the flesh settled into illness, coming very close to death, but the longing of his spirit remained unyielding. He had only one desire, to die as a martyr for Christ's sake, and one concern, one sorrow, one sadness: that he would go forth from the body without shedding his blood for Christ's sake. Because of this, then,

this wise man was such a lover of the truth that he did not forfeit his will completely. He called for a certain person named Qaiouma to stand watch over his illness and serve him in the exhaustion of his infirmity. And he said to him, "Go out into the streets of the city and look around the alleys until you reach the temple of the Arabs and call out the noteworthy people from there, for I need to entrust something to you, and I want them to be witnesses of this pledge." But this was a trick, for he wanted to make a profession and to lay down a noble martyrdom, and he made this a good provision for himself.

Qaiouma then completed this task right away, and very many and the best of the Arabs came. And when they sat down, the holy one began to profess the good confession to them, and he said: "Everyone who hides the truth is an enemy of the truth, and everyone who preaches lies and deception is an adversary of God, and everyone who denies Christ and does not confess him as being God is deceived and heading for destruction. And anyone who calls someone else a prophet after the prophet John the Baptist places himself in error, for 'the Law and the prophets were until John the Baptist' [Luke 16.16], as the Lord clearly proclaims in the gospels. Now do not be deceived and do not boast excessively, for the faith of the Christians alone is true and leading unto eternal life." This and very many similar things he said to them, and when he had sufficiently denounced their blasphemy and godless actions, he caused no small uproar and outrage among them, for he immediately inflamed their fury, like a when fire touches a kindling reed. They were gnashing their teeth and boiling like cauldrons and spitting foam with rage, like the waves of the sea stirred by the wind and crashing on the shore. They were crying out and inciting one another to murder. "Behold the astonishment!" they said. "O the extraordinary audacity! Do you see how he mocks us? Look at how he has made our religion appear dishonored and ridiculed! Should we not kill him? Shall we not bring death upon him prematurely?" And they were about to do this, if they had not seen that he was in his final breath.

Nevertheless, longing for virtue overcame the illness, and he prayed to be killed by them and to die by their hands. How much the desire for martyrdom returned, how much the longing! But the righteous God, the giver of life and lord of death, sentenced him to martyrdom lawfully and clearly, so that the cause of his martyrdom would not be considered an expected death.[11] But it was the beginning of November when this happened, in the twelfth indiction. So then these wild servants of evil went forth from there full of rage and were looking for blood, and they went to their temple of godlessness. And they made known to all those there who shared their unbelief what the holy one did to them, and they rose up with excessive madness, like the sea stirred up by a fierce northerly wind. And if news of the man of God's death had not already gone forth, they would have set upon him with demented rage and torn his body limb from limb. But for the moment this restrained them, for the news of his death extinguished their fire like water. Nevertheless, God, who always reveals the hidden virtue of his servants and grants to his friends the ripened fruit of their aspirations, relieved the holy one's illness and granted health to his body so that it could serve the longing of his spirit. So he rose up from his illness and was restored to his original bodily strength, so that once again he walked about through the streets of the city. . . . [A rhetorical dialogue between Peter and the Devil interrupts the narrative at this point.]

7. Therefore they could not endure his extreme audacity, for it seemed challenging to those who heard his godly witness. That is why they made known the righteous things that had been said to them in writing to ʿUmar, the son of Walid, the tyrant of the Arabs. ʿUmar was a very cruel man with fear flowing from his eyes, who had authority over the Arabs settled in Jordan, and when he received their letter, he wrote to one named Zora, who had been given authority

by him over the Trichora:[12] "Bring forth the holy one and question him as to whether the things that were said about him in writing were true. And if he denies their account, he is to be set free from torture, for you know that many people say many such worthless things through delirium, since it is known that the mind suffers and is enfeebled along with the flesh. But if he seems resolved and insolent, having a steadfast and unchangeable mind, and he confirms these same thoughts and words, lock him up in prison and in chains and then make known what has been said in writing about him." When Zora received this letter and he came to the city of Capitolias, he sat on the throne and ordered them to bring forth the holy one, who came forward having his confession ready from the beginning. Then Zora ordered that the ruler's letter should be read aloud, and after it was read, he said to the holy one: "The emir"—for so they call the ruler of the Arabs—"as an example of his love of humanity, has given you an opportunity to answer here, in order to avoid blame and save your life. It also seems right to us that if, on account of derangement from some illness, someone says something unseemly, not to penalize or impose punishment but instead to pardon him or her on account of the illness. Therefore how much of what they have written to the emir is true, for the law does not punish unintended transgressions? Spare yourself and do not hand over your flesh to torment and your spirit to death, for we have been taken by great concern and sympathy for you. But if you will not save yourself from torture, no one can save you: just deny what they say you said and go home alive." His blood relatives were crying out similar things to him, and his close friends were sorrowfully urging and cautiously pleading: "Do not deliver yourself to death, o beloved!"

Nevertheless, he shut his ears to these sorcerers, and when it became very silent, like a brave royal soldier of Christ, with great boldness and a fearless mind, he said to them: "I am speaking the truth; I am not lying [cf. Rom 9.1]. I do not ever recall any deception of the mind during the time of my illness, and what I said then is true." He said this, and with a great and brilliant voice and with a fearless mind he again professed the good confession, and he said again what he had said before and also added much more to what he had said before. And when Zora heard this, as he had been ordered, he handed over the holy one bound up into prison. And in a letter he informed ʿUmar what had happened and issued a decree that none of the Christians should be allowed to go to him. But even though he was bound and detained in prison, he did not forget charity, and he did not rest from doing good deeds, but being a prisoner for Christ he was bound with the inmates of the prison even more by love, and he used the oil of grace as a coworker, for he knew that as oil makes the fighter fat, so charity also strengthens the soldier spiritually. Therefore while he was accomplishing this, Walid, the previously mentioned ruler of the Arabs, fell into illness and gathered his children and relatives to himself from every region, for the illness was a herald of death and threatening his departure, which occurred two months later. Therefore ʿUmar, the ruler of the Arabs of Jordan went forth to his father. The boldness of the blessed man Peter came to mind, and he told his father, and as iron sharpens iron [cf. Prov. 27.17], for he was also a bloodthirsty and sanguinary man, always breathing murder [cf. Acts 9.1], he ordered that the holy one should be brought forth to him in chains.

8. Thus the one who was to bring him there was sent forth, riding on swift horses, and on the first of January he reached the city of Capitolias. He did as he was ordered by presenting the letter that he had brought from there and by leading forth the holy one in its stead. And the martyr had been locked in the confinement of prison for one month, bound with chains on his neck and with shackles on his hands. Therefore when they completed their journey, they came to Kassia, which is a mountain overlooking the city of Damascus, where once had been the beautiful monastery of Saint Theodore,

which was abounding with virtuous monks, but recently the Arab tyrants took it from their control and built palaces for themselves, where at that time Walid, the tyrant of the Arabs, was found in the throes of illness. . . . [This section concludes with a description of Peter's three-day journey to Damascus in captivity.]

9. But he was ordered to appear before 'Umar at dawn. When the holy one was brought before him, he did not frighten him with rage but took on a calm appearance—not that he had been softened by a spirit of mercy but because he had become the mouth of his father the devil, who desires the perdition of all human beings and that they should not attain understanding of the truth. Then he said to him: "I have heard that you spoke many blasphemies, albeit in the throes of illness, and I believe that you were sick in your spirit on account of an illness of the flesh. But I also know that after your release from this illness you are saying the same things that you said while you were ill. Yet as evidence of my great love of humanity, I offer you a chance to escape judgment. Confess your error, and your mistake will be let go: there will be either life or death for you." When the martyr for Christ heard this, he was neither afraid nor frightened and did not abandon courage of thought, but he responded even more audaciously and fearlessly than before. "I will not cease to worship Christ, whom I call my God. But you, being blind in mind, believe in a false prophet and proclaim him as the messenger of God. Behold, I am ready for the wounds, for crucifixion, for burning, and to delight in every kind of torture: I will delight in them; on account of them I will be joyful."

When the insatiable 'Umar heard this, he roared with his heart like a lion. Then he handed over the holy one to his father Walid, king of the Arabs, who ordinarily was savage and monstrous, but then, on account of illness, had naturally acquired an increase in wrath. He said to the holy one: "Why am I hearing talk about you? So be it if you want to confess Jesus as God, even though he is a man and servant of the Creator. Why have you insulted our religion? Why have you said that our peaceful prophet is the master of deception and the father of lies?" And the holy one said to him: "I have not ceased nor will I cease to confess Christ as my God and Creator, the judge of the living and the dead, as he has authority over all things. Nevertheless this one who calls himself a prophet is called out as a slave of my Christ, as a liar and a deceiver.... [Peter continues to profess his faith before Walid, who in exasperation eventually determines to send him back home where he is to be exectued. The martyrdom then describes, in gruesome detail, Peter's execution by the Umayyad authorities, concluding with a defense of his status as a genuine martyr.]

Commentary

Although this text is a little later than most of the others in this volume, we include it largely because it depicts a remarkable tolerance on the part of the Umayyad authorities for the differing religious faith of their Christian subjects even near the end of the first Islamic century. Likewise, Peter's *Passion* offers an early exemplar of the revival of Christian martyrdoms and martyrdom accounts that coincided with the rise of Islam in the late ancient Near East. As noted in the introduction, during the early Islamic period the martyr's *Passion* reemerged as a popular genre, especially, among the Chalcedonian communities of Syria and Palestine who had remained faithful to the Roman imperial church.[13] Although most of these martyrdoms were originally composed in Greek in the Chalcedonian monasteries of Syria, Palestine, and Sinai, many now survive only in Arabic or Georgian translations. Peter's *Passion*, which survives in Georgian, was certainly written in Greek and probably was translated directly from Greek into Georgian, without an Arabic intermediary as sometimes is the case.

The scale of Christian persecution during the early Islamic period was certainly nothing close to what the early Christians faced at the hands of the Romans and Sasanians, but this renewal of martyrdoms and the revival of martyriological literature is seemingly one of the more interesting features of Christian culture in early Islamic Syria and Palestine. The adaptation of this early Christian genre to new circumstances of political domination during the early middle ages offers a potentially revealing window onto how Christians responded culturally to Islamic imperialism. Interestingly enough, we see repeated in these martyrdoms some of the same patterns that emerge from the early Christian experience of martyrdom: reluctance on the part of the government authorities to execute Christians and the martyrdom of large numbers of Christians primarily through mob violence. Two new themes emerge in this literature, however, both of which have to do with the transgression of community boundaries: several of these neo-martyrs meet their fate either because of their apostasy from Islam or through efforts to proselytize among the Muslim community.

Peter's martyrdom certainly contains many noteworthy features that are deserving of further historical reflection, but I will here note only a few details from the excerpts above that are important for understanding the early history of Islam. Perhaps the single most striking element of this text is the extreme reluctance on the part of the authorities to put Peter to death, a resistance that only is overcome by Peter's relentless desire for the Arabs to execute him so that he could gain the martyr's crown. In this regard, the *Passion* continues a theme that we have seen in other sources in this volume, which indicate that Muhammad's followers were remarkably tolerant, at least in some contexts, of Christians and their faith. And even though we find that such reluctance by the authorities to deliver a capital sentence is a common theme in many Christian martyrdoms from the early Islamic period, in Peter's *Passion* their efforts to avert his execution are exceptional.[14] The Islamic authorities, Walīd and ʿUmar, who are also known from the Islamic tradition, and the local official Zora all seek a way to avoid killing Peter.[15] Even after he has repeatedly denied that illness was the cause of his public denunciations of Muhammad's claims to prophecy, these officials persistently try to convince him to take the easy way out: just say it was the illness, they plead with him, so that they can pardon him. They have no problem with Peter's confession of Christ's divinity, it would seem, and they are willing to allow this, so long as he will stop rebuking their prophet.

Unlike the Roman persecutors before them, the Islamic authorities here show no interest in persuading Peter to renounce his faith; they merely want him to stop publically criticizing their own faith. If only he would show a bit more tact and offer a ready excuse for his impolite ravings, they seem more than happy to allow him to live and to tolerate his profession of a different faith. Thus, the *Passion of Peter of Capitolias* indicates that even into the beginning of the eighth century, as Islamification of Muhammad's religious movement was beginning to take hold, the ruling authorities continued to show remarkable tolerance toward Christians, at least in some regions and in certain instances. Clearly, by this point, Muhammad's followers have come to regard themselves as members of a distinctive "religion" that is different from that of the Christians, and they have explicitly identified Muhammad as their prophet. Yet even at this late date when Muhammad's followers seem to have moved well along the way toward a more sectarian and confrontational identity, these rulers nonetheless are portrayed as doing all that they can to extend great religious generosity to one of their Christian subjects.

As for Peter's behavior in the narrative, his ardent desire to suffer a painful death, seemingly without necessity, undoubtedly strikes most modern readers as bizarre and utterly deranged. Moreover, given the circumstances of his execution, as described in this narrative, it is not entirely clear that Peter is in fact a proper martyr. According to the story of his *Passion*, Peter is put to death not so much for his confession of the Christian faith, which he seemingly is allowed to profess, but rather for his persistent and public critique of the faith held by the ruling authorities. No less significant is the extent to which Peter actively seeks his own martyrdom, even when he is more than once offered the opportunity to preserve his life *without* renouncing his faith. His unwavering pursuit of martyrdom seemingly contradicts the received teaching of the early Church Fathers, who, on the whole, maintained that while Christians must not turn away from martyrdom when the only other alternative is blasphemy and the destruction of the soul, at the same time, martyrdom should not be actively sought. From the early third century onward, the prevailing voice of the orthodox Fathers rejects those who would volunteer themselves for martyrdom.[16]

One must wonder, then, what was the purpose of this martyrdom, which again certainly is not just a straightforward report of actual events from the early eighth century. Rather, we have here a highly stylized account of this martyr's death that was designed to meet certain expectations of its audience and to advance a particular Christian self-understanding in the face of rule by Arab infidels who were promoting a new and blasphemous strain of monotheism. So just what are the values and ideas that this narrative advocates and presumably expects its readers and hearers to embrace? Other Christian martyrdoms from the early Islamic period seem designed to encourage resistance to conversion and to address the delicate issues of Christian apostasy to Islam and Muslim apostates to Christianity (some of whom, we learn from these tales, had originally been Christians, as in the case of George the Black above, chapter 10). Yet these issues seem distant from the present text: no one is guilty of apostasy, and Peter is in no way pressured to convert. To the contrary, the authorities are happy for him to remain a Christian; they merely wish that he would shut up about their religion. It is true that Peter was allegedly inspired to speak out against Islam because he was enraged that some Christians had been lured away from their faith through bribery or even torture. He was greatly disturbed, or so we are told, that others lacked the courage to denounce the errors of the Arabs' false new religion, and thus he felt compelled to speak out boldly and expose its lies. Yet in comparison with other similar texts from this period, the threat of apostasy emerges as a relatively minimal concern here.

Much clearer, however, are the doctrinal issues that the text's author identifies as decisive ideological boundaries dividing the faith of the Christians from that of their new Arab rulers. Time and again, we find Peter insisting on the full divinity of Christ and the illegitimacy of Muhammad's claim to be a prophet. The former point, as we have noted, was seemingly not objectionable to the Muslim authorities when professed by the Christians. Yet one would imagine that this narrative aims to meet fresh doubts about this centerpiece of the Christian faith that had possibly been introduced by the new Islamic teachings about Jesus that were becoming more widely known. Likewise Peter's forceful denunciations of Muhammad's prophetic pretentions were undoubtedly intended to prevent any Christians from being lured away by the notion that "biblical" prophecy had somehow resumed in Muhammad's teachings. After all, several centuries before, Mani had persuaded many Christians to follow in his renewal of prophecy.[17] And amid the political turmoil and urgent eschatological expectations of the late ancient and early Islamic Near East, surely its largely monotheist inhabitants were highly receptive to the idea that God would raise up a new prophet to guide the faithful through these troubled times.[18] Yet Peter's strident rejections of Muhammad's alleged prophetic status served to remind the Christians of early Islamic Palestine that such prophecy had absolutely come to an end with John the Baptist and was no longer possible or even useful after God's incarnation and direct revelation in Jesus Christ. The practical purpose of such rhetoric is relatively easy to grasp.

20 Excerpts from a Lost Seventh-Century Greek Source

The Chronicle of Theophanes (c. 814)

The Chronicle of Agapius (c. 940)

The Chronicle of Michael the Syrian (1195)

The Chronicle of 1234

The following two brief excerpts most likely derive from a now lost Greek historical writing, composed in the seventh century, some of whose contents have been recently identified through the painstaking research of Maria Conterno. Selected contents of this vanished source are witnessed collectively by the four sources named in the title above: the Greek *Chronicle of Theophanes* (c. 814); the Arabic *Chronicle of Agapius* (c. 940); the Syriac *Chronicle of Michael the Syrian* (1195); and the Syriac *Chronicle of 1234*. Since the nineteenth century, scholars have recognized that Theophanes and Michael the Syrian share a common source for their accounts of the seventh and eighth centuries. In the case of Michael's chronicle, we know that he took this material from another now lost source, the Syriac *Chronicle of Dionysius of Tellmahre* (d. 845), which he tells his readers was the only substantial source available to him for the seventh and eighth centuries.[1] When the *Chronicle of Agapius* and the *Chronicle of 1234* were published at the beginning of the twentieth century, scholars quickly recognized that most of the material shared by Theophanes and Michael also occurred in these two chronicles, indicating that they too somehow depend on a now lost common source for events of the seventh and eighth centuries. Agapius, it was determined, depends almost entirely and directly on this shared source for his account of events during the years 630-754, providing a third independent witness to this missing source,[2] while the *Chronicle of 1234* depends, like Michael, on the intermediary transmission of the ninth-century *Chronicle of Dionysius of Tellmahre*.[3]

Early speculation regarding the authorship of this lost chronicle focused on two individuals: John bar Samuel, a little-known Syriac writer of the eighth century who was initially favored for this role by Edward Brooks, and Theophilus of Edessa, on whom scholarly consensus would eventually settle as the author of this vanished source.[4] Theophilus of Edessa (695-785) is a well known Maronite scholar of the eighth century who served as the court astrologer for the Abbasid caliph al-Mahdi (775-85). Theophilus is said to have written several works on astrology, and his knowledge of Greek was such that he translated the *Iliad* and perhaps the *Odyssey* into Syriac, although all of these works are now lost, except for a few surviving fragments and excerpts. Yet, most importantly for the present purposes, Theophilus also is said to have composed a chronicle, and since Agapius writes that he drew some material from "Theophilus the Astrologer," scholars at the end of the twentieth century came to identify Theophilus with confidence as the author of the missing source underlying these four chronicles.[5]

Despite the strong consensus that formed around this hypothesis, some nagging problems remained, not the least of which was how a source written in Syriac (Theophilus's *Chronicle*) could have been used by an author writing in Greek who does not appear to have known Syriac (Theophanes).[6] Theophanes must have somehow accessed the source in a Greek translation, and so the theory required an assumption that Theophilus's *Chronicle* was indeed translated into Greek shortly after its composition, probably in the 780s by some unknown monk living either in Palestine or in the region of Ḥimṣ (Emesa), who also added some additional information to his new Greek version.[7] The only problem with this stipulation is that it is inherently improbable, "since translations from Syriac into Greek are little short of inexistent in the period in question."[8] Accordingly, it would appear that a better solution to the relations among these chronicles remains to be found.

Through careful comparison of the relevant texts, Conterno has now convincingly identified a half dozen or so traditions from these later historical narratives that do not derive from a shared Syriac source written in the middle of the eighth century, but instead take their origin in an earlier Greek source underlying these common accounts. As Conterno rightly notes of the shared material,

> Looking carefully at the material shared by Theophanes, Michael the Syrian, Agapius, and the anonymous author of the *Chronicle of the year 1234*, one will soon notice that there are different degrees of resemblance. In some items, sentences are paralleled almost word for word, which definitely points to a common written source, whereas in other parts the relation is suggested only by the organization of the content. Elsewhere the correspondence is limited to the core of the information, different details are reported, and similarities are minimal, to the extent that the provenance from the same source cannot be taken for granted. Finally, in other cases still, the four chronicles are clearly describing the same events, but their accounts are too dissimilar to derive from a common version.[9]

Conterno's work draws our attention especially to the sections in which the parallels are "almost word for word." These passages all concern events from the seventh century, which they relate from a Byzantine point of view, and, perhaps most importantly, they bear clear evidence of translation from a Greek original. Therefore, she concludes that these particular traditions, including the two translated below, were originally found in a Greek historical source covering the seventh century that Theophilus may (or may not) have used and Theophanes would have known in the Greek original, without a retranslation from Syriac into Greek.[10]

It is difficult to know when to date this lost source, and so largely for this reason we have placed it at the end of this volume. Clearly, however, it belongs to the period in question, the first Islamic century—particularly if we are to imagine that Theophilus might have used it. Conterno notes that the final episode that appears to derive from this Greek source is an "account of the wreck of the entire fleet sent by Justinian II in 705/6 to bring back his wife from the land of the Khazars."[11] On this basis we might propose, then, that the Greek text was written not long after this event, in the first part of the eighth century. Nevertheless, Muriel Debié suggests that Theophanes "used more than one, all-embracing Oriental source," observing that "for the reigns of Constans II (641-68) and Constantine IV (668-85), Theophanes' account is confused, whereas for the following period, from Justinian II to Leo III (685-717), his information is clearer and much more abundant." For this reason she concludes that "Theophanes most probably had two different sources for these two periods."[12] Following her analysis, we might conclude instead that the shared material from before 685, which would include the two traditions below, is from an earlier source, different from the one that supplied the report concerning Justinian II and possibly dated to the later seventh century at the latest. In Glen Bowersock's assessment, these accounts reflect "reports that were either contemporary with the events or were circulated soon afterward and subsequently written down in Greek before being incorporated into the Syriac and Arabic traditions."[13] Conterno herself is a bit more circumspect, concluding that in her opinion, this episode "does not come from a source close to the events . . . but is based on material deriving from the Islamic tradition."[14] Nevertheless, I do not find Conterno's judgments regarding the influence of the Islamic tradition persuasive, particularly since the specific points of this alleged influence are largely found only in the later Syriac chronicles. Presumably, these Syriac adaptations, written during the twelfth and thirteenth centuries, have understandably been colored by the Islamic historical tradition. Accordingly, I think it is more likely that these accounts derive from a Greek source written in the late seventh or early eighth centuries, quite possibly on the basis of early reports, as Bowersock maintains. This would certainly be more consistent, for instance, with the direct identification of the Believer's place of worship with the Temple of Solomon.

Below I translate the two accounts first from Theophanes's Greek, particularly because that was the original language of their composition and also because Theophanes's account is more spare than some of the others. I also translate the parallel accounts from Michael the Syrian's *Chronicle* for comparision, largely because some scholars have proposed that Theophanes introduces polemic into what was originally a more neutrally or even positively toned account that is better witnessed by the Syriac and Arabic sources. Nevertheless, as readers will find in the commentary below, I am not entirely convinced that we should favor the Syriac and Arabic accounts over Theophanes's version. To the contrary, Theophanes's account seems more consistent with what Sophronius himself wrote about the invasion by Muhammad's followers and thus should not be so quickly set aside.

ʿUmar and the Conquest of Jerusalem[15]

THEOPHANES AM 6127 [634/5 CE]   In this year ʿUmar invaded Palestine, and after he beseiged the Holy City for two years, he took it by agreement, for Sophronius the bishop of Jerusalem received a guarantee of security for all of Palestine. And ʿUmar entered the Holy City clothed in filthy garments made of camel's hair, and showing diabolical deceit, he sought the Temple of the Jews, the one built by Solomon, in order to make it a place of worship for his blasphemy. Seeing this, Sophronius said, "Truly this is the abomination of desolation, as Daniel said, standing in a holy place" [Dan 11.31; cf. Matt 24.15]. And with many tears this champion of piety lamented for the Christian people. And while ʿUmar was there, the Patriarch besought him to take cloth garments from him and put them on, but he refused to put them on. Through persistence he persuaded him to wear them until his own clothes were washed, and then he returned them to Sophronius, and he put on his own clothes.

MICHAEL THE SYRIAN   At the end of the year 948, the 26th of Heraclius, and the 15th of the Nomads, King ʿUmar came to Palestine, and Sophronius the bishop of Jerusalem went forth to meet him. And he [Sophronius] received an agreement for the whole land, and he [ʿUmar] wrote a document for him that did not allow Jews to live in Jerusalem.[16] When ʿUmar entered Jerusalem, he ordered a mosque to be built on the place of the Temple of Solomon for their prayer. When Sophronius saw that ʿUmar was wearing dirty clothes, he asked him to take a garment and a cloth. And he had them brought to him and strongly urged him to put them on, but he was not willing, because he had not taken anything from anyone before. And he said, "It is not right for someone to take from another something that God has not given to him, for God has given each person what he knows. . . ."[17] Nevertheless, because the bishop urged him strongly, he answered, "Because you asked me and you have shown me great honor, lend me these belonging to you to wear until you have taken my garments and given them to be washed, and when you return mine, take yours," and thus he did.

Early Construction on the Temple Mount[18]

THEOPHANES: [AM 6135, 642/3 CE]   In this year 'Umar began to build the Temple in Jerusalem, but the structure would not stand and kept falling down. When he inquired about the cause of this, the Jews said to him, "If you do not remove the cross that is above the church on the Mount of Olives, the structure will not stand." On account of this advice the cross was removed from there, and thus was their building made stable. For this reason the enemies of Christ took down many crosses.

MICHAEL THE SYRIAN   At this time, when the Nomads were building the Temple of Solomon in Jerusalem, the structure collapsed. And the Jews said, "If you do not take down the cross placed across from the Temple on the Mount of Olives, the Temple cannot be built." And when they took down the cross, the building was stable.

Commentary

Two important features stand out in these reports. First, we find here yet another testimony indicating that Muhammad's followers set about restoring worship to the Temple Mount very quickly after they captured Jerusalem. By this point, we have seen numerous other reports to this effect; accordingly, it seems that we must recognize that both Jerusalem and its Temple Mount were sacred places of the highest order for Muhammad's earliest followers. Moreover, once again we find that they identified the return of worship to the Temple Mount with a restoration, in some genuine manner, of the Temple of Solomon, which they also revered. And as I have noted both in comments to other texts above and in other publications, the Believers' determination to restore sanctity and worship to the site of the Jewish Temple is directly linked to their imminent eschatological expectations and their resolve to reclaim the Abrahamic patrimony in advance of the final judgment and end of the world. One should also note that, as in many other reports of the Believers' early interest in the Temple Mount, the Jews play an important role in their efforts to restore worship there. Nevertheless, the tale of their advice to remove the cross from the church on the Mount of Olives is of course pure polemic, although presumably it reflects the actual removal of crosses from churches by the authorities, at least in some instances.

The second point is more complicated and has to do with the portrayed attitudes of the patriarch Sophronius and the caliph ʿUmar toward one another. According to Bowersock, for instance, the common account underlying these later chronicles is remarkable for relating the transfer of Jerusalem to Muhammad's followers "by a diplomatic agreement without any bloodshed," thanks to the skillful leadership of these two men, who were "determined to negotiate a peaceful tranfer of power" and to avoid confrontation. Sophronius chose to personally receive ʿUmar and was willing to allow the Arabs sovereignty, so long as the Jews were barred from Jerusalem. The latter stipulation, Bowersock notes, may very well be consequent to the Jewish collaboration with the Persians, who occupied Jerusalem and the Holy Land from 614 until only very recently, in 628, when Roman authority was restored. As Bowersock reads the Arabic and Syriac versions, they attest to ʿUmar's humility, modesty, and piety and the genuine concern between the two leaders to work together peacefully. In these accounts, Sophronius welcomed ʿUmar, personally leading him to the Temple Mount and generously offering him clean clothes in which he could pray there. The more "prejudicial" version of these events related by Theophanes, he maintains, has distorted the original version preserved by the Semitic sources to a polemical end, and is to be effectively disregarded in their favor, a conclusion in which he follows Conterno.[19]

Both Bowersock and Conterno maintain that the more positive portrayal of 'Umar and his shared interest in peaceful coexistence with Sophronius in these later sources is consistent with the patriarch's own words as preserved in his homilies on the Nativity and Epiphany.[20] I must say that I disagree, and I invite readers to return to these texts in the chapter 2 above and reconsider them for themselves. There Sophronius describes the Saracens as "seizing everything as booty with cruel and savage intent and godless and impious boldness" and committing "wanton acts, full of madness." In the Christmas homily, he notes that they were not able to travel to Bethlehem, only ten kilometers distant, on account of fear of "the sword of the savage and barbaric Saracens, which, filled with every diabolical cruelty, striking fear and bringing murder to light, keeps us banished from this blessed vision." These Saracens, he reports, "threaten slaughter and destruction if we should go forth from this holy city and dare to draw near to our longed for and holy Bethlehem." Likewise, according to Sophronius's writings, these Saracens were destroying churches, mocking the cross, and blaspheming against Christ. As he writes, "the God-hating and wretched Saracens—clearly the abomination of the desolation that was prophetically foretold to us [Dan 11.31]—run about through places where they are not allowed, and they plunder cities, mow down fields, burn villages with fire, set flame to the holy churches, overturn the sacred monasteries, stand in battle against the Roman armies, and they raise up trophies in combat and add victory to victory. And increasingly they mock us and increase their blasphemies against Christ and the church and speak iniquitous blasphemies against God. And these adversaries of God boast of conquering the entire world, recklessly imitating their leader the Devil with great zeal."

Sophronius's own words, then, are not consistent with Conterno and Bowersock's reading of a peaceful and amicable meeting between the two leaders in which the patriarch warmly welcomed the humble caliph as they carved out a diplomatic détente in mutual admiration. To be sure, it is not impossible that something like this transpired between the two men at the surrender of Jerusalem, but Sophronius himself describes a situation and a view toward the invaders that is certainly more consistent with what Theophanes relates. Indeed, we should not miss the fact that Sophronius, particularly in the homily on the Epiphany, quotes the passage from Daniel describing the Temple as "the abomination of desolation"; likewise, he more than once accuses Muhammad's followers of not only savage violence but also divine blasphemy and serving the Devil. Sophronius's report that the Christians of Jerusalem could not leave the city to travel to Bethlehem for Christmas in the final days of 634 is also consistent with Theophanes's indication of a two-year siege of Jerusalem before its surrender. One should note that Conterno and Bowersock both maintain that mention of "the abomination of desolation," ʿUmar's blasphemy, his unkempt appearance, and "diabolical deceit" are all additions of Theophanes. Yet each one of these elements occurs in Sophronius's own descriptions of Muhammad's followers in his homilies.

If anything, then, these facts lend a strong air of verisimilitude to Theophanes's account, which seems to reflect the patriarch's own attitudes to the invaders as conferred in his writings. Theophanes's alleged "polemical" additions actually match the words of Sophronius himself closely. The later Semitic chronicles, by comparison, or perhaps their collective source, recall this moment very differently, having adjusted the collective memory of these events to a paradigm of Christian-Muslim relations different from Sophronius's own experiences in the 630s. It is true, as Conterno notes, that Sophronius consistently explains the sufferings wrought by the Saracens against the Christians of Palestine as an instrument of divine punishment. Yet this judgment does not somehow obviate the fact that Sophronius describes Muhammad's followers in terms largely consistent with Theophanes's account of the surrender of Jerusalem. Accordingly, we should not privilege the more irenic tone given to this encounter present in the Semitic chronicles as being somehow reflective of an older or more accurate account. Instead, we find that Theophanes's less "politically correct" version of events stands in strong continuity with the attitudes of Sophronius of Jerusalem himself, as related in his own words. On this basis, I would propose, that Theophanes's *Chronicle* in fact preserves the earliest and least redacted account of this event as transmitted by these four related sources. Furthermore, I think there is warrant to conclude that his version likely reflects the episode as it was described in the Greek source from the late seventh or early eighth century that underlies these four medieval chronicles. Certainly, no aspect of the so-called "polemics" present in his account militates against this conclusion.

Notes

Introduction

1. Wilken, *Christians*, xvii–xix.
2. Eventually published as Brock, "Syriac Views."
3. Crone and Cook, *Hagarism*.
4. See, e.g., such criticisms in Wansbrough, "Review of *Hagarism*."
5. For a range of negative reactions, see e.g., Rahman, *Major Themes of the Qurʾān*, xiii– xiv; Stover, "Orientalism and the Otherness of Islam"; Abdul-Rauf, "Outsiders' Interpretations of Islam"; Rahman, "Approaches to Islam"; Serjeant, "Review of John Wansbrough"; Wansbrough, *Sectarian Milieu*, 116-17.
6. For example, Peters, *Muhammad and the Origins of Islam*; Peters, *Jesus and Muhammad*; Lings, *Muhammad*; Afsaruddin, *The First Muslims*; Safi, *Memories of Muhammad*; Armstrong, *Muhammad*.
7. One can find slightly fuller, although similarly brief accounts of this traditional narrative, with some critical reflections in, e.g., Cook, *Muhammad*, esp. 12-24, 31–41; and Donner, *Muhammad and the Believers*, 39–50.
8. For example, Hawting, *Idea of Idolatry*; Crone, "Religion of the Qurʾānic Pagans."
9. See Shoemaker, *Death of a Prophet*, 73-117, 266-77; Shoemaker, "In Search of ʿUrwa's Sīra"; Shoemaker, "Muhammad"; Shoemaker, "Les vies de Muhammad."
10. See, e.g., Humphreys, *Muʿawiya*, 3-10, 15-19; Hawting, *First Dynasty of Islam*, 2-3, 11-18; Crone, *Slaves on Horses*, 3-8; Hodgson, *Venture of Islam*, 247-51. See also on the history of the Umayyads, Borrut, "The Future of the Past."
11. Shoemaker, "Muḥammad and the Qurʾān," 73-74, 118-19, 154-55; Shoemaker, *Death of a Prophet*. See also Cook, *Muhammad*, 70; Donner, *Narratives of Islamic Origins*, 75-85, esp. 80; Wansbrough and Rippin, *Quranic Studies*, xvii.

12. Brown, *Muhammad*, 96.

13. See, e.g., Brown, *Misquoting Muhammad*, xv–xvii, 236–37, 268–72, 288–90, which is in fact much more a work of apologetics than critical history, even if it is sometimes taken for the latter by some scholars. In all fairness, based on what he writes in this volume, I think that Brown would likely agree that this is in fact a work of theology rather than history.

14. Donner, *Early Islamic Conquests*, although see also now Hoyland, *In God's Path*.

15. Donner, *Muhammad and the Believers*.

16. For example, Crone, *Slaves on Horses*; Crone, *Meccan Trade*; Crone, "The First-Century Concept of Ḥiǧra"; Crone, "What Do We Actually Know about Mohammad?"; Hawting, "The Umayyads and the Ḥijāz"; Hawting, "The Origins of the Muslim Sanctuary at Mecca"; Hawting, "The *hajj* in the Second Civil War"; Hawting, *Idea of Idolatry*.

17. Shoemaker, *Death of a Prophet*; Shoemaker, *Apocalypse of Empire*.

18. Anthony, *Muhammad*.

19. Hoyland, *Seeing Islam*.

20. Penn, *When Christians*.

21. Unlike the present volume, Wilken does not include translations of the various non-Christian witnesses.

22. I thank my colleague in history at the University of Oregon, Lisa Wolverton, for suggesting such a format, while discussing an early draft of some of this material in our Mediterranean studies reading group.

23. Shoemaker, *Death of a Prophet*, 118–30; Shoemaker, *Apocalypse of Empire*, 154–61.

24. Shoemaker, *Death of a Prophet*, 230–40; Shoemaker, *Apocalypse of Empire*, 161–68; Shoemaker, "Dome of the Rock." See also Kaplony, *The Ḥaram*, 351–63.

25. Elad, *Medieval Jerusalem*, 51; Sharon, "Praises of Jerusalem," 60. See also Elad, "Pilgrims and Pilgrimage," esp. 300–302.

26. Elad, *Medieval Jerusalem*, 55.

27. Sharon, "Praises of Jerusalem," esp. 64–65.

28. Donner, "From Believers to Muslims," 9. See also Cook, "The Beginnings of Islam."

29. Donner, "From Believers to Muslims," 10–11. Hints in certain early Islamic apocalyptic traditions of a primitive self-identity as a sort of "new Israel" also could suggest such a community: Livne-Kafri, "Some Notes on the Muslim Apocalyptic Tradition," 85–86.

30. Donner, *Muhammad and the Believers*, 87.

31. For text, translation, and analysis of the most important version, see Lecker, The "Constitution of Medina." See also Wensinck, *Muhammad and the Jews of Medina*; Watt, *Muhammad at Medina*, 221-60; Serjeant, "The *Sunnah*, *Jāmi'ah*"; and Donner, *Muhammad and the Believers*, 227-32.

32. Citing Donner's slight modification of Serjeant's translation: Donner, "From Believers to Muslims," 30-31; cf. Serjeant, "The *Sunnah, Jāmi'ah*," 27.

33. Donner, "From Believers to Muslims," 38. See also Donner, *Muhammad and the Believers*, 230-31.

34. See the discussion of other relevant passages in Donner, "From Believers to Muslims," 30-33.

35. Ibid., 19.

36. See the complete discussion in ibid., 17-24. See also Donner, *Muhammad and the Believers*, esp. 69-71, 74-77, 111-12; and Hoyland, "Sebeos," 95.

37. Donner, "From Believers to Muslims," 18; Donner, *Muhammad and the Believers*, 74.

38. See also the discussion of this hypothesis in Shoemaker, *Death of a Prophet*, 198-240.

39. Hoyland, "New Documentary Texts," 409; cf. Hoyland, *Seeing Islam*, 554-55 which more or less says exactly the same thing. Also, Hoyland, "Sebeos," but see now Hoyland, "Reflections on the Identity," which qualifies his earlier views somewhat. In addition, see Borrut and Donner, eds., *Christians and Others*.

40. Penn, *Envisioning Islam*, esp. 142-82; Tannous, *Making*, esp. 353-99.

41. Tannous, *Making*, 394-96.

42. In fairness to Tannous, Donner's use of "ecumenical" to describe the phenomenon is deeply problematic, as are his efforts to minimize the violence of the invasions and conquest. Yet these issues do not diminish the many important observations he makes regarding the evidence that the early community of the Believers was confessionally complex.

43. For instance, when Robert Hoyland asserts that "Christian Trinitarian views were diametrically opposed to the original monotheism that Muhammad sought to revive" in Hoyland, "Reflections on the Identity," 119. Most Christians, I more than suspect, would reject this characterization of their Trinitarian faith as diametrically opposed to "original monotheism."

44. Tannous, *Making*, 394-95n158, 278-301, esp. 278 and 300. Andrew Marsham also finds this element of the Qur'an, anti-Trinitarian polemic, as evidence for mounting division by the time of Mu'āwiya, yet given the apparent status of the Qur'an at this time, this conclusion is questionable: Marsham, "Architecture of Allegiance," 109.

45. As first demonstrated convincingly in Schacht, *Origins of Muhammadan Jurisprudence*, esp. 224. See also Sinai, "Consonantal Skeleton Part I," 289; Crone, "Two Legal Problems"; as well as the excellent discussion of this matter in Dye, "Le corpus coranique: Canonisation," 883–94

46. Nöldeke and Schwally, *Geschichte des Qorāns*, vol. 2, 7; translation from Nöldeke et al., *History of the Qur'ān*, 217.

47. See esp. van der Velden, "Konvergenztexte," 168–86; van der Velden, "Kotexte im Konvergenzstrang"; Pohlmann, *Entstehung des Korans*; Dye, "Qur'anic Mary"; Dye, "Mapping the Sources."

48. On this topic see also Shoemaker, "Jewish Christianity."

49. John E. Wansbrough, *Quranic Studies: Sources and Methods of Scriptural Interpretation*, London Oriental Series 31 (Oxford: Oxford University Press, 1977), 55.

50. John of Damascus, *On Heresies* 100. The text is most easily accessible in Migne, ed. *Patrologiae cursus completus, Series graeca*, 94, 764A–773A; see also LeCoz, ed., *Écrits sur l'Islam*, 210–27. The best study of John of Damascus's writings on Islam is Schadler, *John of Damascus and Islam*. For a brief, general discussion of this part of John's writings, see Louth, *St John Damascene*, 76–83.

51. Taylor, "Disputation," 200; Hoyland, *Seeing Islam*, 488–89; Dye, "Pourquoi et comment," 93–95. See also de Prémare, "'Abd al-Malik b. Marwān et le Processus," 186–89; trans. de Prémare, "'Abd al-Malik b. Marwān and the Process," 195–97.

52. See, e.g., Schadler, *John of Damascus and Islam*, 99–100.

53. Ibid., 101, 98.

54. de Prémare, "'Abd al-Malik b. Marwān and the Process," 195.

55. Ibid., 196–97. See also the excellent discussion in Schadler, *John of Damascus and Islam*, 132–40; also, the intriguing attempt to reconstruct this ancient Arabian myth in Stetkevych, *Muḥammad and the Golden Bough*.

56. See, e.g., Conrad, "Theophanes and the Arabic Historical Tradition," 43; Conrad, "Conquest of Arwad," 322–48; Hoyland, *Seeing Islam*, 400–405; Palmer, *Seventh Century*, 96–98; Conrad, "Varietas Syriaca," 91–94.

57. Schadler, *John of Damascus and Islam*, 126. See also Hoyland, *Seeing Islam*, 496. For a more thorough discussion of these texts, their relation, and their dating, see my more extended discussion of them in Shoemaker, *Death of a Prophet*, 59–64, which focuses more on the letter of 'Umar and its apparent implication that Muhammad was still alive at the time when his followers began to invade the Roman Near East.

58. Ezeants', ed., Պատմութիւն Ղեւոնդեայ, 45–98; Jeffery, "Ghevond's Text," 281–330; Arzoumanian, *History of Lewond*, 72–105.

59. Schadler, *John of Damascus and Islam*, 126–28.

60. Ezeants', ed., Պատմութիւն Ղեւոնդեայ, 63. The translation is my own, but cf. Jeffery, "Ghevond's Text," 297–98; Arzoumanian, *History of Lewond*, 82.

61. Schadler, *John of Damascus and Islam*, 113.

62. See Shoemaker, *Death of a Prophet*, esp. 136–58; but also see on this subject esp. de Prémare, *Aux origines du Coran*; Dye, "Le corpus coranique: Questions"; Dye, "Le corpus coranique: Canonisation"; Amir-Moezzi, *Silent Qur'an*; Powers, *Muḥammad Is Not the Father*. Look also for more detailed discussion of this matter in my forthcoming monograph *Creating the Qur'an: A Historical Critical Study*.

63. Sinai, "Consonantal Skeleton Part I," 285. The reference given to Motzki "Compilation" (presumably Motzki, "Collection of the Qur'ān,") certainly does not provide sufficient warrant for such dismissal.

64. Hoyland, *Seeing Islam*.

65. See esp. Shoemaker, *Apocalypse of Empire*.

66. See esp. Shoemaker, *Death of a Prophet*, 158–78. See also the important studies by Amir-Moezzi, "Muḥammad the Paraclete"; and Lindstedt, "Last Roman Emperor."

67. See the important study of this topic by Sahner, *Christian Martyrs*.

68. On this topic, see my study Shoemaker, *Death of a Prophet*.

69. Donner, "Review of *In God's Path*," 138.

70. Webb, *Imagining the Arabs*, passim, esp. 8, 48, 111, 139–41, 150. *Nomad* is partly imperfect because, at least according to the traditional accounts, many in the early Islamic polity were said to be oasis dwellers and even merchants rather than nomads.

71. Crone, "Hiğra"; Lindstedt, "*Muhājirūn*"; Webb, *Imagining the Arabs*, esp. 141.

72. See Segovia, "Sourate 3," 141, 154; and Dye and Decharneux, "Sourate 10," 458–59. I thank Guillaume Dye for pointing this out.

73. Chabot, ed., *Incerti auctoris Chronicon*, 195. See also Lindstedt, "Who Is In?," esp. 168; Hoyland, *Seeing Islam*, 414n88. There is, one should note, a tombstone that refers to the "people of Islam" that was dated to the year 71 CE. More recent analysis, however, has favored a date of 171 or even 271 CE instead: see Lindstedt, "Who Is In?," 210–11; and Hoyland, "Content and Context," 87n65.

74. Donner, "From Believers to Muslims," 12, 14–16; Donner, *Muhammad and the Believers*, 57–58, 71–72, 203–4. See also Hoyland, "New Documentary

Texts," 409–10, where something similar is proposed and also Marsham, "Architecture of Allegiance," esp. 107–9.

75. See, e.g., Theissen, *Sociology of Early Palestinian Christianity*, a work which in the German original is more descriptively titled *Soziologie der Jesusbewegung*; also more recently Patterson, *The Lost Way*.

76. Wansbrough, *Quranic Studies*, 55. See also Donner, "From Believers to Muslims," 13–16; Donner, *Muhammad and the Believers*, 69–70, 75–77, 87, 134, 204, 206; Shoemaker, *Death of a Prophet*, 206–11. It is true that the Qur'an refers to Muhammad in one instance as "the seal of the prophets," but originally it seems that this was not understood to identify him as a final prophet but rather was an indication of his confirmation of what the prophets before him had taught. See Friedmann, "Finality of Prophethood"; Powers, *Muḥammad is Not the Father*, esp. 50–57; and Powers, *Zayd*, 109–23.

77. Donner, "From Believers to Muslims," 13–16; Donner, *Muhammad and the Believers*, 69–70, 75–77, 87, 134, 204, 206.

78. For readers wanting more discussion of this often slippery term, for the present historical context, one can consult Shoemaker, *Apocalypse of Empire*, esp. 11–16.

Chapter 1. *The Teaching of Jacob*

1. The most recent edition has been published by Dagron and Déroche, "Juifs et chrétiens," 47–219. The edition has recently been republished with the rest of this article, with the same pagination, in Dagron and Déroche, *Juifs et chrétiens en Orient byzantin*, 47–219. A complete English translation has recently been made available online by Andrew S. Jacobs: http://andrewjacobs.org /translations/doctrina.html.

2. Hoyland, *Seeing Islam*, 59. Here Hoyland argues persuasively against Dagron's suggestion that the text was composed sometime in the early 640s, which seems unlikely: Dagron and Déroche, "Juifs et chrétiens," 246–47. See also, for example, Howard-Johnston, *Witnesses*, 155–56; Kaegi, *Heraclius, Emperor of Byzantium*, 37; McCormick, *Origins of the European Economy*, 179; Olster, *Roman Defeat*, 21; Thümmel, *Frühgeschichte*, 232; Jacobs, "Gender, Conversion." Recently, Sean Anthony has questioned this consensus, but the alternatives that he proposes are not persuasive, while the arguments for the consensus dating fit the text convincingly: see Anthony, "Muhammad," and Anthony, *Muhammad*, 55–58.

3. Olster, *Roman Defeat*, 175.

4. Ibid., 158–75, esp. 159–61.

5. Ibid., 159–64; cf. also Hoyland, *Seeing Islam*, 56; Dagron and Déroche, "Juifs et chrétiens," 240–46. The specific attention given to the cities of Ptolemais and Sykamine in Palestine leads Hoyland and Dagron and Déroche to conclude that the author is likely a native of their environs.

6. Text is from Dagron and Déroche, "Juifs et chrétiens," 209–11.

7. The name Sergius appears only in the Church Slavonic version of the *Teaching of Jacob*, but comparison with other sources suggests that this probably was the name of the Roman official to which the text refers at this point. See the discussion below. On the different versions of the *Teaching of Jacob*, which also survives in Arabic and Ethiopic in addition to Greek and Church Slavonic, see ibid., 47–68.

8. The Greek word used here is Ἑρμόλαος, which is a Greek form of the name Armilus. Armilus is the name given to the Antichrist in Jewish apocalyptic literature of this period. In Christian apocalyptic, Armilus (from Romulus) is instead the name of the emperor who receives the promise of Rome's eternal rule. This is one of the many details that demonstrates the author's considerable knowledge of contemporary Judaism: a Christian would not name the Antichrist Armilus. See Olster, *Roman Defeat*, 173–74. For a contemporary example of such Jewish usage, see the seventh-century *Sefer Zerubbabel*: Lévi, "L'Apocalypse de Zorobabel," at 68 (1914), 136; Himmelfarb, trans., "Sefer Zerubbabel," 75.

9. Found in the so-called *Syriac Common Source*, which until recently has been identified with the lost *Chronicle* of Theophilus of Edessa, and Thomas the Presbyter's *Chronicle*, both of which are discussed later in this volume. Recent research on this *Syriac Common Source*, however, has challenged its assignment to Theophilus, arguing that the textual relations among several medieval chronicles that this hypothetical source alleged to explain are in fact more complicated than previously thought and thus demand a more complicated model in order to understand these relation. See the discussion of this problem and the sources in question in the introduction to the final text included in this volume. See also Donner, *Early Islamic Conquests*, 115–16; Gil, *History of Palestine*, 38–39; Kaegi, *Byzantium and the Early Islamic Conquests*, 88–89; Dagron, "Judaïser," 246n105; Hoyland, *Seeing Islam*, 60 (esp. n. 19), 120; Palmer, *Seventh Century*, 19n119.

10. On this point, see Shoemaker, *Death of a Prophet*.

11. For example, see ibid., 118–96; Shoemaker, *Apocalypse of Empire*, 116–84; Shoemaker, "Muḥammad and the Qurʾān"; Shoemaker, "The Reign of God."

12. See, e.g., Shoemaker, *Apocalypse of Empire*, 90-115; Shoemaker, *Death of a Prophet*, 22, 24, 32, 134, 205. See also Donner, "La question du messianisme"; and Bashear, "The Title 'Fārūq.'"

13. *Secrets of Rabbi Shimʿōn b. Yoḥai* (Jellinek, ed., *Bet ha-midrash*, vol. 3, 78). See also Bashear, "Riding Beasts," and Crone and Cook, *Hagarism*, 3-6.

14. See Shoemaker, "The Reign of God"; Shoemaker, *Apocalypse of Empire*.

15. al-Khaṭīb, ed., *Muʿjam al-qirāʾāt*, vol. 8, 392-93.

16. Anthony, "Muhammad," 248n13; Amir-Moezzi, "Muḥammad the Paraclete," 46-48.

17. Ibid., 31.

18. Cook, *Studies in Muslim Apocalyptic*, 79, 170-73, 178, 202, 212-13, 323-24.

19. *Doctrina Iacobi* V.16 (Dagron and Déroche, "Juifs et chrétiens," 209-11).

20. Anthony, "Muhammad"; Crone and Cook, *Hagarism*, 4.

21. Anthony, "Muhammad," 255-62, although Anthony's proposal for a later dating of the *Teaching of Jacob* is not very convincing, in my opinion.

Chapter 2. *Synodical Letter*, Sophronius of Jeruselm

1. The main literary source for these events is a text known as *The Capture of Jerusalem by the Persians in 614*, attributed to an otherwise unknown "Antiochus Strategius." The text was written in Greek but only survives in Old Georgian and Arabic versions, and my colleague Sean Anthony and I have recently completed the first comparative, critical translation of the two versions, which should soon appear. This text provides some of the most important background information for understanding the rise of Islam in the late ancient Near East.

2. See Di Berardino, ed., *Patrology: The Eastern Fathers*, 298-99.

3. See Booth, *Crisis of Empire*, 228-34.

4. Sophronius, *Synodical Letter* 2.1.5 (Allen, *Sophronius of Jerusalem*, 70); trans. from Booth, *Crisis of Empire*, 234.

5. See Booth, *Crisis of Empire*, 242-44.

6. Gil, *History of Palestine*, 455-56; Booth, *Crisis of Empire*, 295-97.

7. Text from Allen, *Sophronius of Jerusalem*, 152-55.

8. Text from Usener, "Weihnachtspredigt," 506-9, 514-15.

9. Presumably the Nea church that was built under Justinian.

10. Text from Papadopoulos-Kerameus, Ἀνάλεκτα Ἱεροσολυμιτικῆς 5, 166-67.

11. Busse, "ʿOmar b. al-Ḫaṭṭāb," esp. 111-16; Busse, "ʿOmar's Image as the Conqueror," esp. 160-64

12. Donner, *Muhammad and the Believers*, 123.

13. Olster, *Roman Defeat*, 103.

14. Hoyland, *Seeing Islam*, 73.

15. Booth, *Crisis of Empire*, 249.

Chapter 3. *The Believers' Invasion of Syria*

1. The Syriac text is published in Brooks, ed., *Chronica minora II*, vol. 1, 75, but one must also see now the translation in Palmer, *Seventh Century*, 2–3, which draws on an improved reading of the manuscript by Sebastian Brock that has not been published, although the translation is sufficiently technical and annotated that it can easily be compared with Brooks's edition.

2. Palmer, *Seventh Century*, 1; Hoyland, *Seeing Islam*, 117.

3. Text from Brooks, ed., *Chronica minora II*, vol. 1, 76, consulting also Palmer, *Seventh Century*, 2–3.

4. The second part of this name is illegible, and the consonants in the brackets are themselves not entirely certain.

5. *Sakellarios* was an administrative position in the late Roman Empire, and there was, in fact, a *sakellarios* named Theodore Trithyrios in command of the Roman forces at the battle of Gabitha-Yarmuk. Note that the *Khuzistan Chronicle*, which appears later in this volume, also indicates the involvement of this *sakellarios*, although this source mistakes his position for his name. See Kaegi, *Heraclius, emperor of Byzantium*, 237, 240, 242.

6. Wright, *Catalogue of Syriac Manuscripts*, vol. 1, 65 (no. 94), which gives the text and translation. This was also the opinion of Nöldeke, "Zur Geschichte der Araber," who also edited and translated the piece. On the identification of the battle of Gabitha, referred to in this text, with the battle of Yarmuk, see Kaegi, *Byzantium and the Early Islamic Conquests*, 112–13.

Chapter 4. *Letter 14*, Maximus the Confessor

1. Regarding the controversies of Maximus' biography and why this is the most likely narrative, see, e.g., Booth, *Crisis of Empire*, 143–54; and Shoemaker, "Georgian *Life of the Virgin*," 6–13.

2. Sherwood, *Annotated Date-List*, 40–41; Ponsoye and Larchet, eds., *Saint Maxime le Confesseur: Lettres*, 52.

3. Text from PG 91, 537C–540B.

4. See, e.g., Cameron, "Blaming the Jews."

Chapter 5. *Chronicle,* Thomas the Presbyter

1. BL Add. 14643

2. Palmer, *Seventh Century* 5-12; see also the discussion in Palmer, "Une chronique syriaque," 31-46, and esp. 34-37 on the author.

3. Palmer, *Seventh Century,* 5-12; Palmer, "Une chronique syriaque," 39-41; Hoyland, *Seeing Islam,* 118-20.

4. Text from Brooks, ed., *Chronica minora II,* vol. 1, 147-48.

5. Hoyland, *Seeing Islam,* 120.

6. These events were first identified by de Goeje, *Mémoire sur la conquête,* 30-34; see also, e.g., Donner, *Early Islamic Conquests,* 115-16; Gil, *History of Palestine,* 38-39; Kaegi, *Byzantium and the Early Islamic Conquests,* 88-89; Dagron and Déroche, "Juifs et Chrétiens," 246n105; Hoyland, *Seeing Islam,* 60 (esp. n. 19); 120; Palmer, *Seventh Century,* 19n119. The latter two in particular provide the most thorough and up-to-date discussions of the problems with the designation "son of YRDN" or "BRYDN."

Chapter 6. *The Armenian Chronicle of 661*

1. On this attribution, its history, and its inaccuracy see Thomson and Howard-Johnston, *Armenian History,* 1:xxxiii-xxxviii; also Howard-Johnston, *Witnesses,* 71-74. See also Greenwood, "Sasanian Echoes," esp. 325-26.

2. See, e.g., Hoyland, *Seeing Islam,* 124-25; Thomson and Howard-Johnston, *Armenian History,* xxxvn20; Greenwood, "Sasanian Echoes," 326. For reasons identified by Thomson, "Pseudo-Sebeos" is not a possible alternative.

3. See the discussions in Howard-Johnston, *Witnesses,* 80-86; Hoyland, *Seeing Islam,* 125; Thomson and Howard-Johnston, *Armenian History,* xxxviii-xxxix; Greenwood, "Sasanian Echoes," 389.

4. Thomson and Howard-Johnston, *Armenian History,* 1: lxxvii.

5. Ibid., 1:lxv-lxxiv; Greenwood, "Sasanian Echoes," 326-74. On the reliability of Sebeos in general, see also Howard-Johnston, *Witnesses,* 94-99; and Hoyland, *Seeing Islam,* 125-28.

6. Hoyland, *Seeing Islam,* 128.

7. Text from Abgarian, ed., Պատմութիւն Սեբէոսի, 134-40. In the translation by Robert Thomson these passages are found in chapters 42 and 43: Thomson and Howard-Johnston, *Armenian History,* 1:94-103. Extensive commentary on these two passages can be found in volume 2 of the same publication.

8. That is, the land of the Tachiks. *Taçik* is the Armenian equivalent of *Tayyāyē*, deriving similarly from the name of the tribe Ṭai. According to Heinrich Hübschmann, the Armenian term is derived from Persian: Hübschmann, *Armenische Grammatik*, 86-87. Nevertheless, since the Persian term derives ultimately from the Syriac, one wonders if perhaps the Armenian term was drawn directly from Syriac. See Webb, *Imagining the Arabs*, 48.

9. The word translated here as "testament" relates to the idea of inheritance and can also mean, in effect, "will and testament."

10. As Robert Thomson notes, these final remarks seem to come from Sebeos's written source, indicating the original source of the information that was taken from this earlier account.

11. Brooks, Guidi, and Chabot, eds., *Chronica minora III*, 326 (Syr), left column. See also Anthony, *Muhammad*, 59-73.

12. See, e.g., Tannous, *Making*, 278-87, 464-71.

13. Thomson and Howard-Johnston, *Armenian History*, 2:240-42.

14. Shoemaker, *Death of a Prophet*, 223-28.

15. On this point see also Bori, "All We Know."

16. Hoyland, "Sebeos," 97, citing Hoyland's translation. Cf. sura 5.21.

17. Trans. from Donner, *Muhammad and the Believers*, 81.

18. "Remembrance" here translated from *dhikr*, a word that interpreters often identify with the Torah.

19. Rubin, *Between Bible and Qur ʾān*, 11-35, esp. 35.

20. We have omitted these accounts because they do not relate much information about the beliefs and practices of the Believers, and readers interested in these details can readily consult the complete English translation of Sebeos by Robert Thomson. See Thomson and Howard-Johnston, *Armenian History*, 1:97-102.

21. Tannous, *Making*, 477-90, esp.484.

22. For more on this earlier source, see Thomson and Howard-Johnston, *Armenian History*, 1:lxviii-lxx; 102n634; and 2:238-40; Howard-Johnston, *Witnesses*, 85-86.

23. For more on this rock and its relation to the Temple and the Dome, see Shoemaker, *Death of a Prophet*, 231-37, where the evidence for this rock's traditional identity is thoroughly examined.

24. Thomson and Howard-Johnston, *Armenian History*, 1:102n637.

25. See, e.g., Shoemaker, *Death of a Prophet*, 235-36.

1. PG 87.3, 2851–3112.

2. Photius, *Bibliotheca* 199 (Henry, ed., *Photius: Bibliothèque*, 3:96–7).

3. Moschus, *Spiritual Meadow*, x.

4. Booth, *Crisis of Empire*, 91–92.

5. See Garitte, "Histoires édifiantes"; Abulaże, ed., ოთაჲ მოჲსი, 85–118.

6. Garitte, "La version géorgienne du Pré Spirituel," 174–78, 184–85. See also Canart, "Trois groupes," 6; Flusin, "L'esplanade du Temple," 18.

7. Today the city of Morphou in Turkish-occupied Cyprus. See Garitte, "Pré Spirituel," 180.

8. Garitte, "Histoires édifiantes," 397–98

9. Abulaże, ed., ოთაჲ მოჲსი, 93.

10. Garitte, "Histoires édifiantes," 399–400; Garitte, ed., *La prise de Jérusalem*, 1:67–70. Sean Anthony and I have prepared a critical comparative translation of this text that will soon be published.

11. See Garitte, "Histoires édifiantes," 401–6. Although Garitte thought that number twenty-nine in the collection was a story from the tenth-century writer Paul of Monemvasia, Bernard Flusin clarifies that this is not in fact the case, and the story is also likely a part of this same early collection: Flusin, "L'esplanade du Temple," 19n13.

12. Abulaże, ed., ოთაჲ მოჲსი, 118.

13. Flusin, "L'esplanade du Temple," 18–19.

14. Booth, "Gregory," 126–28.

15. Text from Abulaże, ed., ოთაჲ მოჲსი, 100–102. Abulaze's edition of this anecdote is reproduced with French translation and commentary in Flusin, "L'esplanade du Temple," 19–21.

16. This information is supplied from the previous tale, which is assigned to the same individual: Abulaże, ed., ოთაჲ მოჲსი, 99. Some scholars have concluded that this church was probably "part of the complex that included the church of St John the Baptist": see Pringle, *Churches*, 3:384; Vincent and Abel, *Jérusalem nouvelle*, 614. The church of St. John the Baptist is just to the south of the Anastasis. Nevertheless, the indication that this church is outside the city would seem to contradict this identification, and so presumably Robert Schick is correct that this church should be identified as a different structure, most likely on the Mount of Olives: Schick, *Christian Communities of Palestine*, 358; see also Milik, "Notes d'épigraphie," 360–61; Milik, *La topographie*, 185.

17. Presumably the holy mountain is the Mount of Olives, but I cannot identify a monastery by this name. If the location is correct, perhaps this monastery is the one where, the following is alleged to have taken place, according to Strategius, *The Capture of Jerusalem*, in the wake of the Persian conquest: "There was in Jerusalem monastery on the Mount of Olives in which there were four-hundred holy virgins. And the enemies entered the monastery and brought forth the brides of Christ like doves from their nest, these blessed women who were living worthily and pure in virginity. And when they brought them forth from the monastery, they began to butcher them like cattle, and they divided them among themselves and took them away to their own places. Then a grievous thing took place, for they defiled the virgins of Christ by force and forcibly corrupted their virginity." Strategius, *Capture of Jerusalem* XII.2–4 (Garitte, ed., *La prise de Jérusalem*, 1:30).

18. See also Hoyland, *Seeing Islam*, 64–65.

19. See Donner, "From Believers to Muslims"; Donner, *Muhammad and the Believers*, 39–89.

Chapter 8. *The End-Times*, Ps.-Ephrem the Syrian

1. For more detailed discussions of this topic, see Shoemaker, "The Reign of God"; and Shoemaker, *Apocalypse of Empire*. On the Qur'an's use of a particular Syriac apocalyptic text, the *Syriac Alexander Legend*, see esp. van Bladel, "Alexander Legend"; and Tesei, "Prophecy."

2. Palmer, *Seventh Century*, 222–42; Penn, *When Christians*, 108–29; Garstad, *Apocalypse of Pseudo-Methodius*.

3. For further details and a thorough discussion of the relevant scholarship, readers can consult Shoemaker, "The *Tiburtine Sibyl*, the Last Emperor, and the Early Byzantine Apocalyptic Tradition"; Shoemaker, "The *Tiburtine Sibyl*: A New Translation"; Shoemaker, *Apocalypse of Empire*, 42–63.

4. Sackur, *Sibyllinische Texte*, 157–63.

5. Alexander, *Oracle of Baalbek*, 53–55, 63–64. There are, one should note, in the current state of the text lengthy interpolations of medieval king lists, but these are obvious and clearly recognizable medieval interpolations that are easily distinguished from the ancient form of the legend.

6. See, e.g., Bardill, *Constantine*, 338–95; Digeser, "Persecution and the Art of Writing"; Papoutsakis, *Vicarious Kingship*, esp. 192–93.

7. Again, for further details and thorough discussion of the relevant scholarship, readers can consult Shoemaker, "The *Tiburtine Sibyl* (2015)"; Shoemaker,

Apocalypse of Empire, 42–63. Note that since the publication of these works Christopher Bonura has completed a dissertation on imperial eschatology in the Middle Ages that addresses these texts: Bonura, "Roman Empire of the Apocalypse." In it Bonura makes some interesting and important points, but in the main, I find unpersuasive his effort to silo imperial apocalypticism within the Syriac language tradition until *Ps.-Methodius*. To the point in question here, the dissertation brings no new arguments concerning the relationship between the Last Emperor tradition of the *Tiburtine Sibyl* and that of *Ps.-Methodius* beyond what was previously argued in Bonura, "When Did the Legend." Accordingly, I stand by my previous arguments in response to this article in Shoemaker, *Apocalypse of Empire*, 51–52, 191–99 as demonstrating the priority of the *Tiburtine Sibyl*'s Last Emperor tradition.

8. Reinink, ed., *Die Syrische Apokalypse*, 44–45 (Syr). My translation, although see also Reinink's German translation, 73–74; Reinink, "Ps.-Methodius: A Concept of History," 161–62; and Palmer, *Seventh Century*, 240.

9. Alexander, *Byzantine Apocalyptic Tradition*, 168.

10. In Palmer, *Seventh Century*, 233.

11. Text from Beck, ed., *Sermones III*, 1:60–71, and Suermann, *Die geschichtstheologische Reaktion*, 15–21, which reproduces Beck's text.

12. Beck (Beck, ed., *Sermones III*, 2:81), and Suermann after him, interprets this reference to "their ancestral land" as a reference to the Assyrians' ancestral lands ("das Land der Väter [der Assyrer]"), presumably Iraq, which the Romans invaded in their final defeat of the Persian army. Nevertheless, I think it is much more likely that the Christian Romans are hurrying back to take possession of the land of the patriarchs and of their inheritance, the Holy Land. By the beginning of the seventh century, the Roman Empire had identified itself as the New Israel and accordingly saw itself as the rightful heir to the land of divine promise. Moreover, this region was the most contested area of the Persian occupation, and likewise, it is an important focus of the events that follow immediately in the invasion of the Abrahamic offspring of Hagar. Penn understands the passage in similar fashion: "The Romans too will hasten to their fathers' country." Penn, *When Christians*, 41.

13. Lamy, ed., *Sancti Ephraem*, 3:187–212. Regarding the attribution to Ephrem, see p. 197.

14. Nöldeke, "Review of Lamy," 246.

15. Sackur, *Sibyllinische Texte*, 34.

16. Published posthumously in Czeglédy, "Literary Remains of M. Kmosko," 34–35.

17. Caspari, *Briefe*, 429–72, esp. 438–43

18. Suermann, *Die geschichtstheologische Reaktion*, 111–12, 127.

19. Reinink, "Pseudo-Ephraems 'Rede über das Ende,›» esp. 455–62.

20. Hoyland, *Seeing Islam*, 263.

21. Beck, ed., *Sermones III*, 2:ix.

22. Thomas and Roggema, eds., *Christian Muslim Relations*, 160–61.

23. Penn, *When Christians*, 39.

24. Beck, ed., *Sermones III*, 2:84.

25. See, e.g., the specific examples of exactly such payment of tribute by the defeated parties to the Believers in Hoyland, *In God's Path*, 44, 47, 54–55, 74, 79, 83, 90, 96–97, etc.

26. For more on this topic, see esp. Shoemaker, *Apocalypse of Empire*.

27. See also the *Apocalypse of Ps.-Shenoute* included later in this volume, as well as the many other apocalypses inventoried in Hoyland, *Seeing Islam*, 257–335.

28. Ps.-Ephrem, *Homily on the End* 8 (Suermann, *Die geschichtstheologische Reaktion*, 25).

Chapter 9. *Letter 14C*, Isho'yahb III of Adiabene

1. For more on Isho'yahb, see Hoyland, *Seeing Islam*, 174–79.

2. For more on these events, see Healey, "Christians of Qatar"; Healey, "Patriarch Isho'yahb."

3. Text from Duval, *Išo 'yahb Patriarchae III Liber epistularum*, 250–51.

4. See also ibid., 248: "How were the great people of Mrwny', when they saw neither sword nor fire nor torments, seized with desire for only half of their belongings like madmen?"

5. According to Amir Harrack, "This [Radan] is the name of a branch of the Tigris. . . .The river name was given to region east of the Tigris, to the north of Seleucia-Ctesiphon." See Harrak, *Acts of Mār Māri*, 41n99. See also Morony, *Iraq after the Muslim Conquest*, 138–39, 280–82, 386, which notes its importance as a center of Zoroastrianism and "pagan" worship in the late Sasanian period.

6. Firestone, *Jihad*, 51. See also Firestone, "Disparity and Resolution."

7. Assemani, *Bibliotheca*, 3:130.

8. Nau, "Maronites."

9. Ibn Hishām, *Kitāb sīrat Rasūl Allāh*, 1:1021; Guillaume, trans., *Life of Muhammad*, 689.

10. Regarding the problems with these early biographies and their historical reliability, see Shoemaker, "In Search of 'Urwa's Sīra"; and Shoemaker, *Death of a Prophet*, 73–106.

11. From Ibn Isḥāq (d. 767) as quoted by Ibn Hishām above, and from Maʿmar b, Rāshid (d. 770) in ʿAbd al-Razzaq, *al-Muṣannaf*, 10:359–60; and Ibn Saʿd, *Ṭabaqāt*, 2.2:44. For more on this subject, see Munt, "No Two Religions," which casts doubt on whether this actually occurred. Nevertheless, Munt's article specifically concerns the Hijaz, and in this specific context the point seems a fairly moot one, since there is no evidence at all for any Christians in the Hijaz at this point, except for its very northernmost edges, close to the Roman Empire, and to its south in Yemen. Indeed, as Munt himself notes, "Considerable effort in modern scholarship has been devoted to trying to establish the existence of Christians in the Hijaz around Mecca and Medina, but it has to be said that the evidence usually offered for their presence in that area remains poor" (252–53). Calling the evidence "poor" is overly generous. It is in fact nonexistent. The question of what happened to Christians in other areas of the Arabian Peninsula, such as Oman or Qatar, remains another question.

12. Webb, *Imagining the Arabs*, passim, esp. 8, 139–41.

13. The most thorough and convincing discussion of this matter at present is Dye, "Le corpus coranique: Contexte," 762–76. See also Wood, "Christianity in the Arabian Peninsula."

14. Duval, *Išoʿyahb Patriarchae III Liber epistularum*, 97.

15. Crone, "First-Century Concept of Hiǧra"; Lindstedt, "*Muhājirūn*"; Webb, *Imagining the Arabs*, esp. 141.

Chapter 10. *Edifying Tales*, Anastasius of Sinai

1. See, for instance, Haldon, "Works of Anastasius," which is an excellent guide. See also Di Berardino, ed., *Patrology: The Eastern Fathers*, 313–31; and Hoyland, *Seeing Islam*, 92–103.

2. The brief account of Anastasius's biography is based on Hoyland, *Seeing Islam*, 92–103; and Thomas and Roggema, eds., *Christian Muslim Relations*, 193–94.

3. Uthemann, ed., *Viae dux*.

4. Richard and Munitiz, eds., *Quaestiones et responsiones*.

5. Thomas and Roggema, eds., *Christian Muslim Relations*, 201.

6. Regarding these works, see Geerard, *Clavis Patrum Graecorum*, 3:455–62; and in much greater detail Uthemann, *Anastasios Sinaites*.

7. Collection A and some of the tales from Collection BC were edited in Nau, "Le texte grec des récits du moine"; Nau, "Le texte grec des récits utiles"; French

translation in Nau, "Les récits inédits du moine Anastase." These "translations," however, are in some cases more summaries than actual translations.

8. See Flusin, "Démons et Sarrasins," 390–96; Hoyland, *Seeing Islam*, 99; Caner, *History and Hagiography*, 173.

9. Uthemann, *Anastasios Sinaites*, 1:374–463, esp. 456–63. Anastasius's authorship of this collection had previously been challenged by Canart, "Nouveaux récits."

10. Flusin, "Démons et Sarrasins," 390–96; Uthemann, *Anastasios Sinaites*.

11. Binggeli in Thomas and Roggema, eds., *Christian Muslim Relations*, 198–99, which also provides this dating for the stories in the collection. This edition will be based on Binggeli, "Anastase le Sinaïte."

12. Note that an earlier version of these translations and commentaries on anecdotes from the *Edifying Tales* appeared as Shoemaker, "Anastasius."

13. Text from Binggeli, "Anastase le Sinaïte," 219–20, and for the last paragraph, from Nau, "Le texte grec des récits utiles," 64–65.

14. Beginning here the text is also in Nau, "Le texte grec des récits utiles," 64–65.

15. Text from Binggeli, "Anastase le Sinaïte," 225. An almost identical version can be found in Flusin, "L'esplanade du Temple," 25–26.

16. That is, the destruction of the Temple in 70 CE during the Roman destruction of Jerusalem during the Jewish Revolt of 66–73 CE.

17. Text from Binggeli, "Anastase le Sinaïte," 226–28. A similar, slightly shorter version, has been published in Nau, "Le texte grec des récits du moine," 87–89.

18. Specified as the fortress "Pharan" in Nau's version of the text. Regarding this fortress that was nearby the monastery of Sinai, see Caner, *History and Hagiography*, 2, 6–7, 15, etc. Nevertheless, according to Caner, this passage should be understood as a reference to "the fortified Mount Sinai monastery and the church within it": 197n129.

19. Concerning these martyrs of Sinai from the early Christian period, see ibid., 141–71, which includes an English translation and discussions of the various versions of their martyrdom.

20. Text from Binggeli, "Anastase le Sinaïte," 231.

21. Text from ibid., 233–34.

22. Story II.3 in the collection. According to this anecdote, the demon who was tormenting Sartabias informed him that he would be leaving him temporarily to accompany the Arabs on their way to Constantinople, because the demons were allied with the Arabs.

23. Klysma was an important Roman port at the north end of the Red Sea, which is today the city of Suez at the southern end of the Suez canal.

24. Byzantine title for a certain class of military scouts with special knowledge of the local terrain: see Haldon, *Warfare, State, and Society*, 155.

25. The location of In is not at all clear, although one imagines that it, like Klysma, may have been in Egypt somewhere in or near the Sinai Peninsula.

26. Text from Binggeli, "Anastase le Sinaïte," 252.

27. This was seemingly first proposed by Goitein in Goitein and Grabar, "al-Ḳuds," 325, although this position has been most clearly argued in Grabar, "Meaning of the Dome," 148–51 (originally published in *Medieval Studies at Minnesota* 3 (1988), pp. 1–10). Recently, Beatrice St. Laurent has developed Grabar's argument further in a paper "The Dome of the Rock: Muʾāwiya's Vision to Unify the Three Religions of the Book," which was presented at the conference on Marking the Sacred: The Temple Mount/Haram al-Sharif in Jerusalem at Providence College, 5–7 June 2017. This should soon be published in the conference volume, Joan Branham and Beatrice St. Laurent, eds., *Marking the Sacred: The Temple Mount / Haram al-Sharif in Jerusalem* (University Park: Pennsylvania State University Press, 2020). See also Flusin, "L'esplanade du Temple," 31; St. Laurent and Awwad, "Archaeology and Preservation," 451.

28. Grabar, "Meaning of the Dome," 149.

29. Ibid., 149–51.

30. For more on this point, see Shoemaker, *Death of a Prophet*, 214–15, as well as the many studies on this topic signaled in the notes. See also Donner, *Muhammad and the Believers*, 14–15.

31. Hoyland, *Seeing Islam*, 100–101.

32. Flusin, "L'esplanade du Temple," 30–31.

33. Ibid., 31

34. Tannous badly misreads this passage, attributing the reference to a belief that the Dome of the Rock was a church. Nevertheless, the persistent associations between the Dome of the Rock and the Temple in Christian, Jewish, and early Islamic writings make clear that this "Temple of God," refers to the reconstruction of the Temple and not a church. This identification is made explicit as Anastasius continues, "For how could the Temple of God be built in that place? A prohibition has been laid down for the Jews: 'Behold, this house is left desolate' [cf. Matt 23.38]. 'It is left,' said Christ: that is to say, it will remain desolate forever. For this was 'the final splendor of this house' [Hag 2.9] that was incinerated by Titus." Cf. Tannous, *Making*, 383–84.

35. See Hoyland, *Seeing Islam*, 354.

36. See ibid., 352–53, where a number of sources reporting this policy are mentioned in relation to this anecdote.

37. See, e.g., Shoemaker, *Death of a Prophet*, ch. 4. In contrast to Anthony, "Meccan Sanctuary?," 35–36, which identifies this shrine confidently as the Ka'ba.

38. Even Bell was forced to acknowledge this problem in his rather ironically titled *The Origin of Islam in Its Christian Environment*: "There is no good evidence of any seats of Christianity in the Hijaz or in the near neighbourhood of Mecca or even of Medina." Bell, *Origin of Islam*, 42–43. Likewise, Peters, *Muhammad and the Origins of Islam*, 1: "There were Christians at Gaza, and Christians and Jews in the Yemen, but none of either so far as we know at Mecca." See also Hawting, *Idea of Idolatry*, 14–16; Dye, "Le corpus coranique: Contexte," 762–76; and Wood, "Christianity in the Arabian Peninsula."

39. Binggeli, "Anastase le Sinaïte," 546.

40. Crone, *Meccan Trade*.

41. Crone, "How Did the Quranic Pagans Make a Living?," 395–97. In the case that one might look to the tradition of the so-called "first hijra" to Ethiopia as evidence of seafaring, I would note that this tradition appears very late and with very bad support in the Islamic historical tradition. I have seen no trustworthy evidence that such a migration ever actually occurred, despite its acceptance by the Islamic tradition and scholarship that is deferential toward it. For more details, see my extended discussion of this event and its status within the early Islamic historical tradition in Shoemaker, "In Search of 'Urwa's Sīra," 270–303.

42. See also Hoyland, *Seeing Islam*, 352.

43. Uthemann, *Anastasios Sinaites*, 2:792–94. An Arabic version of the homily survives and has been published in Cheikho, [no title], with a translation in Sheicho, "Eine verlorene Homilie." Nevertheless, according to Uthemann the Arabic version is a very poor translation of the original (personal correspondence, 8 November 2017).

44. Uthemann, *Anastasios Sinaites*, 1:357–58.

45. Text from Uthemann, ed., *Viae dux*, 9 and 169–70.

46. See Shoemaker, *Death of a Prophet*, esp. 240–64; and Webb, *Imagining the Arabs*, passim, esp. 8, 139–41.

47. Richard and Munitiz, eds., *Quaestiones et responsiones*, 131.

48. See 2.34 in the translation of Arberry, *The Koran Interpreted*, 5. See also 7.11–34; 17.61–62.

49. *Pace* Griffith, "Anastasios of Sinai," 55–58. See also Schadler, *John of Damascus and Islam*, 119–24.

Chapter 11. *The Khuzistan Chronicle*

1. In earlier scholarship, the chronicle has also been called the "*Anonymous Guidi*" after its first editor. See the discussions in Hoyland, *Seeing Islam*, 182–85; Howard-Johnston, *Witnesses*, 128–29.

2. Hoyland, *Seeing Islam*, 183.

3. For example, Nautin, "L'auteur de la 'Chronique Anonyme.'"

4. Hoyland, *Seeing Islam*, 184–85, whose reasoning is persuasive. Howard-Johnston, however, understands this section as the work of a continuator: Howard-Johnston, *Witnesses*, 128.

5. Text from Guidi, ed., *Chronica minora I*, 1:30–3, 35–9. Reprinted with English translation in al-Kaʿbī, *Short Chronicle*, 76–85, 94–115.

6. *Mrwny'* in the manuscript, although Guidi, and following him al-Kaʿbī, read instead *Mrwzy'*, which they then read as Merv, particularly since Yazdgerd III is known to have died there. Nevertheless, elsewhere in the text Merv appears less ambiguously as *Mrw*. Note also the discussion of the puzzling use of *Mrwny'* above in the commentary on Ishoʿyahb III's letter.

7. According to al-Kaʿbī, this reflects a custom of "establishing new cities using the gates of their predecessors": see al-Kaʿbī, *Short Chronicle*, 82n209.

8. Beth Lapaṭ was Gundeshapur, a major city and center of learning in Sasanian Khuzistan, and Karka of Ledan was an episcopal diocese within the metropolitan province of Beth Lapaṭ / Gundeshapur. It is not entirely clear what the fortress of Shushan is. Perhaps it refers to some fortification near Susa?

9. Two important cities in ancient Khuzistan. Susa survives today as the small city of Shush, as does Shushtar, which is a larger city.

10. The founder of the Sasanian dynasty, Ardashir I (180–242).

11. The legendary wife of the King Nimrod.

12. Darius the Great (550–486 BCE), who ruled the Persian Empire at its greatest extent.

13. This figure is also known from the Islamic historical tradition, according to which he became a Muslim sometime before the conquest of Mecca in 629 and was placed in charge of certain military operations by Muhammad. He was named Amir of Yemen and was active in the Ridda wars on the Arabian Peninsula under Abu Bakr. During the reigns of ʿUmar and Uthmān, he served as Amir of

Kufa. Although it is not clear from these sources that he oversaw the construction of Basra, he was reportedly its first ruler. For more information and for references to the Islamic sources, see al-Ka'bī, *Short Chronicle*, 96–98nn244–45.

14. Sa'd ibn Abī Waqqāṣ is also known from the Islamic historical tradition, which identifies him among the earliest converts and also as the leader of the conquest of Iraq, who built the city of Kufa. Again, see ibid., 100n248.

15. Presumably Prat is Prat d-Mayshan, or Prat of Mayshan, which is Basra. The precise location of Ulay is not known.

16. This theft by the Believers of what were believed to be the remains of the prophet Daniel is also reported in the Islamic tradition. See al-Ka'bī, *Short Chronicle*, 102n253.

17. Such a betrayal by one of the city's inhabitants is also reported in the Islamic historical tradition, as is the massacre of the city's inhabitants following its capture. See ibid., 104nn255–56

18. The ancient and modern capital of Khuzistan, today the city of Ahvaz.

19. That is, the Wādī 'Araba/Aravah, a part of the Jordan Rift Valley that runs between the Dead Sea and Aqaba/Eilat and forms the border between modern Israel and Jordan. This Khālid ibn al-Walīd is also known from the early Islamic historical tradition, according to which he participated in the battle of Mecca and the expedition to Mu'ta (which is near Arabah), as well as the conquest of Iraq and Palestine. For more information, see al-Ka'bī, *Short Chronicle*, 104n258.

20. Here the author seems to have mistaken this person's position for his name: *sakellarios* was an administrative position in the late Roman Empire. There was, in fact, a *sakellarios* named Theodore Trithyrios in command of the Roman forces at the battle of Gabitha-Yarmuk, which is most likely the engagement referenced here. Note that the "Syriac Fragment concerning the Islamic Conquest of Syria," the third item in this volume, also indicates the involvement of this *sakellarios*. See Kaegi, *Heraclius, Emperor of Byzantium*, 237, 240, 242.

21. Ḥira was the capital of the Lakhmid dynasty, a kingdom of Christian Nomads [*ṭayyāyē*] that was a vassal of the Sasanians, allied with them against the Romans, and had been given authority over all of the other Nomads/Saracens in the Persian lands. It was located just south of Kufa.

22. This is in contrast to the Islamic historical tradition, which reports that the patriarch of Alexandria at the time, Cyrus, was cooperative with the invaders and even sympathetic to them: see al-Ka'bī, *Short Chronicle*, 108n267.

23. Although the phrase here is often translated as "dome of Abraham," and this is not incorrect, we follow the precedent of biblical formulation "tent of Abraham." The alternative, "tabernacle," seems by comparison much too loaded with other meanings in modern English, connected with Christian worship, whereas in Latin, *tabernaculum* signifies a tent. I thank Sean Anthony for suggesting this: see Anthony, "Why Does the Qur'ān Need the Meccan Sanctuary?," 35-36.

24. An ancient city in the Upper Galilee in modern Israel.

25. An ancient city in northwestern Saudi Arabia.

26. We follow Hoyland in understanding the *Hgry'* as a reference to the inhabitants of Hajar, which is modern Bahrain, which seems the most plausible interpretation: Hoyland, *Seeing Islam*, 188n48. Nevertheless, other alternatives have been suggested, regarding which see al-Kaʿbī, *Short Chronicle*, 112n278. Hagarene certainly is not entirely out of the question; yet, although these Nomads are identified as sons of Abraham and Ishmael, Hagar does not otherwise come into view in this account, nor does their identity as Hagarenes. The Arabic *Muhājirūn*, "Emigrants," is perhaps an outside possibility, since this is a name that Muhammad's follows appear to have called themselves from early on. Nevertheless, in that case we would expect instead *Mhgry'*, which is the Syriac equivalent, a term also not used in this text. Others have sought to identify this term with a specific city, although without much success. In any case, it does seem that some specific region, rather than the lands of these invaders in general seems to be in view.

27. In the modern Emirates: see Hoyland, *Arabia and the Arabs*, 31-32. See also al-Kaʿbī, *Short Chronicle*, 112n279.

28. Oman: see Hoyland, *Arabia and the Arabs*, 32. See also al-Kaʿbī, *Short Chronicle*, 112n280.

29. A desert region in the center of modern Saudi Arabia.

30. According to Hoyland, Ṭawf is most likely al-Ṭaff, a desert area to the east of Ḥira: Hoyland, *Arabia and the Arabs*, 324. Al-Kaʿbi suggests, less plausibly, that *Twp* should instead be identified with the city of Ṭāʾif near Mecca: al-Kaʿbī, *Short Chronicle*, 114n282. Clearly, however, the context suggests that *Twp* is associated with and nearby Ḥira.

31. Al-Mundhir III ibn al-Nuʿman was one of the most famous and longest reigning of the Lakhmid kings, who was known for being a formidable warrior. According to Procopius (*Wars* 1.17, 2.1), the Sasanian authorities had given him authority over all the Saracens in the Persian lands: see, e.g., Robin, "Arabia and Ethiopia," 296; and Hoyland, *Arabia and the Arabs*, 81-82.

32. Hoyland, *Seeing Islam*, 185; Howard-Johnston, *Witnesses*, 132.

33. The information given in this account does not warrant the conclusion drawn by Howard-Johnston and Anthony that this sacred place is a reference to the Ka'ba, even if one cannot, to be sure, completely exclude this possibility. Howard-Johnston, *Witnesses*, 132; Anthony, "Meccan Sanctuary?," 35–36.

34. So Hoyland also concludes: Hoyland, *Seeing Islam*, 188n48; Hoyland, *Arabia and the Arabs*, 32, 81–82.

Chapter 12. *The Apocalypse of Rabbi Shim'ōn b. Yohai*

1. In addition to *The Secrets of Rabbi Shim'ōn b. Yohai*, from which we translate the most important passage below, this tradition is also witnessed in the *Ten Kings* Midrash, and *The Prayer of Rabbi Shim'ōn b. Yohai*. See the discussion of these sources and their relations in Reeves, *Trajectories*, 77–78.

2. Text from Jellinek, ed., *Bet ha-midrash*, 3:78–79.

3. Cf. 1 Kings 4.31; Ps 89.1. In rabbinic tradition, however, Ethan the Ezrahite was identified with Abraham.

4. This would be the Caliph 'Umar (634–44).

5. Most likely Mu'āwiya (661–80).

6. On the Kenite's identification with the descendants of Ishmael, see Crone and Cook, *Hagarism*, 35–37.

7. See the discussions of this passage in Lewis, "An Apocalyptic Vision," 323–24; Crone and Cook, *Hagarism*, 4–5; Gil, *History of Palestine*, 63; Hoyland, *Seeing Islam*, 310–11; Reeves, *Trajectories*, 80–81. See also the broader analysis of these traditions in Bashear, "Riding Beasts."

8. Reeves, *Trajectories*, 76–88 and online at https://clas-pages.uncc.edu/john-reeves/research-projects/trajectories-in-near-eastern-apocalyptic/nistarot-secrets-of-r-shimon-b-yohai-2/.

9. For example, Even-Shmuel, ed., *Midreshe ge'ulah*, 167–69, 175–77; Lewis, "An Apocalyptic Vision," 323; Baron, *A Social and Religious History of the Jews*, 3:93, 274n27; Crone and Cook, *Hagarism*, 4–5; Dagron and Déroche, "Juifs et Chrétiens," 43; Gil, *History of Palestine*, 61–62; Hoyland, "Sebeos," 92; Hoyland, *Seeing Islam*, 308; Reeves, *Trajectories*, 77. Sean Anthony, however, suggests instead that the text should be understood in the context of an eighth-century Jewish messianic movement that he reconstructs from a range of later sources. Nevertheless, I am not persuaded that this provides the most probable context for these traditions. See Anthony, "Who Was the Shepherd?"

10. Crone and Cook, *Hagarism*, 4.

Chapter 13. *Pirqe de-Rabbi Eliezer*

1. The similarities have been explored most thoroughly in McDowell, "L'histoire sainte," but see also Spurling and Grypeou, "Pirke de-Rabbi Eliezer"; and Reeves, *Trajectories*, 67.

2. See, e.g., Reeves, *Trajectories*, 67; Adelman, *Return of the Repressed*, 35–42.

3. The best discussion of these traditions is in Bakhos, *Ishmael on the Border*, 85–128, esp. 104–16, which also includes a translation of section 30 at 106–9.

4. Several of the various efforts to date this apocalypse are discussed in Adelman, *Return of the Repressed*, 35–42, who opts for around 750 CE as the likely date.

5. Translation based on the critical edition of this passage published in ibid., 279 and the synoptic edition published in Reeves, *Trajectories*, 74–75.

6. The verse from Daniel continues, according to the New Revised Standard Version, ". . . that shall never be destroyed, nor shall this kingdom be left to another people. It shall crush all these kingdoms and bring them to an end, and it shall stand forever."

7. See Shoemaker, *Apocalypse of Empire*, 64–115. With respect to Jewish apocalypticism and messianic expectations during this time, see, e.g., Himmelfarb, *Jewish Messiahs*; Newman, "Dating Sefer Zerubavel"; Sivertsev, *Judaism and Imperial Ideology*; Hoyland, *Seeing Islam*, 307–21; Reeves, *Trajectories*.

8. Hoyland, *Seeing Islam*, 316. Adelman, *Return of the Repressed*, 39 also identifies the first two events with ʿAbd al-Malik's reign.

9. Reeves, *Trajectories*, 69; Rubin, *Between Bible and Qurʾān*, 33–34.

10. Lewis, "An Apocalyptic Vision," 331.

11. Hoyland, *Seeing Islam*, 178.

12. Silver, *Messianic Speculation*, 40–41.

13. See, e.g., the discussion of Muʿāwiya's campaigns against Constantinople in Hoyland, *In God's Path*, 105–10.

14. See Humphreys, *Muʿawiya*, 11–12, 21–22, 89–96. Whether or not Ziyād was actually Muʿāwiya's bastard brother or not (there is some dispute), Muʿāwiya nonetheless proclaimed him to be such, which surely was all that mattered to all but the highest-ranking and most politically connected of his subjects.

Chapter 14. *The Maronite Chronicle*

1. For example, Tannous, "In Search of Monotheletism."

2. Nöldeke, "Zur Geschichte," 82.

3. Palmer, *Seventh Century*, 29, 35; Brock, "Syriac Sources," 18–19. See also Hoyland, *Seeing Islam*, 137–39; Howard-Johnston, *Witnesses*, 175–76.

4. Text from Brooks, ed., *Chronica minora II*, 69–72.

5. The text here is incomplete since it stands at the beginnings of one of the various fragments.

6. The final folio of the manuscript describes three military engagements between the Romans and Muhammad's followers, which are primarily of interest for understanding the early history of this conflict.

7. Humphreys, *Muʿawiya*, 28–33, 45–50.

8. See, e.g., Shoemaker, *Death of a Prophet*, 1–114.

9. See, e.g., Tannous, *Making*, 433.

10. See, e.g., Humphreys, *History of al-Ṭabarī*, esp. 75n130.

11. Penn, *Envisioning Islam*, 62, 134; Penn, *When Christians*, 54–55.

12. Penn, *When Christians*, 54–55; Tannous, *Making*, 115–17; also 162; Penn, *Envisioning Islam*, 70, 134–39.

13. Adomnán, *On the Holy Places* I.9, in Geyer, *Itinera*, 235–38).

14. Thus Arietta Papaconstaninou seems to interpret the passage: Papaconstantinou, "Between *Umma* and *Dhimma*," 137.

15. This possibility is also noted in Humphreys, *Muʿawiya*, 126.

16. Ibid., 102.

17. Ibid., 9, 126.

18. See, e.g., ibid., 3–10, 15–19; Hawting, *First Dynasty of Islam*, 2–3, 11–18; Crone, *Slaves on Horses*, 3–8; Hodgson, *Venture of Islam*, 247–51.

19. In addition to the other sources included in this volume that present Muʿāwiya in highly positive terms, one should also see *The Armenian Chronicle of 682*, which describes him as having "worldly humility and human kindness": Movses Daskhowrantsʻi, *History of the Caucasian Albanians* 2.27 (Shahnazariantsʻ, Ս̆ուսէ Կաղանկատուացի, vol. 1, 315). Although the chronicle in which this report occurs is itself later, dating to the 990s, here it draws on a much earlier source from the later seventh century: see Howard-Johnston, *Witnesses*, 105–28.

20. Humphreys, *Muʿawiya*, 61, 63, 97; Donner, *Muhammad and the Believers*, 176–77, 182; Hoyland, *Seeing Islam*, 690–92.

21. Shoemaker, *Death of a Prophet*, 218–65.

22. Howard-Johnston, *Witnesses*, 177.

23. Donner oddly fails to consider this report, even though he is generally interested in other evidence of the Believers worshiping in Christian churches. Donner, "From Believers to Muslims," 51–52; Donner, *Muhammad and the Believers*, 115.

24. Tannous, *Making*, 305, 379; Howard-Johnston, *Witnesses*, 178.

25. Donner, "From Believers to Muslims," 51–52; Donner, *Muhammad and the Believers*, 115. See also Creswell and Allen, *Short Account*, 65–67. In Jerusalem, the Church of the Ascension on the Mount of Olives was similarly appropriated and transformed into a mosque: Murphy-O'Connor, *Holy Land*, 124–25. Likewise, during the early Islamic period, a *mihrab* was added to the Church of the Kathisma, an early Nativity Shrine dedicated to the Virgin Mary midway between Jerusalem and Bethlehem, and it was converted into a mosque. Nevertheless, although Rina Avner and Leah Di Segni have argued that Christians and Muslims shared usage of this sacred shrine during the early Islamic period, in fact the evidence does not support this conclusion, but rather contradicts it, as I explain in a forthcoming article on the Kathisma shrine: Shoemaker, "Mary between Bible and Quran." See Di Segni, "Christian Epigraphy," 248–49; Di Segni, "Greek Inscription"; Avner, "Recovery of the Kathisma Church," 180–81; Avner, "Kathisma: Christian and Muslim Pilgrimage," 550.

26. Busse, "'Omar b. al-Ḥaṭṭāb"; Busse, "'Omar's Image as the Conqueror"; Busse, "Die 'Umar-Moschee."

27. Bashear, "Qibla Musharriqa," 267-8, 274-77.

28. Ibid., 267–68, 277–78

29. Ibid., 268, 280–81.

30. For more on the inclusion of a cross on early Arab-Byzantine coins, see esp. Foss, *Arab-Byzantine Coins*, 42–55, 117.

31. See, e.g., Robinson, *'Abd al-Malik*, 72–78.

32. Metcalf, "Three Seventh-Century Byzantine Gold Hoards," esp. 99n7.

33. Foss, "Syrian Coinage," 362–63.

Chapter 15. *On the Holy Places*, Adomnán / Arculf

1. Bede, *Ecclesiastical History* V.15.

2. A recent example in this vein is Nees, *Perspectives*, esp. 33–57. Nevertheless, in my estimation this study is marred by a strong materialist bias and regular dismissal of textual evidence, which is treated with much greater skepticism than is warranted. Nevertheless, as is so often the case, Nees treats Islamic texts with greater deference, such as, for instance, in the case of Mecca. For a thoughtful response to this sort of hyper-skepticism, see, e.g., Hoyland and Waidler, "Adomnán's De Locis Sanctis."

3. Adomnán, *On the Holy Places* I.9, in Geyer, *Itinera*, 235–38).

4. Text is from Adomnán, *On the Holy Places* I.1 (ibid., 226-27).

5. Perhaps most famously Creswell, *A Short Account*, 10; and Creswell, *Early Muslim Architecture, vol. 1*, pt. 1, 33-34. Hoyland concludes that the building is a mosque on account of the mention of prayer: Hoyland, *Seeing Islam*, 221n18. Nevertheless, such conclusions, in my opinion, presume that later Islamic patterns of worship, especially regarding where one would pray, were already firmly in place by this time, which is not entirely certain.

6. St. Laurent and Awwad, "Archaeology and Preservation"; St. Laurent and Awwad, "Marwani Musalla."

7. See, e.g., Shoemaker, *Death of a Prophet*, 235-36.

8. See, e.g., Nees, *Perspectives*, 49-56.

9. Hoyland and Waidler, "Adomnán's De Locis Sanctis," 798.

10. On this see esp. Shoemaker, *Death of a Prophet*, 231-40; Shoemaker, *Apocalypse of Empire*, 161-68.

11. See the accounts by Sibṭ Ibn al-Jawzī's *Mir'āt al-Zamān*, published with extensive analysis in Elad, "Why Did 'Abd al-Malik Build," and Wāsiṭī, *Faḍā'il al-Bayt al-Muqaddas*, 82-83. Much of Elad's article is reproduced in Elad, *Medieval Jerusalem*, 51-61, which lacks the Arabic text, however. See also Kaplony, *The Ḥaram*, 321-82, esp. 321-28, 351-63; Sharon, "Praises of Jerusalem," 60-65; Elad, "Pilgrims and Pilgrimage," esp. 300-302. Even as the site's primary significance shifted to be located in Muhammad's Night Journey and Ascent, the location of the Dome and its Rock remained identified with the Jewish Temple.

12. Elad, *Medieval Jerusalem*, 55.

Chapter 16. *The Apocalypse of Ps.-Shenoute*

1. Lubomierski, *Die Vita Sinuthii*, esp. 170, 205-11.

2. Ibid., esp. 113-15, 183, 205-11. See also Amélineau, *Monuments*, vii-ix; Amélineau, *Les moines*, 230.

3. Amélineau, *Monuments*, 338-51; Colin, *La version éthiopienne*, 17-27 (Eth) and 11-18 (Fr). On the latter, see Suciu, "More Sahidic Fragments," although the fragment in question does not preserve the part of this tradition that interests us.

4. Amélineau, *Monuments*, lvi-lviii; Frankfurter, *Elijah in Upper Egypt*, 25-26; Davis, *Early Coptic Papacy*, 114; Lubomierski, *Die Vita Sinuthii*, 209; Thomas and Roggema, eds., *Christian Muslim Relations*, 182-85. Regarding the possibility of an earlier date, see below as well as Hoyland, *Seeing Islam*, 281-82.

5. Thomas and Roggema, eds., *Christian Muslim Relations*, 183. See also Frankfurter, *Elijah in Upper Egypt*, 25.

6. Shoemaker, *Apocalypse of Empire*, esp. 35-36, 39, 60.

7. Text from Amélineau, *Monuments*, 340-41.

8. I thank Stephen Davis for suggesting this translation, although the lexica also suggest "having authority" or "acting at will": *mutaṣarrifīn*.

9. Lubomierski, *Die Vita Sinuthii*, esp. 170, 205-11; Lubomierski, "The Vita Sinuthii"; Lubomierski, "Towards a Better Understanding"; Lubomierski, "The Coptic Life of Shenoute."

10. Goldziher, *Muslim Studies*, 2:44-47. See also Besant and Palmer, *Jerusalem*, 80-86; Wellhausen, *The Arab Kingdom and Its Fall*, 212-16; Caetani, *Annali dell'Islām*, 3:773. More recently, see Elad, "Why Did ʿAbd al-Malik Build," 40-48.

11. See, e.g., Hawting, *First Dynasty of Islam*, 2-3, 11-18; Crone, *Slaves on Horses*, 3-8; Hodgson, *Venture of Islam*, 247-51.

12. For example, Goldziher, *Muslim Studies*, 2:44-47; Caetani, *Annali dell'Islām*, 3:773; Elad, "Why Did ʿAbd al-Malik Build," 40-48.

13. As was first demonstrated in particular by Goitein, "The Sanctity of Palestine"; Goitein, "The Historical Background." These two articles form the basis of Goitein, "The Sanctity of Jerusalem." The acceptance of this view as a new *status quaestionis* can be seen, e.g., in the following studies: Hirschberg, "The Sources of Moslem Tradition," 319-21; Grabar, "The Umayyad Dome of the Rock," 36, 45; Busse, "Der Islam und die biblischen Kultstätten," 124; Busse, "The Sanctity of Jerusalem," 454; Kessler, "ʿAbd al-Malik's Inscription," 11; Peters, *Jerusalem and Mecca*, 94-95; Rosen-Ayalon, *Early Islamic Monuments*, 14; Gil, *History of Palestine*, 93n105. The only major dissent to this consensus comes in Elad, *Medieval Jerusalem*, 147-63, but see Shoemaker, *Death of a Prophet*, 242-57.

14. Goitein, "The Sanctity of Jerusalem," 138.

15. Ibid., 147.

16. Hoyland, *Seeing Islam*, 281-82. One should note, however, that objection to taxation is a common theme of the tradition of imperial apocalypticism before the rise of Islam: see Shoemaker, *Apocalypse of Empire*, 194n63.

17. Thomas and Roggema, eds., *Christian Muslim Relations*, 183.

18. Citing Griffith's translation in Griffith, *Bible in Arabic*, 37.

19. Ibid., 37-38, 88-89

20. For example, 3:55; 5:117; 19:33. See also Ayoub, "Towards an Islamic Christology," 106.

21. Colin, *La version éthiopienne*, 19 (Eth) and 12-13 (Fr).

22. Amélineau, *Monuments*, lvi, 341.

23. Hoyland, *Seeing Islam*, 280n68, citing Périer, "Lettre de Pisuntios," 308 and 319.

24. Shoemaker, *Apocalypse of Empire*, 41, 95, 99, 100, 113, 158.

25. Reeves, *Trajectories*, esp. 69. See also Cohen, "Esau as Symbol"; de Lange, "Jewish Attitudes."

26. Papaconstantinou, "Between *Umma* and *Dhimma*," 137. Note that while Papaconstantinou mistakenly identifies this court official as Manṣūr ibn Sarjūn, John of Damascus's grandfather, surely she meant to indicate Sarjūn ibn Manṣūr instead. On John's family tree, see Anthony, "Fixing John Damascene's Biography."

Chapter 17. *Book of Main Points*, John Bar Penkaye

1. After his death, al-Mukhtār's followers would organize into an early Shi'i group known as the Kaysānīyya or Kaysanites.

2. Text is from Mingana, *Sources syriaques*, 141–43, 145–47, 155–58, 167.

3. Literally "Meṣrīn," which is an Aramaic word for Egypt.

4. An unknown place, but, as Brock notes, "it represents the furthest south, just as the 'Gates of Alan' designate the furthest north." Brock, "North Mesopotamia," 58n.e.

5. That is, the Caucasian Gates or the Darial Pass in the Darial Gorge on the modern Georgian and Russian border.

6. Brock, "North Mesopotamia," 62.

7. Brock says that 'Abd al-Raḥmān is clearly an error here, since he was the governor of Khorasan and the brother of 'Ubayd Allāh, who led the "westerners" in this theater of the Second Civil War. Ibid., 64.

8. According to Brock, an otherwise unknown figure: ibid.

9. Also an otherwise unknown figure, according to Brock: ibid.

10. Perhaps we must understand here instead bar Zāyāt? See the discussion in the commentary below.

11. Brock, "North Mesopotamia," 74.

12. Hoyland, "New Documentary Texts," 409. See also Crone, *Slaves on Horses*, 237–38n362.

13. Hoyland, *In God's Path*, 98–102; Humphreys, *Mu'awiya*, esp. 93–97; Donner, "Formation"; Hoyland, "New Documentary Texts."

14. Brock, "Syriac Views," 14; Donner, *Muhammad and the Believers*, 111.

15. Donner, "From Believers to Muslims," 13-16; Donner, *Muhammad and the Believers*, 69-70, 75-77, 87, 134, 204, 206; Wansbrough, *Quranic Studies*, 55.

16. On this, see also Kister, ". . . *illā bi-ḥaqqihi . . . .*"

17. Donner, *Muhammad and the Believers*, 61-69. See also on eschatology esp. Shoemaker, "The Reign of God"; Shoemaker, *Apocalypse of Empire*.

18. Hoyland, "New Documentary Texts," 409-10.

19. Hoyland, *Seeing Islam*, 480-89; Anthony, "Fixing John Damascene's Biography"; Donner, *Muhammad and the Believers*, 176-77, 180-81, 192-93, 222.

20. Donner, *Muhammad and the Believers*, 177; Hawting, *First Dynasty of Islam*, 46.

21. Hawting, "The *ḥajj* in the Second Civil War," 36.

22. Hoyland, *Seeing Islam*, 552-53; Robinson, *'Abd al-Malik*, 37-38; Rubin, *Between Bible and Qur'ān*, 36-7; Goitein, "The Sanctity of Jerusalem," 148. See also Shoemaker, *Death of a Prophet*, 253-57.

23. Brock, "North Mesopotamia," 64

24. Ibid.

25. See Anthony, *The Caliph and the Heretic*, 282-85. Brock's speculation that the name should be understood as "the *šurāt*, who had 'sold' their life for the cause of God (Qur'an IV.76), rather than the *šurṭa* (bodyguard)," is not correct: Brock, "North Mesopotamia," 66.

Chapter 18. *Fourth Letter*, Jacob of Edessa

1. Such is the assessment offered in Wright, *Short History of Syriac Literature*, 143. This was repeated more recently in Albert et al., *Christianismes orientaux*, 357: "a tenu en Orient une place équivalente à celle de Jérome dans le monde latin."

2. His considerable oeuvre is discussed in Wright, *Short History of Syriac Literature*, 141-54. Of all the authors covered in this work, only the discussion of Bar Hebraeus is as lengthy.

3. This text is unedited, but I thank Kristian Heal for sharing a digital reproduction of the manuscript containing this letter with me. The complete letter is found in BL Add 12,172 ff. 121b-126b. The section translated above occurs on f. 124a. Another letter responding to eighteen questions from the same John the Stylite immediately precedes this letter in the manuscript.

4. On the use of this term as a self-designation by Muhammad's early followers, see the discussion of Isho'yahb above.

5. Note that instead of "and those in the land of Babel and in Ḥira and Basra pray to the west. And the Muhājirūn there also pray to the west toward the Kaʿba," Penn's translation has "and also the Hagarenes there worship toward the east, toward the Kaʿba," which is clearly a mistake: see Penn, *When Christians*, 172.

6. See Shoemaker, *Death of a Prophet*, 223–30. See also "Sacred Direction in Islam," in Hoyland, *Seeing Islam*, 560–73, which also makes similar arguments using the same sources for early prayer in the direction of Jerusalem (and elsewhere) and the late adoption of a Meccan *qibla*.

7. Sura 2.142–44; trans. from Hoyland, *Seeing Islam*, 560.

8. Ibn Hishām, *Kitāb sīrat Rasūl Allāh*, 1:381; al-Ṭabarī, *Annales*, 1:1280.

9. See, e.g., Neuwirth, "Erste Qibla—Fernstes Masǧid?," 232–38.

10. Bashear, "Qibla Musharriqa," 282.

11. Ibid., 269–73.

12. Andræ, *Die person Muhammeds*, 293; Andræ, "Der Ursprung des Islams," 152; Andræ, *Les origines de l'Islam*, 10–11; Buhl, *Das Leben Muhammeds*, 218. Barthold, who does not appear to engage Andrae's earlier hypothesis, supposes that the earliest Muslims believed that Muhammad's night journey took him to a heavenly sanctuary somewhere in the east, and thus they directed their prayers in this direction. Also, because the earliest mosques were entered by a western door, Barthold concludes that they must have faced east. Barthold, "Die Orientierung." Regarding an early tradition of Muhammad's night journey to a heavenly mosque, cf. Busse, "Jerusalem in the Story of Muḥammad's Night Journey," 35–37.

13. Again, see, e.g., Bell, *Origin of Islam*, 42–43, Peters, *Muhammad and the Origins of Islam*, 1; Hawting, *Idea of Idolatry*, 14–16; Dye, "Le corpus coranique: Contexte," 762–76; and Wood, "Christianity in the Arabian Peninsula."

14. Sharon, "The Umayyads as *Ahl al-Bayt*."

15. Sharon, "Birth of Islam in the Holy Land," 230–32, quotation at 232. Barthold's observation regarding the western entrance of the earliest mosques could also support this hypothesis: Barthold, "Die Orientierung," 246–48.

16. Hoyland, *Seeing Islam*, 565n89 proposed the idea of a converted church, citing in support of this position Beno Rothenberg's suggestion that the structure was "a 'symbolic' early Christian church in Rothenberg, *Timna*, 221–22. Nevertheless, Hoyland seems to have overlooked that Rothenberg later adopted Sharon's position that the building was indeed a mosque: Rothenberg, "Early Islamic Copper Smelting," 3–4. Moreover, in the excavation report for the site, the excavators observe that "while one might suggest that this was a symbolic open church, it

would be the only such example in the world." Sharon, Avner, and Nahlieli, "An Early Islamic Mosque," 113.

17. The main sources are cited in Sharon, "Birth of Islam in the Holy Land," 230; see also Crone and Cook, *Hagarism*, 24-25.

18. Al-Balādhurī, *Futūḥ al-buldān*, 276; al-Ṭabarī, *Annales*, 1:2488-92. See Hoyland, *Seeing Islam*, 561-62, where the sources are discussed.

19. See, e.g., Crone and Cook, *Hagarism*, esp. 21-26; Crone, *Meccan Trade*, esp. 186-99; Hawting, "The Origins of the Muslim Sanctuary at Mecca"; Hawting, *Idea of Idolatry*, 10-13.

Chapter 19. *The Passion of Peter of Capitolias*

1. Theophanes, *Chronicle* AM 6234 (de Boor, ed., *Theophanis chronographia*, 417).

2. Kekeliże, "Житіе Петра," 2-3. The work is not included in the *Clavis Patrum Graecorum*, even under "dubia" or "spuria," although one finds there that John was indeed otherwise involved in the composition of hagiographies: Geerard and Noret, *Clavis Patrum Graecorum*; Geerard et al., *Clavis Patrum Graecorum: Supplementum*.

3. Anthony, "Fixing John Damascene's Biography."

4. al-Samʿānī, *Biographie*, 29-30. The information and reference are from Anthony, "Fixing John Damascene's Biography." Since with this source we reach the early seventh century, at this point it seems appropriate to refer to Muhammad's new religious community as Islam, Islamic, and Muslim.

5. Auzépy, "De la Palestine," 184-85.

6. Louth, "St John Damascene," 248-49. Anthony, "Fixing John Damascene's Biography," also appears to continue with the tradition that John became a monk at Mar Saba.

7. Hoyland, *Seeing Islam*, 354-90.

8. Theophanes, *Chronicle* AM 6234 (de Boor, ed., *Theophanis chronographia*, 416-17).

9. Text and translation in Shoemaker, *Three Christian Martyrdoms*, 22-41.

10. Or "blasphemies."

11. That is, a death from "natural causes."

12. The Trichora is the three cities of Capitolias, Gadara, and Abila in northern Jordan, which were part of the ancient Decapolis in this region.

13. See now the important study of this topic and these texts by Sahner, *Christian Martyrs*.

14. Swanson, "Martyrdom of ʿAbd al-Masīḥ," 119.

15. The identities of these early Islamic authorities are well correlated with the early Islamic tradition in Anthony, *Crucifixion*, 56–57. The identity of Zora, however, remains more uncertain.

16. See, e.g., De Ste. Croix, *Christian Persecution*, 153–200; Moss, "Discourse of Voluntary Martyrdom."

17. See "Manichaeism and the Biblical Forefathers," in Reeves, *Heralds*, 5–30.

18. Shoemaker, "The Reign of God"; Shoemaker, *Apocalypse of Empire*.

Chapter 20. *Excerpts from a Lost Greek Source*

1. These points were demonstrated definitively in Brooks, "Sources of Theophanes." The history of the investigation of Theophanes' "eastern sources" is briefly surveyed in Conrad, "Theophanes and the Arabic Historical Tradition," 5–6.

2. See Hoyland, *Seeing Islam*, 440–43.

3. Palmer, *Seventh Century*, 90, 101–3; Conrad, "Conquest of Arwad," 328–34, 347–48.

4. Brooks, "Sources of Theophanes," 583–86. On Theophilus's authorship, see Conrad, "Theophanes and the Arabic Historical Tradition," 43; Conrad, "Conquest of Arwad," 322–48; Hoyland, *Seeing Islam*, 401–2; Palmer, *Seventh Century*, 96–98; Howard-Johnston, *Witnesses*, 194–99. "Of John [bar Samuel] nothing is known apart from his place of activity, namely 'the Western regions and the islands.' He is not cited anywhere else and nothing's survived of his chronicle": Debié, "Theophanes' 'Oriental Source,'" 366–67.

5. Agapius, *Chronicle* (Vasiliev, ed., *Kitab al-ʿUnvan / Histoire universelle*, 3:525); Conrad, "Varietas Syriaca," 91–94; Conrad, "Conquest of Arwad," 331; Hoyland, *Seeing Islam*, 400–401.

6. It is true that Lawrence Conrad demonstrated that Theophanes knew certain elements of the developing early Islamic historical tradition, but there is no evidence that his knowledge of these traditions derives from a written source in a language other than Greek, as dependence on Theophilus would require. One imagines that what Theophanes knows of the emerging Islamic collective memory is mediated, very likely by oral transmission I would imagine, given the general rather than specific nature of what he knows. See Conrad, "Theophanes and the Arabic Historical Tradition."

7. For example, Brooks, "Sources of Theophanes," 586–87; Conrad, "Conquest of Arwad," 336–40; also Howard-Johnston, *Witnesses*, 295–99.

8. Debié, "Theophanes' 'Oriental Source,'" 366.

9. Conterno, "Theophilos, 'the more likely candidate'?," 385–86.

10. See esp. Conterno, *La "descrizione dei tempi,"* 39–75 and Conterno, "Theophilos, 'the more likely candidate'?," 385–93.

11. Conterno, "Theophilos, 'the more likely candidate'?," 386.

12. Debié, "Theophanes' 'Oriental Source,'" 377–78.

13. Bowersock, *The Crucible of Islam*, 123. See also Bowersock, *Empires in Collision*, 74.

14. Conterno, *La "descrizione dei tempi,"* 75; Conterno, «'L'abominio della desolazione,'» 14.

15. Translated from Theophanes, *Chronicle* AM 6127 and AM 6135 (de Boor, ed., *Theophanis chronographia*, 339) and Michael the Syrian, *Chronicle* (Chabot, ed., *Chronique de Michel le Syrien*, 4:419–20). But see also *Chronicle of 1234* (Chabot, ed., *Chronicon ad annum Christi 1234*, vol. 1, 254–5); Agapius, *Chronicle* (Vasiliev, ed., *Kitab al-ʿUnvan / Histoire universelle*, 3:475). Translations of all four passages are available for comparison in Hoyland, *Theophilus of Edessa*, 114–17.

16. This statement prohibiting Jews from living in Jerusalem is absent from Theophanes but is present in the other three sources. Agapius relates this point at much greater length.

17. As Hoyland notes, here Michael the Syrian adds a brief encomium on the simplicity of ʿUmar's lifestyle unrelated to the original source material. Hoyland also omits this from his translation: Hoyland, *Theophilus of Edessa*, 116n264.

18. Translated from Theophanes, *Chronicle* AM 6127 and AM 6135 (de Boor, ed., *Theophanis chronographia*, 342) and Michael the Syrian, *Chronicle* (Chabot, ed., *Chronique de Michel le Syrien*, 4:420–21). See also *Chronicle of 1234* (Chabot, ed., *Chronicon ad annum Christi 1234*, 1:260–61). Note that a report about the building of the Temple is not found in Agapius, although a closely related version can be found in the tenth-century Arabic *Chronicle of Siirt* 104 (Scher, ed., *Histoire nestorienne*, 4:624). Translations of all four passages are available for comparison in Hoyland, *Theophilus of Edessa*, 126–27.

19. Bowersock, *The Crucible of Islam*, 120–23; Bowersock, *Empires in Collision*, 73–74; Conterno, "'L'abominio della desolazione,'" 14.

20. Bowersock, *The Crucible of Islam*, 121; Bowersock, *Empires in Collision*, 72; Conterno, "'L'abominio della desolazione,'" 16–18.

Bibliography

ʿAbd al-Razzaq al-Sanʿani. *al-Muṣannaf*. Edited by Ḥabīburraḥmān Aʿẓamī. 11 vols. Beirut: al-Maktab al-Islāmī, 1983.

Abdul-Rauf, Muhammad. "Outsiders' Interpretations of Islam: A Muslim's Point of View." In *Approaches to Islam in Religious Studies*, edited by Richard C. Martin, 179–88. Tucson: University of Arizona Press, 1985.

Abgarian, Gevorg V., ed. Պատմութիւն Սեբէոսի [*Patmut ʿiwn Sebeosi*]. Erevan: Haykakan SSH Gitut'yunneri Akademiayi Hratarakch'ut'yun, 1979.

Abulaże, Ilia, ed. იოანე მოსხი. ლიმონარი [*Ioane Mosxi. Limonari*]. T'bilisi, Georgia: Mec'niereba, 1960.

Adelman, Rachel. *The Return of the Repressed: Pirqe de-Rabbi Eliezer and the Pseudepigrapha*. Leiden: Brill, 2009.

Afsaruddin, Asma. *The First Muslims: History and Memory*. Oxford: Oneworld, 2008.

Albert, Micheline, Robert Beylot, René-G. Coquin, Bernard Outtier, and Charles Renoux. *Christianismes orientaux: Introduction à l'étude des langues et des littératures*. Initiations au christianisme ancien. Paris: Éditions du Cerf, 1993.

Alexander, Paul J. *The Byzantine Apocalyptic Tradition*. Berkeley: University of California Press, 1985.

———. *The Oracle of Baalbek: The Tiburtine Sibyl in Greek Dress*. Dumbarton Oaks Studies 10. Washington, DC: Dumbarton Oaks Center for Byzantine Studies, 1967.

Allen, Pauline. *Sophronius of Jerusalem and Seventh-Century Heresy: The Synodical Letter and Other Documents*. Oxford Early Christian Texts. Oxford: Oxford University Press, 2009.

Amélineau, Émile. *Les moines égyptiens: Vie de Schnoudi*. Bibliothèque de vulgari-
sation 1. Paris: Leroux, 1889.

———. *Monuments pour servir à l'histoire de l'Égypte chrétienne aux IVe et Ve (aux
IVe, Ve, VIe et VIIe) siècles*. Mémoires publiés par les membres de la Mission
Archéologique Française au Caire. tom. 4. Paris: Librarie de la société
asiatique, 1888.

Amir-Moezzi, Mohammad Ali. "Muḥammad the Paraclete and ʿAlī the Messiah:
New Remarks on the Origins of Islam and of Shiʿite Imamology." *Der Islam*
95 (2018): 30–64.

———. *The Silent Qurʾan and the Speaking Qurʾan: Scriptural Sources of Islam
between History and Fervor*. New York: Columbia University Press, 2016.

Andræ, Tor. *Les origines de l'Islam et le Christianisme*. Translated by Jules Roche.
Initiation à l'Islam 8. Paris: Adrien-Maisonneuve, 1955.

———. *Die person Muhammeds in lehre und glauben seiner gemeinde*. Archives
d'études orientales, Stockholm 16. Stockholm: Kungl. boktryckeriet.
P. A. Norstedt & söner, 1918.

———. "Der Ursprung des Islams und das Christentum." *Kyrkohistorisk Årsskrift*
23 (1923): 149–206; 24 (1924): 213–92; 25 (1925): 45–112.

Anthony, Sean W. *The Caliph and the Heretic: Ibn Sabaʾ and the Origins of
Shiʿism*. Leiden: Brill, 2012.

———. *Crucifixion and Death as Spectacle: Umayyad Crucifixion in its Late Antique
Context*, American Oriental Series 96. New Haven, CT: American Oriental
Society, 2014.

———. "Fixing John Damascene's Biography: Historical Notes on His Family
Background." *Journal of Early Christian Studies* 23 (2015): 607–27.

———. *Muhammad and the Empires of Faith*. Berkeley: University of California
Press, 2020.

———. "Muhammad, the Keys to Paradise, and the Doctrina Iacobi: A Late
Antique Puzzle." *Der Islam* 91 (2014): 243–65.

———. "Who Was the Shepherd of Damascus? The Enigma of Jewish and
Messianist Responses to the Islamic Conquests in Marwānid Syria and
Mesopotomia." In *The Lineaments of Islam: Studies in Honor of Fred McGraw
Donner*, edited by Paul Cobb, 19–59. Leiden: Brill, 2012.

———. "Why Does the Qurʾān Need the Meccan Sanctuary? Response to Professor Gerald Hawting's 2017 Presidential Address." *Journal of the International
Qurʾanic Studies Association* 3 (2018): 25–41.

Arberry, A. J. trans. *The Koran Interpreted*. London: Oxford University Press, 1983.

Armstrong, Karen. *Muhammad: A Biography of the Prophet*. New York: Harper-SanFrancisco, 1993.

Arzoumanian, Zaven, trans. *History of Lewond, The Eminent Vardapet of the Armenians*. Wynnewood, PA: St. Sahag and St. Mesrob Armenian Church, 1982.

Assemani, Giuseppe Simone. *Bibliotheca orientalis Clementino-vaticana*. 3 vols. Rome: Typis Sacrae Congregationis de Propaganda Fide, 1719–28.

Auzépy, Marie-France. "De la Palestine à Constantinople (VIIIe–IXe siècles): Etienne le Saba'ite et Jean Damascène." *Travaux et Mémoires* 12 (1994): 183–218.

Avner, Rina. "The Kathisma: A Christian and Muslim Pilgrimage Site." *ARAM* 18–19 (2006–07): 541–57.

———. "The Recovery of the Kathisma Church and Its Influence on Octagonal Buildings." In *One Land—Many Cultures: Archaeological Studies in Honor of Stanislao Loffreda, O.F.M.*, edited by G. C. Bottini, L. D. Segni and D. Chrupcala, 173–88. Jerusalem: Franciscan Printing Press, 2003.

Ayoub, Mahmoud M. "Towards an Islamic Christology II: The Death of Jesus, Reality or Delusion." *The Muslim World* 70 (1980): 91–121.

Bakhos, Carol. *Ishmael on the Border: Rabbinic Portrayals of the First Arab*. SUNY series in Judaica. Albany: State University of New York Press, 2006.

al-Balādhurī, Aḥmad ibn Yaḥyā. *Futūḥ al-buldān*. Edited by M. J. de Goeje. Leiden: E. J. Brill, 1866.

Bardill, Jonathan. *Constantine, Divine Emperor of the Christian Golden Age*. Cambridge: Cambridge University Press, 2012.

Baron, Salo Wittmayer. *A Social and Religious History of the Jews*. 2nd ed. 18 vols. Philadelphia: Jewish Publication Society of America, 1952–83.

Barthold, W. "Die Orientierung der ersten muhammedanischen Moscheen." *Der Islam* 18 (1929): 245–50.

Bashear, Suliman. "Qibla Musharriqa and Early Muslim Prayer in Churches." *The Muslim World* 81 (1991): 267–82.

———. "Riding Beasts on Divine Missions: An Examination of the Ass and Camel Traditions." *Journal of Semitic Studies* 37 (1991): 37–75.

———. "The Title 'Fārūq' and Its Association with 'Umar I." *Studia Islamica* 72 (1990): 47–70.

Beck, Edmund, ed. *Des Heiligen Ephraem des Syrers Sermones III*. Corpus Scriptorum Christianorum Orientalium 320–21, Scriptores Syri 138–39. Louvain: Secrét. du CSCO, 1972.

Bell, Richard. *The Origin of Islam in Its Christian Environment*. London: Macmillan and Co., 1926.

Besant, Walter, and Edward Henry Palmer. *Jerusalem, the City of Herod and Saladin*. London: R. Bentley and Son, 1871.

Binggeli, André. "Anastase le Sinaïte: "Récits sur le Sinaï "et "Récits utiles à l'âme: Edition, traduction, commentaire." PhD diss., Paris-Sorbonne, 2001.

Bonura, Christopher. "The Roman Empire of the Apocalypse: History, Eschatology, and the Four Kingdoms of Daniel in Late Antiquity, the Early Medieval Middle East, and Byzantium." PhD diss., University of California, Berkeley, 2019.

———. "When Did the Legend of the Last Emperor Originate: A New Look at the Textual Relationship between the *Apocalypse of Pseudo-Methodius* and the *Tiburtine Sibyl*." *Viator* 47, no. 3 (2016): 47–100.

Booth, Phil. *Crisis of Empire: Doctrine and Dissent at the End of Late Antiquity*: Berkeley: University of California Press, 2014.

———. "Gregory and the Greek East." In *A Companion to Gregory the Great*, edited by Bronwen Neil and Matthew J. Dal Santo, 109–31. Leiden: Brill, 2013.

Bori, Caterina. "'All We Know Is What We Have Been Told': Reflections on Emigration and Land as Divine Heritage in the Qur'ān." In *The Coming of the Comforter: When, Where, and to Whom?*, edited by Carlos A. Segovia, 303–42. Piscataway, NJ: Gorgias Press, 2012.

Borrut, Antoine. "The Future of the Past: Historical Writing in Early Islamic Syria and Umayyad Memory." In *Power, Patronage, and Memory in Early Islam: Perspectives on Umayyad Elites*, edited by Alain George and Andrew Marsham, 275–300. Oxford: Oxford University Press, 2018.

Borrut, Antoine, and Fred McGraw Donner, eds. *Christians and Others in the Umayyad State*. Late Antique and Medieval Islamic Near East (LAMINE) 1. Chicago: Oriental Institute of the University of Chicago, 2016.

Bowersock, G. W. *The Crucible of Islam*. Cambridge, MA: Harvard University Press, 2017.

———. *Empires in Collision in Late Antiquity*. The Menahem Stern Jerusalem Lectures. Waltham, MA: Brandeis University Press, 2012.

Brock, Sebastian P. "North Mesopotamia in the Late Seventh Century: Book XV of John Bar Penkāyē's *Riš Mellē*" *Jerusalem Studies in Arabic and Islam* 9 (1987): 51–75.

———. "Syriac Sources for Seventh-Century History." *Byzantine and Modern Greek Studies* 2 (1976): 17–36.

———. "Syriac Views of Emergent Islam." In *Studies on the First Century of Islam*, edited by G. H. A. Juynboll, 9–21, 199–203. Carbondale: Southern Illinois University Press, 1982.

Brooks, E. W., ed. *Chronica minora II*. 2 vols. Corpus Scriptorum Christianorum Orientalium 3–4, Scriptores Syri 3–4. Paris: E Typographeo Reipublicae, 1904.

———. "The Sources of Theophanes and the Syriac Chroniclers." *Byzantinische Zeitschrift* 15 (1906): 578–87.

Brooks, E. W., I. Guidi, and I.-B. Chabot, eds. *Chronica minora III*. 2 vols. Corpus Scriptorum Christianorum Orientalium 5–6, Scriptores Syri 5–6. Paris: E Typographeo Reipublicae, 1905.

Brown, Jonathan A. C. *Misquoting Muhammad: The Challenge and Choices of Interpreting the Prophet's Legacy*. London: Oneworld, 2014.

———. *Muhammad: A Very Short Introduction*. Oxford; New York: Oxford University Press, 2011.

Buhl, Frants. *Das Leben Muhammeds*. Translated by Hans Heinrich Schaeder. Leipzig: Quelle & Meyer, 1930.

Busse, Heribert. "Der Islam und die biblischen Kultstätten." *Der Islam* 42 (1966): 113–43.

———. "Jerusalem in the Story of Muḥammad's Night Journey and Ascension." *Jerusalem Studies in Arabic and Islam* 14 (1991): 1–40.

———. "'Omar b. al-Ḫaṭṭāb in Jerusalem." *Jerusalem Studies in Arabic and Islam* 5 (1984): 73–119.

———. "'Omar's Image as the Conqueror of Jerusalem." *Jerusalem Studies in Arabic and Islam* 8 (1986): 149–68.

———. "The Sanctity of Jerusalem in Islam." *Judaism* 17 (1968): 441–68.

———. "Die ʿUmar-Moschee im östlichen Atrium der Grabeskirche." *Zeitschrift des deutschen Palästina-Vereins* 109 (1993): 73–82.

Caetani, Leone. *Annali dell'Islām*. 10 vols. Milano: U. Hoepli, 1905–26.

Cameron, Averil. "Blaming the Jews: The Seventh-Century Invasions of Palestine in Context." *Travaux et Mémoires* 14 (Mélanges Gilbert Dagron) (2002): 57–78.

Canart, Paul. "Nouveaux récits du moine Anastase." In *Actes du XIIe congrés internationale d'études byzantines*, 2:263–71. Belgrade: Comité Yougoslave des Etudes Byzantines, 1964.

———. "Trois groupes de récits édifiants byzantins." *Byzantion* 36 (1966): 5–25.

Caner, Daniel F. *History and Hagiography from the Late Antique Sinai*. Translated Texts for Historians. Liverpool: Liverpool University Press, 2010.

Caspari, Carl Paul. *Briefe, Abhandlungen und Predigten aus den zwei letzten Jahrhunderten des kirchlichen Alterthums und dem Anfang des Mittelalters. Theils zum ersten, theils zum zweiten Male herausgegeben und mit Anmerkungen und Abhandlungen.* Christiania: Mallingsche Buchdruckerei, 1890.

Chabot, J. B., ed. *Chronicon ad annum Christi 1234 pertinens.* Corpus Scriptorum Christianorum Orientalium 81-82, Scriptores Syri 36-37. Paris: E. Typographeo Reipublicae, 1916-20.

———, ed. *Chronique de Michel le Syrien, patriarche jacobite d'Antioche (1166-99).* 4 vols. Paris: Ernest Leroux, 1899-1910.

———, ed. *Incerti auctoris Chronicon anonymum Pseudo-Dionysianum vulgo dictum.* 2 vols. Corpus Scriptorum Christianorum Orientalium 91, 104, Scriptores Syri 43, 53. Paris: E Typographeo Reipublicae, 1927.

Cheikho, L. [no title]. *Al-Masriq* 15 (1912): 264-80.

Cohen, Gerson D. "Esau as Symbol in Early Medieval Thought." In *Jewish Medieval and Renaissance Studies*, edited by Alexander Altmann, 19-48. Cambridge, MA: Harvard University Press, 1967.

Colin, Gérard. *La version éthiopienne de la vie de Schenoudi.* 2 vols. Corpus Scriptorum Christianorum Orientalium 444-45, Scriptores Aethiopici 75-76. Lovanii: E. Peeters, 1982.

Conrad, Lawrence I. "The Conquest of Arwad: A Source-Critical Study in the Historiography of the Early Medieval Near East." In *The Byzantine and Early Islamic Near East: Papers of the First Workshop on Late Antiquity and Early Islam*, edited by Averil Cameron and Lawrence I. Conrad, 317-401. Princeton, NJ: Darwin Press, 1992.

———. "Theophanes and the Arabic Historical Tradition: Some Indications of Intercultural Transmission." *Byzantinische Forschungen* 15 (1990): 1-44.

———. "Varietas Syriaca: Secular and Scientific Culture in the Christian Communities of Syria after the Arab Conquest." In *After Bardaisan: Studies on Continuity and Change in Syriac Christianity in Honour of Professor Han J. W. Drijvers*, edited by G. J. Reinink and A. C. Klugkist, 85-105. Leuven: Uitgeverij Peeters en Departement Oosterse Studies, 1999.

Conterno, Maria. "'L'abominio della desolazione nel luogo santo': l'ingresso di 'Umar I a Gerusalemme nella Cronografia di Teofane Confessore e in tre cronache siriache." In *Luoghi del desiderio: Gerusalemme medievale*, 9-24. Verona: Cierre, 2010.

———. *La "descrizione dei tempi" all'alba dell'espansione islamica: Un'indagine sulla storiografia greca, siriaca e araba fra VII e VIII secolo.* Millennium-Studien / Millennium Studies 47. Berlin: De Gruyter, 2014.

———. "Theophilos, 'the more likely candidate'? Towards a Reappraisal of the Question of Theophanes' Oriental source(s)." In *Studies in Theophanes*, edited by Marek Jankowiak and Federico Montinaro, 383–400. Paris: Association des Amis du Centre d'Histoire et Civilisation de Byzance, 2015.

Cook, David. "The Beginnings of Islam as an Apocalyptic Movement." *Journal of Millennial Studies*, no. 1 (2001). http://www.bu.edu/mille/publications /winter2001/cook.html.

———. *Studies in Muslim Apocalyptic.* Studies in Late Antiquity and Early Islam 21. Princeton, NJ: Darwin Press, 2002.

Cook, Michael. *Muhammad.* Oxford: Oxford University Press, 1983.

Creswell, K. A. C. *Early Muslim Architecture.* 2nd ed. 2 vols. Vol. 1, *Umayyads, A.D. 622–750.* Oxford: Clarendon Press, 1969.

———. *A Short Account of Early Muslim Architecture.* Harmondsworth, UK: Penguin Books, 1958.

Creswell, K. A. C., and James W. Allen. *A Short Account of Early Muslim Architecture.* Rev. and enl. ed. Aldershot: Scolar, 1989.

Crone, Patricia. "The First-Century Concept of Hiğra." *Arabica* 41 (1994): 352–87.

———. "How Did the Quranic Pagans Make a Living?" *Bulletin of the School of Oriental and African Studies* 68 (2005): 387–99.

———. *Meccan Trade and the Rise of Islam.* Princeton, NJ: Princeton University Press, 1987.

———. "The Religion of the Qur'ānic Pagans: God and the Lesser Deities." *Arabica* 57 (2010): 151–200.

———. *Slaves on Horses: The Evolution of the Islamic Polity.* Cambridge: Cambridge University Press, 1980.

———. "Two Legal Problems Bearing on the Early History of the Qur'ān." *Jerusalem Studies in Arabic and Islam* 18 (1994): 1–37.

———. "What Do We Actually Know about Mohammad?" *openDemocracy* (2006), http://www.opendemocracy.net/faith-europe_islam/mohammed_3866.jsp.

Crone, Patricia, and M. A. Cook. *Hagarism: The Making of the Islamic World.* Cambridge: Cambridge University Press, 1977.

Czeglédy, K. "Monographs on Syriac and Muhammadan Sources in the Literary Remains of M. Kmosko." *Acta Orientalia* 4 (1954): 19–91.

Dagron, Gilbert, and Vincent Déroche. "Juifs et chrétiens dans l'Orient du VIIe siècle." *Travaux et mémoires* 11 (1991): 17–273.

———. *Juifs et chrétiens en Orient byzantin.* Paris: Association des amis du Centre d'histoire et civilisation de Byzance: Ouvrage publié avec le concours de la Foundation Ebersolt du Collège de France, 2010.

Davis, Stephen J. *The Early Coptic Papacy: The Egyptian Church and Its Leadership in Late Antiquity*. Popes of Egypt 1. Cairo: American University in Cairo Press, 2004.

de Boor, Carolus, ed. *Theophanis chronographia*. 2 vols. Leipzig: Teubner, 1883-85.

de Goeje, Michael Jan, ed. *Mémoire sur la conquête de la Syrie*. 2nd ed. Leiden: E. J. Brill, 1900.

de Lange, N. R. M. "Jewish Attitudes to the Roman Empire." In *Imperialism in the Ancient World*, edited by C. R. Whittaker and P. D. A. Garnsey, 255-82. Cambridge: Cambridge University Press, 1979.

de Prémare, Alfred-Louis. "'Abd al-Malik b. Marwān and the Process of the Qurʾān's Composition." In *The Hidden Origins of Islam: New Research into Its Early History*, edited by Karl-Heinz Ohlig and Gerd-R. Puin, 189-221. Amherst, NY: Prometheus Books, 2010.

———. "'Abd al-Malik b. Marwān et le Processus de Constitution du Coran." In *Die dunklen Anfänge: Neue Forschungen zur Entstehung und frühen Geschichte des Islam*, edited by Karl-Heinz Ohlig and Gerd-R. Puin, 179-210. Berlin: Verlag Hans Schiler, 2005.

———. *Aux origines du Coran: Questions d'hier, approches d'aujourd'hui*, L'Islam en débats. Paris: Téraèdre, 2004.

De Ste. Croix, G. E. M. *Christian Persecution, Martyrdom, and Orthodoxy*. Oxford: Oxford University Press, 2006.

Debié, Muriel. "Theophanes' 'Oriental Source': What Can We Learn from Syriac Historiography?" In *Studies in Theophanes*, edited by Marek Jankowiak and Federico Montinaro, 365-82. Paris: Association des Amis du Centre d'Histoire et Civilisation de Byzance, 2015.

Di Berardino, Angelo, ed. *Patrology: The Eastern Fathers from the Council of Chalcedon (451) to John of Damascus (750)*. Cambridge: James Clarke & Co., 2006.

Di Segni, Leah. "Christian Epigraphy in the Holy Land: New Discoveries." *Aram* 15 (2003): 247-67.

———. "A Greek Inscription in the Kathisma Church." In *One Land—Many Cultures: Archaeological Studies in Honor of Stanislao Loffreda, O.F.M.*, edited by G. C. Bottini, L. D. Segni and D. Chrupcala, 187-88. Jerusalem: Franciscan Printing Press, 2003.

Digeser, Elizabeth Depalma. "Persecution and the Art of Writing between the Lines: *De vita beata*, Lactantius, and the Great Persecution." *Revue belge de Philologie et d'Histoire* (2014): 167-85.

Donner, Fred M. *The Early Islamic Conquests*. Princeton, NJ: Princeton University Press, 1981.

———. "The Formation of the Islamic State." *Journal of the American Oriental Society* 106 (1986): 283-96.

———. "From Believers to Muslims: Confessional Self-Identity in the Early Islamic Community." *al-Abḥāth* 50-51 (2002): 9-53.

———. *Muhammad and the Believers: At the Origins of Islam.* Cambridge, MA: Harvard University Press, 2010.

———. *Narratives of Islamic Origins: The Beginnings of Islamic Historical Writing.* Studies in Late Antiquity and Early Islam, 14. Princeton, NJ: Darwin Press, 1998.

———. "La question du messianisme dans l'islam primitif." In *Mahdisme et millénarisme en Islam*, edited by Mercedes García-Arenal, 17-27. Aix-en-Provence: Édisud, 2001.

———. "Review of Robert Hoyland, *In God's Path*." *Al-ʿUṣūr al-Wusṭā* (2015): 134-40.

Duval, Rubens. *Išoʿyahb Patriarchae III Liber epistularum.* Corpus Scriptorum Christianorum Orientalium 11-12. Paris: E Typographeo Reipublicae, 1904.

Dye, Guillaume. "Le corpus coranique: Contexte, chronologie, composition, canonisation." In *Le Coran des historiens*, edited by Mohammad Ali Amir-Moezzi and Guillaume Dye, vol. 1, 733-846. Paris: Les éditions du Cerf, 2019.

———. "Le corpus coranique: Questions autour de sa canonisation." In *Le Coran des historiens*, edited by Mohammad Ali Amir-Moezzi and Guillaume Dye, vol. 1, 847-918. Paris: Les éditions du Cerf, 2019.

———. "Mapping the Sources of the Qur'anic Jesus." In *The Study of Islamic Origins: New Perspectives and Contexts*, edited by Mette Bjerregaard Mortensen, Guillaume Dye, Isaac Oliver and Tommaso Tesei. Berlin: Walter de Gruyter, 2020.

———. "Pourquoi et comment se fait un texte canonique? Quelques réflexions sur l'histoire du Coran." In *Hérésies: Une construction d'identités religieuses*, edited by G. Dye, A. Van Rompaey and C. Brouwer, 55-104. Brussels: Editions de l'Université de Bruxelles, 2015.

———. "The Qurʾanic Mary and the Chronology of the Qurʾān." In *Early Islam: The Sectarian Milieu of Late Antiquity?*, edited by Guillaume Dye. Chicago: University of Chicago Press, 2020.

Dye, Guillaume, and Julien Decharneux. "Sourate 10: Yūnus (Jonas)." In *Le Coran des historiens*, edited by Mohammad Ali Amir-Moezzi and Guillaume Dye, vol. 2, 419-82. Paris: Les éditions du Cerf, 2019.

Elad, Amikam. *Medieval Jerusalem and Islamic Worship: Holy Places, Ceremonies, Pilgrimage*. Islamic History and Civilization. Studies and Texts 8. Leiden: E. J. Brill, 1995.

———. "Pilgrims and Pilgrimage to Jerusalem during the Early Muslim Period." In *Jerusalem: Its Sanctity and Centrality to Judaism, Christianity, and Islam*, edited by Lee I. Levine, 300–14. New York: Continuum, 1999.

———. "Why Did ʿAbd al-Malik Build the Dome of the Rock? A Re-examination of the Muslim Sources." In *Bayt al-Maqdis: ʿAbd al-Malik's Jerusalem*, edited by Julian Raby and Jeremy Johns, 33–58. Oxford: Oxford University Press, 1992.

Even-Shmuel, Yehuda, ed. *Midreshe geʾulah*. Rev. ed. Jerusalem: Mosad Byaliḳ ʿal yede "Masadah," 1953.

Ezeants', Karapet, ed. Պատմութիւն Ղեւոնդեայ մեծի Վարդապետի Հայոց [*Patmut'iwn Ghewondeay Metsi Vardapeti Hayots'*]. 2nd ed. St. Petersburg: I Tparani I.N. Skorokhodovi, 1887.

Firestone, Reuven. "Disparity and Resolution in the Qurʾānic Teachings on War: A Reevaluation of a Tradition's Problems." *Journal of Near Eastern Studies* 56 (1997): 1–19.

———. *Jihad: The Origin of Holy War in Islam*. New York: Oxford University Press, 1999.

Flusin, Bernard. "Démons et Sarrasins: L'auteur et le propos des Diègèmata Stèriktiká d'Anastase le Sinaïte." *Travaux et mémoires* 11 (1991): 381–409.

———. "L'esplanade du Temple à l'arrivée des arabes d'après deux récits byzantins." In *Bayt al-Maqdis: ʿAbd al-Malik's Jerusalem*, edited by Julian Raby and Jeremy Johns, 17–31. Oxford: Oxford University Press, 1992.

Foss, Clive. *Arab-Byzantine Coins: An Introduction with a Catalogue of the Dumbarton Oaks Collection*. Washington, DC: Dumbarton Oaks Research Library and Collection, 2008.

———. "A Syrian Coinage of Muʾawiya?" *Revue Numismatique* 6 (2002): 353–65.

Frankfurter, David. *Elijah in Upper Egypt: The Apocalypse of Elijah and Early Egyptian Christianity*. Studies in Antiquity and Christianity. Minneapolis: Fortress Press, 1993.

Friedmann, Yohanan. "Finality of Prophethood in Sunnī Islam." *Jerusalem Studies in Arabic and Islam* 7 (1986): 177–215.

Garitte, Gérard, "Histoires édifiantes géorgienne." *Byzantion* 36 (1966): 396–423.

———, ed. *La prise de Jérusalem par les Perses en 614*. 2 vols. Corpus Scriptorum Christianorum Orientalium, 202–3, Scriptores Iberici, 11–12. Louvain: Secrétariat du CorpusSCO, 1960.

———. "La version géorgienne du Pré Spirituel." In *Mélanges Eugène Tisserant*, 171-85. Vatican: Biblioteca Apostolica Vaticana, 1964.

Garstad, Benjamin. *Apocalypse of Pseudo-Methodius: An Alexandrian World Chronicle*. Dumbarton Oaks Medieval Library 14. Cambridge, MA: Harvard University Press, 2012.

Geerard, Maurice. *Clavis Patrum Graecorum*. 5 vols. Corpus Christianorum. Turnhout, Belgium: Brepols, 1974.

Geerard, Maurice, and Jacques Noret. *Clavis Patrum Graecorum*. 3 vols. Corpus Christianorum. Turnhout, Belgium: Brepols, 2003.

Geerard, Maurice, Jacques Noret, F. Glorie, and Jean-Pierre Desmet. *Clavis Patrum Graecorum: Supplementum*. Corpus Christianorum. Turnhout, Belgium: Brepols, 1998.

Geyer, Paul. *Itinera hierosolymitana saecvli IIII-VIII*. Corpus Scriptorum Ecclesiasticorum Latinorum 39. Vienna: F. Tempsky, 1898.

Gil, Moshe. *A History of Palestine, 634-1099*. Translated by Ethel Broido. New York: Cambridge University Press, 1992.

Goitein, S. D. "The Historical Background of the Erection of the Dome of the Rock." *Journal of the American Oriental Society* 70 (1950): 104-8.

———. "The Sanctity of Jerusalem and Palestine in Early Islam." In *Studies in Islamic History and Institutions*, 135-48. Leiden: E. J. Brill, 1966.

———. "The Sanctity of Palestine in Moslem Piety." *Bulletin of the Jewish Palestine Exploration Society* 12 (1945-46): 120-26 (in Hebrew).

Goitein, S. D., and Oleg Grabar. "al-Ḳuds." In *Encyclopaedia of Islam*, 322-44. Leiden: Brill, 1960-2005.

Goldziher, Ignác. *Muslim Studies*. Translated by C. R. Barber and S. M. Stern. Edited by S. M. Stern. 2 vols. London: Allen & Unwin, 1967-71.

Grabar, Oleg. "The Meaning of the Dome of the Rock in Jerusalem." In *Jerusalem, Volume IV: Constructing the Study of Islamic Art*, 143-58. Hampshire, UK: Ashgate, 2005.

———. "The Umayyad Dome of the Rock in Jerusalem." *Ars Orientalis* 3 (1959): 33-62.

Greenwood, Tim W. "Sasanian Echoes and Apocalyptic Expectations: A Reevaluation of the Armenian History Attributed to Sebeos." *Le Muséon* 115 (2003): 323-97.

Griffith, Sidney H. "Anastasios of Sinai, the Hodegos, and the Muslims." *Greek Orthodox Theological Review* 32 (1987): 341-58.

———. *The Bible in Arabic: The Scriptures of the "People of the Book" in the Language of Islam*. Princeton, NJ: Princeton University Press, 2013.

Guidi, Ignazio, ed. *Chronica minora I*. 2 vols. Corpus Scriptorum Christianorum Orientalium 1-2, Scriptores Syri 1-2. Paris: E Typographeo Reipublicae, 1903.

Guillaume, Alfred, trans. *The Life of Muhammad*. London: Oxford University Press, 1955.

Haldon, John. "The Works of Anastasius of Sinai: A Key Source for the History of Seventh-Century East Mediterranean Society and Belief." In *The Byzantine and Early Islamic Near East, Volume I: Problems in the Literary Source Material*, edited by Averil Cameron and Lawrence I. Conrad, 107-47. Princeton, NJ: Darwin, 1992.

Haldon, John F. *Warfare, State, and Society in the Byzantine World 565-1204*. Warfare and History. London: University College London Press, 1999.

Harrak, Amir. *The Acts of Mār Māri the Apostle*. Writings from the Greco-Roman World 11. Atlanta: Society of Biblical Literature, 2005.

Hawting, Gerald R. *The First Dynasty of Islam: The Umayyad Caliphate AD 661-750*. 2nd ed. London: Routledge, 2000.

———. "The ḥajj in the Second Civil War." In *Golden Roads: Migration, Pilgrimage and Travel in Mediaeval and Modern Islam*, edited by Ian Richard Netton, 31-42. Richmond, UK: Curzon, 1993.

———. *The Idea of Idolatry and the Emergence of Islam: From Polemic to History*. Cambridge Studies in Islamic Civilization. Cambridge: Cambridge University Press, 1999.

———. "The Origins of the Muslim Sanctuary at Mecca." In *Studies on the First Century of Islamic Society*, edited by G. H. A. Juynboll, 23-47. Carbondale: Southern Illinois University Press, 1982.

———. "The Umayyads and the Ḥijāz." *Proceedings of the Seminar for Arabian Studies* 2 (1972): 39-46.

Healey, J. F. "The Christians of Qatar in the 7th Century A.D." In *Studies in Honour of Clifford Edmund Bosworth, Volume I, Hunter of the East: Arabic and Semitic Studies*, edited by I. Netton, 222-37. Leiden: Brill, 2000.

———. "The Patriarch Ishoʿyahb III and the Christians of Qatar in the First Islamic Century." In *The Christian Heritage of Iraq*, edited by E. C. D. Hunter, 1-9. Piscataway, NJ: Gorgias Press, 2009.

Henry, René, ed. *Photius: Bibliothèque*. 9 vols. Paris: Les Belles lettres, 1959-91.

Himmelfarb, Martha. *Jewish Messiahs in a Christian Empire: A History of the Book of Zerubbabel*. Cambridge, MA: Harvard University Press, 2017.

———., trans. "Sefer Zerubbabel." In *Rabbinic Fantasies: Imaginative Narratives from Classical Hebrew Literature*, edited by David Stern and Mark Jay Mirsky, 67-90. Philadelphia: The Jewish Publication Society, 1990.

Hirschberg, J. W. "The Sources of Moslem Tradition Concerning Jerusalem." *Rocznik Orientalistyczny* 17 (1951-52): 314-50.

Hodgson, Marshall G. S. *The Venture of Islam: Conscience and History in a World Civilization*. 3 vols. Vol. 1, *The Classical Age of Islam*. Chicago: University of Chicago Press, 1974.

Howard-Johnston, James. *Witnesses to a World Crisis: Historians and Histories of the Middle East in the Seventh Century*. Oxford: Oxford University Press, 2010.

Hoyland, Robert G. *Arabia and the Arabs: From the Bronze Age to the Coming of Islam*. London: Routledge, 2001.

———. "The Content and Context of Early Arabic Inscriptions." *Jerusalem Studies in Arabic and Islam* 21 (1997): 77-102.

———. *In God's Path: The Arab Conquests and the Creation of an Islamic Empire*: Oxford University Press, 2015.

———. "New Documentary Texts and the Early Islamic State." *Bulletin of the School of Oriental and African Studies* 69 (2006): 395-416.

———. "Reflections on the Identity of the Arabian Conquerors of the Seventh-Century Middle East." *Al-ʿUṣūr al-Wusṭā* 25 (2017): 113-40.

———. "Sebeos, the Jews, and the Rise of Islam." *Studies in Muslim-Jewish Relations* 2 (1995): 89-102.

———. *Seeing Islam as Others Saw It: A Survey and Evaluation of Christian, Jewish and Zoroastrian Writings on Early Islam*. Studies in Late Antiquity and Early Islam 13. Princeton, NJ: Darwin Press, 1997.

———. *Theophilus of Edessa's Chronicle and the Circulation of Historical Knowledge in Late Antiquity and Early Islam*. Translated Texts for Historians 57. Liverpool: Liverpool University Press, 2011.

Hoyland, Robert G., and Sarah Waidler. "Adomnán's De Locis Sanctis and the Seventh-Century Near East." *The English Historical Review* 129, no. 539 (2014): 787-807.

Hübschmann, Heinrich. *Armenische Grammatik*. Vol. 1, *Armenische Etymologie*. Bibliothek indogermanischer Grammatiken 6. Leipzig: Breitkopf & Härtel, 1897.

Humphreys, R. Stephen, trans. *The History of al-Ṭabarī (Ta'rīkh al-rusul wa'l-mulūk), Volume 15: The Crisis of the Early Caliphate*. Albany: State University of New York Press, 1990.

———. *Muʿawiya Ibn Abi Sufyan: From Arabia to Empire*. Oxford: Oneworld, 2006.

Ibn Hishām, ʿAbd al-Malik. *Kitāb sīrat Rasūl Allāh [Das leben Muhammed's nach Muhammed ibn Ishâk bearbeitet von Abd el-Malik ibn Hischâm]*. Edited by Ferdinand Wüstenfeld. 2 vols. Göttingen: Dieterichsche Universitäts-Buchhandlung, 1858-60.

Ibn Saʿd, Muḥammad. *Ṭabaqāt* [*Biographien Muhammeds, seiner Gefährten und der späteren Träger des Islams, bis zum Jahre 230 der Flucht*]. Edited by E. Sachau. 9 vols. Leiden: E. J. Brill, 1904-28.

Jacobs, Andrew S. "Gender, Conversion, and the End of Empire in the Teaching of Jacob, Newly Baptized." *Journal of Early Christian Studies* 28 (2020): forthcoming.

Jeffery, Arthur. "Ghevond's Text of the Correspondence between ʿUmar II and Leo III." *Harvard Theological Review* 37 (1944): 269-332.

Jellinek, Adolph, ed. *Bet ha-midrash: Sammlung kleiner Midraschim und vermischter Abhandlungen aus der ältern jüdischen Literatur.* 6 vols. Leipzig: F. Nies, 1853-77.

al-Kaʿbī, Naṣīr. *A Short Chronicle on the End of the Sasanian Empire and Early Islam 590-660 A.D.* Gorgias Chronicles of Late Antiquity. Piscataway, NJ: Gorgias Press, 2016.

Kaegi, Walter E. *Byzantium and the Early Islamic Conquests.* Cambridge: Cambridge University Press, 1992.

———. *Heraclius, Emperor of Byzantium.* Cambridge: Cambridge University Press, 2003.

Kaplony, Andreas. *The Ḥaram of Jerusalem, 324-1099: Temple, Friday Mosque, Area of Spiritual Power.* Stuttgart: Franz Steiner Verlag, 2002.

Kekeliże, Korneli. "Житіе Петра Новаго, мученика Капетолійскаго." Христіанскій Востокъ [*Khristīanskiĭ Vostok*] 4 (1915): 1-71.

Kessler, C. "ʿAbd al-Malik's Inscription in the Dome of the Rock: A Reconsideration." *Journal of the Royal Asiatic Society* n. s. 1 (1970): 2-14.

al-Khaṭīb, ʿAbd al-Laṭīf Muḥammad, ed. *Muʿjam al-qirāʾāt.* Damascus: Dār Saʿd al-Dīn, 2010.

Kister, M. J. "... *illā bi-ḥaqqihi* ... : A Study of an Early *Ḥadīth*" *Jerusalem Studies in Arabic and Islam* 5 (1984): 33-52.

Lamy, Thomas Joseph, ed. *Sancti Ephraem Syri hymni et sermones.* 4 vols. Mechliniæ: H. Dessain, 1882-1902.

Lecker, Michael. *The "Constitution of Medina": Muhammad's First Legal Document.* Studies in Late Antiquity and Early Islam 23. Princeton, NJ: Darwin Press, 2004.

LeCoz, Raymond, ed. *Johannes Damascenus: Écrits sur l'Islam.* Sources chrétiennes 383. Paris: Éd. du Cerf, 1992.

Lévi, Israel. "L'Apocalypse de Zorobabel." *Revue des Études Juives* 68; 69; 71 (1914; 1919; 1920): 129-60; 108-21; 57-65.

Lewis, Bernard. "An Apocalyptic Vision of Islamic History." *Bulletin of the School of Oriental and African Studies* 13 (1950): 308-38.

Lindstedt, Ilkka. "The Last Roman Emperor, the Mahdī, and Jerusalem." In *Understanding the Spiritual Meaning of Jerusalem in Three Abrahamic Religions*, edited by Antti Laato, 205-25. Leiden: Brill, 2019.

———. "*Muhājirūn* as a Name for the First/Seventh Century Muslims." *Journal of Near Eastern Studies* 74 (2015): 67-73.

———. "Who Is In, Who Is Out? Early Muslim Identity through Epigraphy and Theory." *Jerusalem Studies in Arabic and Islam* 46 (2019): 147-246.

Lings, Martin. *Muhammad: His Life Based on the Earliest Sources*. Rochester, VT: Inner Traditions International, 1983.

Livne-Kafri, Ofer. "Some Notes on the Muslim Apocalyptic Tradition." *Quaderni di Studi Arabi* 17 (1999): 71-94.

Louth, Andrew. "St John Damascene: Preacher and Poet." In *Preacher and Audience: Studies in Early Christian and Byzantine Homiletics*, edited by Pauline Allen and Mary Cunningham, 247-66. Leiden: Brill, 1998.

———. *St John Damascene: Tradition and Originality in Byzantine Theology*. Oxford Early Christian Studies. Oxford: Oxford University Press, 2002.

Lubomierski, Nina. "The Coptic Life of Shenoute." In *Christianity and Monasticism in Upper Egypt*, edited by Gawdat Gabra and Hany N Takla, 91-98. Cairo: The American University in Cairo Press, 2008.

———. *Die Vita Sinuthii: Form- und Überlieferungsgeschichte der hagiographischen Texte über Schenute den Archimandriten*. Studien und Texte zu Antike und Christentum 45. Tübingen: Mohr Siebeck, 2007.

———. "The Vita Sinuthii (The Life of Shenoute): Panegyric or Biography?" *Studia Patristica* 39 (2006): 417-21.

———. "Towards a Better Understanding of the So-Called 'Vita Sinuthii.'" In *Actes du huitième Congrès international d'études coptes: Paris, 28 juin-3 juillet 2004*, edited by Nathalie Bosson and Anne Bouvarel-Boud'hors, 527-35. Leuven: Peeters, 2007.

Marsham, Andrew. "The Architecture of Allegiance in Early Islamic Late Antiquity: The Accession of Muʿāwiya in Jerusalem, ca. 661 CE." In *Court Ceremonies and Rituals of Power in Byzantium and the Medieval Mediterranean: Comparative Perspectives*, edited by Alexander Beihammer, Stavroula Constantinou and Maria Parani, 87-112. Leiden: Brill, 2013.

McCormick, Michael. *Origins of the European Economy: Communications and Commerce A.D. 300–900.* Cambridge: Cambridge University Press, 2001.

McDowell, Gavin. "L'histoire sainte dans l'Antiquité tardive: Les *Pirqé de-Rabbi Eliézer* et leur relation avec le *Livre des Jubilés* et la *Caverne des trésors*." PhD diss., École Pratique des Hautes Études, 2017.

Metcalf, William E. "Three Seventh-Century Byzantine Gold Hoards." *American Numismatic Society Museum Notes* 25 (1980): 87–108.

Migne, J. P., ed. *Patrologiae cursus completus, Series graeca.*161 vols. Paris: Excecudebatur et venit apud J.-P. Migne, 1857.

Milik, Józef Tadeusz. "Notes d'épigraphie et de topographie palestiniennes." *Revue Biblique* 67 (1960): 354–67.

———. *La topographie de Jérusalem vers la fin de l'époque byzantine.* Beirut: Imprimerie Catholique, 1961.

Mingana, Alphonse. *Sources syriaques.* Vol. 1. Leipzig: Harrassowitz, 1908.

Morony, Michael G. *Iraq after the Muslim Conquest.* Princeton, NJ: Princeton University Press, 1984.

Moschus, John. *The Spiritual Meadow.* Translated by John Wortley. Kalamazoo, MI: Cistercian Publications, 1992.

Moss, Candida R. "The Discourse of Voluntary Martyrdom: Ancient and Modern." *Church History* 81 (2012): 531–51.

Motzki, Harald. "The Collection of the Qurʾān: A Reconsideration of Western Views in Light of Recent Methodological Developments." *Der Islam* 78 (2001): 1–34.

Munt, Harry. "'No Two Religions': Non-Muslims in the Early Islamic Ḥijāz." *Bulletin of the School of Oriental and African Studies* 78, no. 2 (2015): 249–69.

Murphy-O'Connor, Jerome, O.P. *The Holy Land: An Oxford Archaeological Guide from Earliest Times to 1700.* 4th ed. Oxford Archaeological Guides. Oxford: Oxford University Press, 1998.

Nau, François. "Maronites, Mazonites et Maranites." *Revue de l'Orient Chrétien* 9 (1904): 268–76.

———. "Les récits inédits du moine Anastase. Contribution à l'histoire du Sinai au commencement du VIIe siècle." *Revue de l'Institut Catholique de Paris* (1902): 1–26, 110–51.

———. "Le texte grec des récits du moine Anastase sur les saints pères du Sinai." *Oriens Christianus* 2 (1902): 58–89.

———. "Le texte grec des récits utiles à l'âme d'Anastase." *Oriens Christianus* 3 (1903): 56–90.

Nautin, Pierre. "L'auteur de la 'Chronique Anonyme de Guidi:' Elie de Merw." *Revue de l'histoire des religions* 199 (1982): 303-14.

Nees, Lawrence. *Perspectives on Early Islamic Art in Jerusalem*. Arts and Archaeology of the Islamic World 5. Leiden: Brill, 2016.

Neuwirth, Angelika. "Erste Qibla—Fernstes Masǧid? Jerusalem im Horizont des historischen Muḥammad." In *Zion, Ort der Begegnung: Festschrift für Laurentius Klein zur Vollendung des 65. Lebensjahres*, edited by Ferdinand Hahn, Frank-Lothar Hossfeld, Hans Jorissen and Angelika Neuwirth, 227-70. Bodenheim: Athenäum, Hahn, Hanstein, 1993.

Newman, H. I. "Dating Sefer Zerubavel: Dehistoricizing and Rehistoricizing a Jewish Apocalypse of Late Antiquity." *Adamantius* 19 (2013): 324-36.

Nöldeke, Theodor. "Review of Thomas Joseph Lamy, *Sancti Ephraem Syri hymni et sermones*, vol. III." *Wiener Zeitschrift für die Kunde des Morgenlandes* 4 (1890): 245-51.

———. "Zur Geschichte der Araber im 1. Jahrh. d.H. aus syrischen Quellen." *Zeitschrift der Deutschen Morgenländischen Gesellschaft* 29 (1875): 76-98.

Nöldeke, Theodor, and Friedrich Schwally. *Geschichte des Qorāns*. 2nd ed. 2 vols. Leipzig: Dieterich, 1909-19.

Nöldeke, Theodor, Friedrich Schwally, Gotthelf Bergsträsser, and O. Pretzl. *The History of the Qur'ān*. Translated by Wolfgang Behn, Texts and Studies on the Qur'ān 8. Leiden: Brill, 2013.

Olster, David M. *Roman Defeat, Christian Response, and the Literary Construction of the Jew*. Middle Ages Series. Philadelphia: University of Pennsylvania Press, 1994.

Palmer, Andrew. "Une chronique syriaque contemporaine de la conquête arabe." In *La Syrie de Byzance à l'Islam VIIe-VIIIe siècles: Actes du colloque interational Lyon—Maison de l'Orient méditerranéen, Paris—Institut du monde arabe, 11-15 Septembre 1990*, edited by Pierre Canivet and Jean-Paul Rey-Coquais, 31-46. Damascus: Institut français de Damas, 1992.

———. *The Seventh Century in West-Syrian Chronicles*. Translated Texts for Historians 15. Liverpool: Liverpool University Press, 1993.

Papaconstantinou, Arietta. "Between *Umma* and *Dhimma*: The Christians of the Middle East under the Umayyads." *Annales Islamologiques* 42 (2008): 127-56.

Papadopoulos-Kerameus, Athanasios. Ἀνάλεκτα Ἱεροσολυμιτικῆς σταχυολογίας (*Analekta hierosolymitikēs stachyologias*) 5. St. Petersburg: Kirsbaum, 1898.

Papoutsakis, Emmanuel. *Vicarious Kingship: A Theme in Syriac Political Theology in Late Antiquity*. Studien und Texte zu Antike und Christentum 100. Tübingen: Mohr Siebeck, 2017.

Patterson, Stephen J. *The Lost Way: How Two Forgotten Gospels Are Rewriting the Story of Christian Origins*. San Francisco: HarperOne, 2014.

Penn, Michael Philip. *Envisioning Islam: Syriac Christians and the Early Muslim World*, Divinations: Rereading Late Ancient Religion. Philadelphia: University of Pennsylvania Press, 2015.

———. *When Christians First Met Muslims: A Sourcebook of the Earliest Syriac Writings on Islam*. Oakland: University of California Press, 2015.

Périer, Augustin. "Lettre de Pisuntios, évêque de Qeft, à ses fidèles." *Revue de l'Orient Chrétien* 19 (1914).

Peters, F. E. *Jerusalem and Mecca: The Typology of the Holy City in the Near East*. New York University Studies in Near Eastern Civilization 11. New York: New York University Press, 1986.

———. *Jesus and Muhammad: Parallel Tracks, Parallel Lives*. New York: Oxford University Press, 2011.

———. *Muhammad and the Origins of Islam*. Albany: State University of New York Press, 1994.

Pohlmann, Karl-Friedrich. *Die Entstehung des Korans: Neue Erkenntnisse aus Sicht der historisch-kritischen Bibelwissenschaft*. 2. unveränd. Aufl. ed, WBG— Wissen verbindet. Darmstadt: WBG (Wiss. Buchges.), 2013.

Ponsoye, Emmanuel, and Jean-Claude Larchet, eds. *Saint Maxime le Confesseur: Lettres*. Paris: Éd. du Cerf, 1998.

Powers, David S. *Muḥammad Is Not the Father of Any of Your Men: The Making of the Last Prophet*. Philadelphia: University of Pennsylvania Press, 2009.

———. *Zayd: The Little Known Story of Muḥammad's Adopted Son*. Philadelphia: University of Pennsylvania Press, 2014.

Pringle, Denys. *The Churches of the Crusader Kingdom of Jerusalem: A Corpus*. 3 vols. Cambridge: Cambridge University Press, 1993–2007.

Rahman, Fazlur. "Approaches to Islam in Religious Studies: Review Essay." In *Approaches to Islam in Religious Studies*, edited by Richard C. Martin, 189–202. Tucson: University of Arizona Press, 1985.

———. *Major Themes of the Qur'ān*. Minneapolis: Bibliotheca Islamica, 1980.

Reeves, John C. *Heralds of that Good Realm: Syro-Mesopotamian Gnosis and Jewish Traditions*. Nag Hammadi and Manichaean Studies 41. Leiden: Brill, 1996.

———. *Trajectories in Near Eastern Apocalyptic: A Postrabbinic Jewish Apocalypse Reader*. Leiden: Brill, 2006.

Reinink, Gerrit J. "Pseudo-Ephraems 'Rede über das Ende' und die syrische eschatologische Literatur des siebten Jahrhunderts." *Aram* 5 (1993): 437–63.

———. "Ps.-Methodius: A Concept of History in Response to the Rise of Islam." In *The Byzantine and Early Islamic Near East: Papers of the First Workshop on Late Antiquity and Early Islam*, edited by Averil Cameron and Lawrence I. Conrad, 149–87. Princeton, NJ: Darwin Press, 1992.

———, ed. *Die Syrische Apokalypse des Pseudo-Methodius*. 2 vols. Corpus Scriptorum Christianorum Orientalium 540–41, Scriptores Syri 220–21. Louvain: Peeters, 1993.

Richard, Marcel, and Joseph A. Munitiz, eds. *Anastasii Sinaitae: Quaestiones et responsiones*. Corpus Christianorum. Series Graeca 59. Turnhout, Belgium: Brepols, 2006.

Robin, Christian Julien. "Arabia and Ethiopia." In *The Oxford Handbook of Late Antiquity*, edited by Scott F. Johnson, 247–332. New York: Oxford University Press, 2012.

Robinson, Chase F. ʿAbd al-Malik. Makers of the Muslim World. Oxford: Oneworld, 2005.

Rosen-Ayalon, Myriam. *The Early Islamic Monuments of al-Ḥaram al-Sharīf: An Iconographic Study*. Qedem 28. Jerusalem: Institute of Archaeology, The Hebrew University of Jerusalem, 1989.

Rothenberg, Beno. "Early Islamic Copper Smelting and Worship at Beer Orah." *Institute for Archaeo-Metallurgical Studies* 12 (1988): 1–4.

———. *Timna: Valley of the Biblical Copper Mines*. New Aspects of Antiquity. London: Thames and Hudson, 1972.

Rubin, Uri. *Between Bible and Qurʾān: The Children of Israel and the Islamic Self-Image*. Studies in Late Antiquity and Early Islam 17. Princeton, NJ: Darwin Press, 1999.

Sackur, Ernst. *Sibyllinische Texte und Forschungen: Pseudomethodius, Adso und die tiburtinische Sibylle*. Halle, Germany: M. Niemeyer, 1898.

Safi, Omid. *Memories of Muhammad: Why the Prophet Matters*. New York: HarperCollins, 2009.

Sahner, Christian C. *Christian Martyrs under Islam: Religious Violence and the Making of the Muslim World*. Princeton, NJ: Princeton University Press, 2018.

al-Samʿānī, Mikhāʾīl. *Biographie de Saint Jean Damascène: Texte original arabe*. Edited by Constantin Bacha. Harissa: Imprimerie Grecque Melchite de Saint Paul, 1912.

Schacht, Joseph. *The Origins of Muhammadan Jurisprudence*. Oxford: Clarendon Press, 1950.

Schadler, Peter. *John of Damascus and Islam: Christian Heresiology and the Intellectual Background to Earliest Christian-Muslim Relations*. Leiden: Brill, 2018.

Scher, Addai, ed. *Histoire nestorienne (Chronique de Séert)*. 4 vols. Patrologia Orientalis 4, 5, 7, 13. Paris: Firmin-Didot, 1910–19.

Schick, Robert. *The Christian Communities of Palestine from Byzantine to Islamic Rule: A Historical and Archaeological Study*. Studies in Late Antiquity and Early Islam 2. Princeton, NJ: Darwin Press, 1995.

Segovia, Carlos A. "Sourate 3: Āl ʿImrān (La famille de ʿImrān)." In *Le Coran des historiens*, edited by Mohammad Ali Amir-Moezzi and Guillaume Dye, vol. 2, 131–68. Paris: Les éditions du Cerf, 2019.

Serjeant, R. B. "Review of John Wansbrough, *Quranic Studies: Sources and Methods of Scriptural Interpretation* and Patricia Crone and Michael Cook, *Hagarism: The Making of the Islamic World*." *Journal of the Royal Asiatic Society* (1978): 76–79.

———. "The *Sunnah*, *Jāmiʿah*, Pacts with the Yathrib Jews, and the *Taḥarīm* of Yathrib: Analysis and Translation of the Documents Comprised in the So-called 'Constitution of Medina.'" *Bulletin of the School of Oriental and African Studies* 41 (1978): 1–42.

Shahnazariantsʿ, Karapet. Սոյսէս Կաղանկատուացի: Պատմութիւն Աղուանից (*Movsēs Kaghankatuatsʿi: Patmutʿiwn Aghuanits*). 2 vols. Badmutʿiwn Aghuanitsʿ. Paris: I Gortsatan K.V.Shahnazarean, 1860.

Sharon, Moshe. "The Birth of Islam in the Holy Land." In *Pillars of Smoke and Fire: The Holy Land in History and Thought*, edited by Moshe Sharon, 225–35. Johannesburg: Southern Book Publishers, 1988.

———. "Praises of Jerusalem as a Source for the Early History of Islam." *Bibliotheca orientalis* 49 (1992): 55–67.

———. "The Umayyads as *Ahl al-Bayt*." *Jerusalem Studies in Arabic and Islam* 14 (1991): 115–52.

Sharon, Moshe, Uzi Avner, and Dov Nahlieli. "An Early Islamic Mosque Near Beʾer Ora in the Southern Negev: Possible Evidence for an Early Eastern *Qiblah*?" ʿAtiqot 30 (1996): 107–14.

Sheicho, L. "Eine verlorene Homilie des heiligen Anastasius von Sinai." *Theologisch-praktische Quartalschrift* 65 (1912): 780–95.

Sherwood, Polycarp. *An Annotated Date-List of the Works of Maximus the Confessor*. Studia Anselmiana philosophica theologica 30. Rome: "Orbis Catholicus," Herder, 1952.

Shoemaker, Stephen J. "Anastasius of Sinai and the Beginnings of Islam." *Journal of Orthodox Christian Studies* 1 (2018): 137–54.

———. *The Apocalypse of Empire: Imperial Eschatology in Late Antiquity and Early Islam.* Divinations: Rereading Late Ancient Religion. Philadelphia: University of Pennsylvania Press, 2018.

———. *The Death of a Prophet: The End of Muhammad's Life and the Beginnings of Islam.* Divinations: Rereading Late Ancient Religion. Philadelphia: University of Pennsylvania Press, 2012.

———. "The Dome of the Rock and Early Islamic Eschatology." In *Marking the Sacred: The Temple Mount / Haram al-Sharif in Jerusalem,* edited by Joan Branham and Beatrice St. Laurent. University Park: Pennsylvania State University Press, forthcoming.

———. "The Georgian *Life of the Virgin* attributed to Maximus the Confessor: Its Authenticity(?) and Importance." In *Mémorial R.P. Michel van Esbroeck, S.J.,* edited by Alexey Muraviev and Basil Lourié, 307-28. St. Petersburg: Vizantinorossika, 2006.

———. "In Search of 'Urwa's Sīra: Some Methodological Issues in the Quest for 'Authenticity' in the Life of Muḥammad." *Der Islam* 85, no. 2 (2009-11): 257-344.

———. "Jewish Christianity, Non-Trinitarianism, and the Beginnings of Islam." In *Jewish Christianity and Early Islam,* edited by Francisco del Río Sánchez. Turnhout, Belgium: Brepols, 2018.

———. "Mary between Bible and Qur'an: Apocrypha, Archaeology, and the Memory of Mary in Late Ancient Palestine." In *Extracanonical Traditions and the Holy Land,* edited by Harald Buchinger, Andreas Merkt and Tobias Nicklas, forthcoming. Tübingen: Mohr Siebeck, 2021.

———. "Muhammad." In *The Routledge Handbook on Early Islam,* edited by Herbert Berg, 49-64. London: Routledge, 2018.

———. "Muḥammad and the Qur'ān." In *The Oxford Handbook of Late Antiquity,* edited by Scott F. Johnson, 1078-108. New York: Oxford University Press, 2012.

———. "The Reign of God Has Come: Eschatology and Empire in Late Antiquity and Early Islam." *Arabica: Journal of Arabic and Islamic Studies* 61 (2014): 514-58.

———. *Three Christian Martyrdoms from Early Islamic Palestine: Passion of Peter of Capitolias, Passion of the Twenty Martyrs of Mar Saba, Passion of Romanos the Neomartyr.* Eastern Christian Texts. Provo, Utah: Brigham Young University Press, 2016.

———. "The *Tiburtine Sibyl,* the Last Emperor, and the Early Byzantine Apocalyptic Tradition." In *Forbidden Texts on the Western Frontier: The Christian Apocrypha in North American Perspectives,* edited by Tony Burke, 218-44. Eugene, OR: Cascade Books, 2015.

———. "The *Tiburtine Sibyl*: A New Translation and Introduction." In *New Testament Apocrypha: More Noncanonical Scriptures,* edited by Tony Burke and Brent Landau, 506–21. Grand Rapids, MI: Eerdmans, 2016.

———. "Les vies de Muhammad." In *Le Coran des historiens,* edited by Mohammad Ali Amir-Moezzi and Guillaume Dye, vol. 1, 183–245. Paris: Les éditions du Cerf, 2019.

Silver, Abba Hillel. *A History of Messianic Speculation in Israel, From the 1st through the 17th Centuries.* New York: The Macmillan Company, 1927.

Sinai, Nicolai. "When Did the Consonantal Skeleton of the Quran Reach Closure? Part I." 77, no. 2 (2014): 273–92.

Sivertsev, Alexei. *Judaism and Imperial Ideology in Late Antiquity.* Cambridge: Cambridge University Press, 2011.

Spurling, Helen, and Emmanouela Grypeou. "Pirke de-Rabbi Eliezer and Eastern Christian Exegesis." *Collectanea Christiana Orientalia* 4 (2007): 217–43.

St. Laurent, Beatrice, and Isam Awwad. "Archaeology and Preservation of Early Islamic Jerusalem: Revealing the 7th Century Mosque on the Haram Al-Sharif." In *Proceedings of the 9th International Congress on the Archaeology of the Ancient Near East,* edited by Susanne Bickel, 441–53. Wiesbaden: Harrassowitz, 2016.

———. "The Marwani Musalla in Jerusalem: New Findings." *Jerusalem Quarterly* 54 (2013): 7–30.

Stetkevych, Jaroslav. *Muḥammad and the Golden Bough: Reconstructing Arabian Myth.* Bloomington: Indiana University Press, 1996.

Stover, Dale. "Orientalism and the Otherness of Islam." *Studies in Religion / Sciences Religieuse* 17 (1988): 27–40.

Suciu, Alin. "More Sahidic Fragments from the Life of Shenoute Attributed to Besa." In *Zeitschrift für Antikes Christentum / Journal of Ancient Christianity* 17, no. 3 (2013): 424–27.

Suermann, Harald. *Die geschichtstheologische Reaktion auf die einfallenden Muslime in der edessenischen Apokalyptik des 7. Jahrhunderts.* Europäische Hochschulschriften Reihe XXIII, Theologie 256. Frankfurt am Main: Peter Lang, 1985.

Swanson, Mark N. "The Martyrdom of ʿAbd al-Masīḥ, Superior of Mount Sinai (Qays al-Ghassānī)." In *Syrian Christians under Islam: The First Thousand Years,* edited by David Thomas, 107–29. Leiden: Brill, 2001.

al-Ṭabarī, Muḥammad ibn Jarīr. *Annales.* Edited by M. J. de Goeje, J. Barth, Theodor Nöldeke, P. de Jong, Eugen Prym, Heinrich Thorbecke, Siegmund

Fränkel, Ignazio Guidi, David Heinrich Müller, M. Th Houtsma, Stanislas Guyard and V. R. Rozen. 15 vols. Leiden: E. J. Brill, 1879-1901.

Tannous, Jack. "In Search of Monotheletism." *Dumbarton Oaks Papers* 68 (2014): 29-67.

———. *The Making of the Medieval Middle East: Simple Believers and Everyday Religion.*Princeton, NJ: Princeton University Press, 2018.

Taylor, David G. K. "The Disputation between a Muslim and a Monk of Bēt Ḥālē: Syriac Text and Annotated English Translation." In *Christsein in der islamischen Welt: Festschrift für Martin Tamcke zum 60. Geburtstag,* edited by Sidney H. Griffith and Sven Grebenstein, 187-242. Wiesbaden: Harrassowitz, 2015.

Tesei, Tommaso. "The Prophecy of Ḏū-l-Qarnayn (Q 18:83-102) and the Origins of the Qurʾānic Corpus." *Miscellanea Arabica* (2013-14): 273-90.

Theissen, Gerd. *Sociology of Early Palestinian Christianity.* Philadelphia: Fortress Press, 1978.

Thomas, David, and Barbara Roggema, eds. *Christian Muslim Relations: A Bibliographical History, Volume 1 (600-900).* History of Christian-Muslim Relations 11. Leiden: Brill, 2009.

Thomson, Robert W., and James Howard-Johnston, trans. *The Armenian History Attributed to Sebeos.* 2 vols. Translated Texts for Historians 31. Liverpool: Liverpool University Press, 1999.

Thümmel, Hans Georg. *Die Frühgeschichte der ostkirchlichen Bilderlehre: Texte und Untersuchungen zur Zeit vor dem Bilderstreit.* Texte und Untersuchungen zur Geschichte der altchristlichen Literatur 139. Berlin: Akademie Verl., 1992.

Usener, Hermann. "Die Weihnachtspredigt des Sophronios." *Rheinisches Museum für Philologie* 41 (1886): 500-516.

Uthemann, Karl-Heinz, ed. *Anastasii Sinaitae: Viae dux.* Corpus Christianorum. Series Graeca 8. Turnhout, Belgium: Brepols, 1981.

———. *Anastasios Sinaites: Byzantinisches Christentum in den ersten Jahrzehnten unter arabischer Herrschaft.* 2 vols. Arbeiten zur Kirchengeschichte 125. Berlin: De Gruyter, 2015.

van Bladel, Kevin. "The Alexander Legend in the Qurʾān 18.83-102." In *The Qurʾān in Its Historical Context,* edited by Gabriel Said Reynolds, 175-203. New York: Routledge, 2007.

van der Velden, Frank. "Konvergenztexte syrischer und arabischer Christologie: Stufen der Textentwicklung von Sure 3, 33-64." *Oriens Christianus* 91 (2007): 164-203.

———. "Kotexte im Konvergenzstrang—die Bedeutung textkritischer Varianten und christlicher Bezugstexte für die Redaktion von Sure 61 und Sure 5, 110–19." *Oriens Christianus* 92 (2008): 213–46.

Vasiliev, Alexandre, ed. *Kitab al-ʿUnvan / Histoire universelle.* 4 vols. Patrologia Orientalis 5.4, 7.4, 8.3, 11.1. Paris: Firmin-Didot, 1910–15.

Vincent, Hugues, and F. M. Abel. *Jérusalem nouvelle. Fascicule 1 et 2, Aelia Capitolina, le Saint-Sepulcre et le Mont des Oliviers.* Paris: Victor Lecoffre, 1914.

Wansbrough, John E. *Quranic Studies: Sources and Methods of Scriptural Interpretation.* London Oriental Series 31. Oxford: Oxford University Press, 1977.

———. "Review of Patricia Crone and Michael Cook, *Hagarism: The Making of the Islamic World.*" *Bulletin of the School of Oriental and African Studies* 41 (1978): 155–56.

———. *The Sectarian Milieu: Content and Composition of Islamic Salvation History.* London Oriental Series 34. Oxford: Oxford University Press, 1978.

Wansbrough, John E., and Andrew Rippin. *Quranic Studies: Sources and Methods of Scriptural Interpretation.* Amherst, NY: Prometheus Books, 2004.

Wāsiṭī, Abū Bakr Muḥammad ibn Aḥmad. *Faḍāʾil al-Bayt al-Muqaddas.* Edited by Isaac Hasson. The Max Schloessinger Memorial Series 3. Jerusalem: The Magnes Press, The Hebrew University, 1979.

Watt, W. Montgomery. *Muhammad at Medina.* Oxford: Clarendon Press, 1956.

Webb, Peter. *Imagining the Arabs: Arab Identity and the Rise of Islam.* Edinburgh: Edinburgh University Press, 2016.

Wellhausen, Julius. *The Arab Kingdom and Its Fall.* Translated by Margaret Graham Weir. Calcutta: University of Calcutta, 1927.

Wensinck, A. J. *Muhammad and the Jews of Medina.* Islamkundliche Materialien. Freiburg im Breisgau: K. Schwarz, 1975.

Wilken, Robert Louis. *The Christians as the Romans Saw Them.* New Haven, CT: Yale University Press, 1984.

Wood, Philip. "Christianity in the Arabian Peninsula." In *Early Islam: The Sectarian Milieu of Late Antiquity?*, edited by Guillaume Dye. Chicago: University of Chicago Press, forthcoming.

Wright, William. *Catalogue of Syriac Manuscripts in the British Museum Acquired since the Year 1838.* 3 vols. London: British Museum, 1870–72.

———. *A Short History of Syriac Literature.* London: Adam and Charles Black, 1894.

Index

Anastasius of Sinai (*continued*)
of Satan's fall, 127; travels among
Christians, 101-2, 104; writings of,
101-4. *See also Edifying Tales* (Anastasius of Sinai)
Andrae, Tor, 206
animal sacrifice, 110, 120-21, 133, 136
Anthony, Sean, 8, 42, 43, 210
Antiochus Strategius, 75, 242n1,
247n17
Apocalypse of Elijah, 173
Apocalypse of Ps.-Methodius: Christian
apocalypticism and, 82-83; Christian reactions to Believers in, 82;
Last Emperor tradition in, 82-84;
pagan conversion to Christianity
in, 83-84; post-Islamic apocalypses
and, 81; Psalm 68.31 in, 83-84
Apocalypse of Ps.-Shenoute, The:
Christ's revelations and, 172-73;
on construction of Temple Mount
sanctuary, 175, 177-79; dating the
composition of, 174-76, 178-79;
imperial eschatology and, 173;
Islamic origins and, 176; managing
church affairs in, 181, 184; reference
to Christ's crucifixion in, 179-80;
sons of Esau and, 181-84; versions
of, 171-72
apocalypticism: Christians and,
28-29, 81-84, 88, 91-92; imperial
eschatology, 173; Islamic origins
and, 28, 42; Jews and, 28, 81, 182;
messianic deliverance and, 28, 141-
43, 147; Zoroastrians and, 81
al-Aqsā Mosque, 161, 166-67
Arab identity, 31-32, 99, 120
Arculf, 164-65, 169-70
Aristotle, 203
Ark of the Covenant, 13, 71
Armenia, 62

Armenian Chronicle of 661: on Believer
worship at Temple Mount, 71-72;
composition of, 62; defeat of
Romans, 68; historical value of,
63; inter-confessional community
Believers in, 27, 68; on Jewish alli-
ance with Ishmaelites, 64-69; on
Jewish plot to slaughter Christians,
65-66, 71; reclaiming Promised
Land in, 15, 68-71; rise of Muham-
mad's religious movement in,
62-68, 70, 72
Assemani, Joseph, 97
Auzépy, Marie-France, 211
Avner, Rina, 260n25
Awwad, Isam, 166

bar Niṭrōn, 200
Barthold, Vasily, 206, 265n12
bar Zāyāt, 200
Bashear, Suliman, 161, 206
Battle of Dathin, 51, 61
Battle of Gabitha-Yarmuk, 56
Battle of Khazir, 201
Beck, Edmund, 89-90, 248n12
Be'er Orah, 207
Believers' Invasion of Syria (Syriac
fragment), 55-56, 243n5
Belus, 129
Besa, 171
Bibliotheca (Photius), 73
Binggeli, André, 104, 114, 121
Bonura, Christopher, 248n7
Book of Main Points, The (John bar
Penkaye): on Christian commu-
nities, 187-88, 196-97; coming of
the eschaton and, 186; on conflicts
among Christians, 189; dating the
composition of, 185; early history
of the Believers in, 186-92, 195-97;
on invasion of the Nomads, 186-88,

192–93; on Muhammad as guide, 195; regard for Muʿāwiya in, 188–89, 193; on rival factions in Believers, 189–91, 193; Second Civil War and, 193, 197–201; on tolerance for Christians, 193

Booth, Phil, 74–75

Bousset, Wilhelm, 88

Bowersock, Glen, 227–28, 231–33

Brock, Sebastian, 2, 84, 151, 189, 199, 243n1

Brooks, Edward, 225

Brown, Jonathan, 7

Buhl, Frants, 206

Busse, Heribert, 52, 160

Caesarea, 52

Capture of Jerusalem by the Persians in 614, The (Antiochus Strategius), 75, 242n1, 247n17

Caspari, C. P., 88

Chalcedonian Christians, 29, 183–84, 219

Christianity. *See* Christians/ Christianity

Christian Saracens, 118–20

Christians as the Romans Saw Them, The (Wilken), 2, 10

Christians/Christianity: apocalypticism and, 28–29, 81–84, 91–92, 241n8; apologetic works, 104; Chalcedonian, 29, 183–84, 219; in the Community of the Believers, 16, 18–19, 22–23, 29, 33–34, 68, 183–84, 196; Constitution of Medina and, 19; contemporary sources on origins of, 1–2; conversion to Islam, 33–34; Dome of the Rock and, 14; forced baptism of Jews, 37–38; forced conversion of captive, 123–24; in Jerusalem, 45; leadership of

Muhammad and, 20; martyrdom and, 29; Muslim relations, 104, 156, 233; persecution by Muhammad's followers, 97; response to Islamic imperialism, 220; tolerance by Muhammad's followers, 94–100; Trinitarianism and, 20, 22, 237n43. *See also* Syriac Christians

Chronicle (Jacob of Edessa), 66

Chronicle (Theophanes), 209

Chronicle (Thomas the Presbyter), 60–61

Chronicle of 1234, 224–26

Chronicle of Agapius, 224

Chronicle of Dionysius of Tellmahre, 224–25

Chronicle of Łewond, 25

Chronicle of Michael the Syrian, 224, 228–32

Chronicle of Sebeos. See Armenian Chronicle of 661

Chronicle of Theophanes, 224–26, 228–34

Chronicle of Zuqnin, 33

Church of St. John the Baptist, 246n16

Church of the Ascension, 260n25

Church of the Kathisma, 260n25

coinage: ʿAbd al-Malik and, 148; Islamic, 162; Muʿāwiya and cross imagery, 149, 162–63; production of, 162–63; silver, 162–63; withdrawal of, 146, 149

Columba, 164

Community of the Believers: Abrahamic descent and, 15–19; animal sacrifice and, 120–21; ban on alcoholic beverages in, 67; called Hagarenes, 32, 46, 53, 65, 100, 169; called Ishmaelites, 53, 100; Christian members of, 16, 18–19, 22–23, 29, 33–34, 68, 183–84, 196; Christian reactions to, 82; Dome of

Howard-Johnston, James, 63, 72, 134, 159–60

Hoyland, Robert, 8–9, 19–20, 26, 30, 53, 61–63, 68, 89, 123, 129, 148, 167, 178, 182, 196, 207, 211, 268n17

Hübschmann, Heinrich, 245n8

Ḥusayn ibn ʿAlī, 197, 199

Ibn Shihāb al-Zuhrī, 99

Ibrāhīm ibn al-Ashtar, 201

In God's Path (Hoyland), 30

Iona Abbey, 164

Ishmael, 5

Ishmaelites: eschatological expectation and, 92; identity of Nomads as, 32, 100; messianic deliverance and, 138, 141, 143; Muhammad's followers as, 53, 66; reclaiming Promised Land by, 67–68; seizure of Holy of Holies, 71

Ishoʿyahb II, Catholicos, 134, 137

Ishoʿyahb III of Adiabene: on efforts to secede from Catholicos authority, 94–96, 98; on forfeiture of Christian belongings, 95–96, 98, 100, 249n4; *Letter 14C*, 94–100; on life under Sasanian dominion, 93; on Muhammad's followers as *mhaggrāyē*, 100; on people of Mrwny', 95–98, 100, 249n4; on treatment of Christians under Muhammad's followers, 94–100, 134, 137, 197

Islamicization, 32, 99, 208

Islamic origins: Abbasid Empire and, 7; Abrahamic monotheism and, 15–23; anti-Umayyad bias in, 7, 176; apocalypticism and, 42–44; Christian conversion and, 120; Christian response to, 220; Christian sources on, 2, 7; confessional identity and,

22; conversion to and from, 29; eschatological expectation and, 28; importance of Jerusalem to, 11, 168, 177; inclusion of Jews and, 16; Islamic accounts of, 3, 33, 71–72; liberation of Holy Land, 69; Muhammad and, 3–11, 195; non-Islamic witnesses to, 1–4, 7–10, 23–33, 63, 71–72; Qur'an and, 7, 21, 23–27; *sīra* traditions and, 6–7; Syriac writings on, 8–9; terminology of, 32–34; as true religion of Abraham, 5. *See also* Community of the Believers; Muhammad's followers

Islamic sacred geography: Christian sources on, 12; desert shrine, 12; Dome of the Rock and, 13–14; Hijaz and, 176; Holy Land and, 158–59; Jerusalem and, 11–13, 158–59, 198; Jewish Temple and, 12–14; Mecca in, 12, 121, 158, 198–99, 206; Medina (Yathrib) in, 5–6, 158; non-Islamic witnesses to, 13–14; Temple Mount, 12–13

Jacob (the newly baptized), 38–40. *See also Teaching of Jacob the Newly Baptized, The*

Jacob of Edessa: *Chronicle*, 66; on direction of prayer, 203–8; *Fourth Letter to John the Stylite*, 203–8; on Muhājirūn, 100, 203–4; on religious practices of Muhammad's followers, 203; Syrian Miaphysite tradition and, 202; work in canon law, 202

Jerusalem: Christians in, 45, 79; as direction of prayer, 69, 203–8; eschatological expectation and, 28, 81–83; importance to Muhammad's followers, 11–13, 28, 69, 158–59, 176–77, 208, 230–31; liberation from

Roman occupation, 28, 52; Saracen control of, 45, 52–53, 232–34; Sophronius and, 46–47. *See also* Holy Land

Jesus Christ: crucifixion and, 179–80; divinity of, 21–22, 123, 126; as Messiah, 41–44; return at the eschaton, 42–43

Jewish Temple: Ark of the Covenant and, 13; Dome of the Rock and, 167–70, 261n11; Holy of Holies and, 13, 71–72, 167; Islamic restoration of, 12–15, 28, 71–72, 114, 116, 124–25; ritual practices and, 15. *See also* Temple Mount

Jews/Judaism: Abrahamic descent and, 16; apocalypticism and, 28, 81, 241n8; in the Community of the Believers, 16–19, 22; Constitution of Medina and, 17–19; conversion to Islam, 33–34; direction of prayer, 203–4; Dome of the Rock and, 14–15; as followers of Muhammad, 59; forced Christian baptism and, 37–38; leadership of Muhammad and, 20; in Medina (Yathrib), 5–6, 17; Persian collaboration and, 231; prayer toward the Jerusalem Temple, 204; Temple Mount restoration and, 125, 231

John bar Penkaye: on Believer sanctuary in the south, 205; on Believer tolerance for Christians, 193, 196–97; chronicle of world history by, 185–86; on Community of Believers, 195–97; regard for Muʿāwiya, 193, 195; on the Second Civil War, 30, 193, 197–201; on theodicy and divine Providence, 186, 193. *See also Book of Main Points, The* (John bar Penkaye)

John bar Samuel, 225

John Climacus, 101, 103

John of Damascus: monastery of Mar Saba and, 210–11; Muʿāwiya administration and, 183, 197; *Passion of Peter of Capitolias*, 209–12; on the Qurʾan, 23–26; writing of hagiographies, 209–10, 266n2

John of Fenek, 185. *See also* John bar Penkaye

John of Philadelphia, 47

John the Baptist, 214, 223

John the Stylite, 203

Jordan, 52

Judaism. *See* Jews/Judaism

Justinian II, 227

Justus, 38–40

Kaʿba: as direction of prayer, 6, 12, 203–5, 208; Islamic prayer and, 5–6, 12; Meccan location of, 5–6, 12, 121–22, 135, 204–5; Palestinian location of, 204–5

Kalb tribe, 197–98

Kaysānīyya, 263n1

Kekeliże, 209–10

Khālid ibn al-Walīd, 132, 255n19

Khuzistan Chronicle: on animal sacrifices, 133, 136; on Believers' invasion of Iran, 128–30, 133–34; on Believers' invasion of Khuzistan, 128–32, 134–35; on Believers' invasion of Syria and Palestine, 132–33, 135; chronological sequence in, 128–29; on death and destruction by the Believers, 136–37; Khālid ibn al-Walīd and, 132, 255n19; on Muhammad as leader of sons of Ishmael, 133–34; Saʿd ibn Abī Waqqās and, 131, 255n14; on tent of Abraham, 132–33, 135–36, 205, 256n23; on territories under Believers' control,

monotheism: Abrahamic, 26, 33–34, 158; Christian Trinitarianism and, 237n43; Community of the Believers and, 17, 19–20, 22, 79, 196; *jihād* state and, 194; Muhammad and, 5–6, 17, 19, 22, 195; prophets and, 195, 223

Monothelitism, 150

Moschus, John, 46, 73. *See also Spiritual Meadow* (Moschus)

Mount of Olives, 230, 246n16, 247n17

Mount Sinai, 73, 102–3, 108, 118

Mrwny', 95–98, 100, 249n4

Mu'āwiya: coinage with cross imagery and, 149, 162–63; coronation of, 151, 153, 158; development of state apparatus, 194–95; Dome of the Rock construction and, 113, 117, 148, 166; Jacobite tribute and, 152; Jerusalem and, 158–59; leadership of interconfessional community, 158–59; leadership of the Believers, 153–54, 159–60; marriage to Christian woman, 158, 197; mediation of Christian disputes, 156–57; Sarjūn ibn Manṣūr and, 24, 183; Temple Mount restoration and, 117; tolerance of Christian faith, 157–61, 183, 196–97; Umayyad dynasty and, 155; victory in First Civil War, 62, 152; worship at Christian shrines, 153, 159–61; Ziyād ibn Abī Sufyān and, 149

Muhājirūn, 32, 100, 203–4. *See also* Muhammad's followers

Muhammad: Abrahamic movement and, 15–16, 30; on Arabian peninsula monotheism, 98–99, 250n11; Christian descriptions of, 195; Community of the Believers and, 16–17, 19, 34–35; Constitution of Medina and,

17–19; death of, 4–6, 31; expansion of followers, 8; imminent eschatology and, 41–43; Islamic accounts of, 30–31; Islamic origins and, 3–11; leadership of Jews and Christians, 16, 20; liberation of Holy Land, 30–31; Mecca and, 5–6, 100; Medina (Yathrib) and, 5–6, 100; monotheism and, 5–6, 17, 19, 22; non-Islamic witnesses to, 9, 30–31; prophetic status of, 4, 6–7, 19–23, 31, 35, 39–40, 43, 141–42, 195, 221, 223; *qibla* and, 206; Qur'an and, 4–5; *sīra* traditions and, 6–7; writings of, 24, 26

Muhammad and the Believers (Donner), 8

Muhammad and the Empires of Faith (Anthony), 8

Muḥammad b. Abi Ḥudhayfa, 154

Muḥammad ibn al-Ḥanafiyyah, 185, 199–200

Muhammad's followers: absence of Qur'an among, 21, 23; apocalypticism and, 28–29; arrival in the Roman Near East, 37–40, 87–88; attitudes toward other religious confessions, 27; as confederation of Abrahamic monotheists, 17, 20; conversion to Islam, 33–34; direction of prayer, 6, 11–12, 66, 69, 203–8; Dome of the Rock construction and, 113–14, 117; expansion outside Arabian Peninsula, 8, 178–79; First Civil War (*Fitna*), 62, 152, 193, 197; importance of Jerusalem to, 11–14, 28, 69, 176–77, 208, 230–31; importance of Palestine to, 176; invasion of Mesopotamia, 60, 68; Islam as revival of older faith, 5; Jews and, 59; *jihād* state and, 194; liberation of Holy Land, 15, 30; military

Muhammad's followers (*continued*)
activity and, 29–30; as Muhājirūn,
32, 100, 203–4; Muhammad's leadership and, 35; Muhammad's writings and, 23–24, 26; Qur'an and, 4,
26; Second Civil War, 30, 193, 197–
201; Sophronius on, 47–52; Temple
Mount restoration and, 12–14, 78,
117, 124–25, 165–68, 175, 177, 230–31;
terminology and, 31–32; tolerance
of Christian faith, 94–100, 220–21;
use of Christian churches, 160–61,
259n23, 260n25. *See also* Community of the Believers
al-Mukhtār, 185, 199–201, 263n1
Al-Mundhir III ibn al-Nu'man, 136,
256n31
Munt, Harry, 250n11
Muslims: Christian relations with,
104, 156, 233; on Christ's crucifixion, 179; Constitution of Medina
and, 17–18; Dome of the Rock
and, 113; Islamic accounts of, 33,
52; messianic deliverance and,
70; non-Islamic witnesses to, 63,
97; non-Qur'anic reference to, 33;
Qur'an and, 26, 196; terminology
and, 33–34. *See also* Muhammad's
followers

Nau, François, 98, 114
Ninus, 129
Nisibis, 200–201
Nöldeke, Theodor, 21, 88, 151
nomads, 31–32

Olster, David, 39, 53
On the Holy Places (Adomnán): dating the composition of, 165; on
Mu'āwiya and Jewish-Christian
debate, 156; on occupation of Holy

Land, 164; on Temple Mount building activity, 165–70

pagans: Christian influence on,
94–96; on Christianity, 2; conversion prophecy, 84; conversion to
Abrahamic monotheism, 34; conversion to Christianity, 83–84;
Ka'ba shrine in Mecca, 5–6
Palestine: arrival of Muhammad's
followers in, 39–40, 43–44, 46–50,
61, 70; battle of Dathin, 61; Chalcedonian Christians in, 29, 184,
219; direction of prayer, 204–5,
208; expansion of Believers in, 178;
importance to Muhammad's followers, 176; Modestus and church
of, 45; religious life in, 73; Saracen
control of, 52. *See also* Holy Land
Palmer, Andrew, 55, 60, 151
Papaconstaninou, Arietta, 183
Passion of Peter of Capitolias: authorship of, 209–12; martyrdom in,
211–23; Peter's critique of Islam in,
221–23; Peter's desire for painful
death in, 218, 220–21; rejection of
Muhammad as prophet, 218, 221,
223; religious dissent and, 30; tolerance of Christian faith in, 219–21
Penn, Michael, 8–9, 20, 89, 155–56, 160
Persia/Persians: attacks on Believers,
137; Believer conquest of, 30, 70,
100, 129–30, 136, 186–88, 193; conquest and occupation of Egypt,
172–74; occupation of Jerusalem,
45–46, 75, 147, 231, 242n1; occupation of Sinai, 103; on treatment of
Christians under Muhammad's followers, 94
Peter of Capitolias, 209–12. *See also*
Passion of Peter of Capitolias